No. 482
$12.95

MODERN RADIO BROADCASTING

Management & Operation in Small-to-Medium Markets

By Robert H. Coddington

TAB BOOKS
BLUE RIDGE SUMMIT, PA. 17214

FIRST EDITION

FIRST PRINTING — AUGUST 1969

Copyright © 1969 by TAB BOOKS

Printed in the United States
of America

Library of Congress Card Number: 68-56096

Preface

Radio, in the sense of wireless signal transmission, was not discovered; it was predicted. Its nature was suggested by the mathematical investigations of James Clerk Maxwell and experimentally confirmed in the laboratories of Karlsruhe Polytechnic Institute by Heinrich Rudolph Hertz in the late 1880s. However, I discovered radio, in the form of a vital American public medium, when it stood at the threshhold of its so-called Golden Era. If most Americans were greatly captivated by the sounds of the world wafting into their homes, I must have been even more so, for I saw broadcasting as my future. If it is true that teenagers suffer untold torment and anguish in their indecision over the choice of lifelong occupations, I was spared. I was "broadcasting" to hapless captive audiences of as many as three individuals at the age of fourteen!

Now, with over twenty years in the industry behind me—years spent in village and metropolis; in AM "peanut-whistle" and maximum-power VHF TV, I must admit that reality did not conform to the future I had envisioned. Recognizing even then the inevitability of television, I failed to foresee that radio would capitulate, rather than compete. I failed to anticipate the general attrition of those elements of talent and variety that had made radio exciting, just as I also did not envision the proliferation of radio stations to the point where competitive strangulation worked to the detriment of programming in general.

In consequence, radio has not been as vital, as interesting a profession as I would have found it ten years earlier. Yet television, which deprives the viewer of the boundless reach of imaginary visualization, cannot usurp the fascination radio has held for me, and I am encouraged to see the aural medium slowly emerging from its TV-induced doldrums.

It is to the newcomers who will add impetus to radio's re-emergence as a major American influence that this book is directed. If it is true that, unlike the fool who must learn from his own, the wise man learns from the mistakes of others, these pages may be instructive. Any kernels of wisdom they contain must derive from twenty years of my own mistakes; I certainly make no claim to infallibility.

Since I am a jack-of-all radio trades, and therefore master of none, a book based on my experiences must be deficient in some respects. While they are pertinent to any comprehensive treatise on radio, such topics as detail bookkeeping, directional AM antennas, stereo techniques, and others receive but passing notice here because my acquaintance with them is only peripheral. Conversely, some episodes from my experience are detailed for the sake of illustrating a point, and historical references are intended to clarify current practices for the reader who may be new to radio.

This book is not intended to be objective. Underlying every page is a persistent idealism, an idealism scarred through the broadcasting years from the blows of imperfect reality; often submerged, perforce—but never subdued. It is this idealism that insists that radio serves a loftier purpose than a narrow profit motive admits; that a station's first objective is to be a constructive force in its community; and that this goal is best pursued by striving for the highest level of professionalism within reach.

It is not my expectation to convert the experienced broadcaster whose concept of success is limited to financial profit. If anything, radio needs greater diversity, especially as measured by its air product, than it now enjoys, and the experienced broadcaster may find here some statement that provokes him to new accomplishments in justification of his views. The result is bound to enrich the medium.

It is to the newcomer to the field that I state my philosophical case, in a fond hope that I may infect him with a jot of idealism that will contribute to radio's future level of professionalism. For it is to this concept—professionalism in radio—that this book is dedicated.

R. H. Coddington

CONTENTS

Chapter 1

The Unique Requirements of the Small Market

Two typically American traits have set the course of radio broadcasting in the United States virtually since its inception 45-odd years ago. They are technical ingenuity and commercial enterprise. Commercial broadcasting, supported by advertising, is a result of the fusion of our inventive genius and our profit motivation, giving us a radio service that has survived the scorn generated in other countries where broadcasting is government-operated. It not only has survived; it has excelled so that some other nations now are licensing commercial operations to compete with their own national systems.

In the meantime, our own radio system has outgrown the major cities and has invaded the small towns, thereby providing channels for local expression and local advertising. With that expansion has come an awareness among broadcasters that small markets impose their own conditions.

HOW SMALL IS A SMALL MARKET?

10,000 population? Even 5,000—or less?

This book is developed around a typical radio operation: a 1000-watt Amplitude Modulation (AM) station licensed to operate during daylight hours. It is non-directional, radiating its signal equally in all directions from a single tower. (The kilowatt non-directional daytimer is perhaps the largest single category today, representing 22% of all AM stations in the United States.) It is assigned to a population center of from 5,000 to 10,000 persons, or 15,000 at the most—the typical trading center for a substantial and reasonably prosperous rural area.

The market probably is penetrated by radio and TV signals from the nearest metropolitan center, and towns in the 10,000-

to-15,000 size range may have one already established station. There may be one or two newspapers, weekly or semi-weeking but probably not daily. Of course, there will be a motion picture theater or two, and a throw-away shoppers' guide competing for the local advertising dollar. The 1000-watt daytimer classification is not rigid; most small market techniques are applicable to other typical stations, including full-time operations of 100, 250, 500, or 1,000 watts.

Emphasis on the increasing importance of Frequency Modulation (FM) radio is made throughout the book for two reasons: 1. nearly all AM broadcasters will, as FM listenership inevitably increases, find it advantageous to add FM facilities at the earliest feasible date, and 2. while AM today remains the only expedient means to reach large rural audiences in most areas, a very real shortage of AM frequencies for nondirectional stations is forcing many new applicants to choose between multi-tower directional AM—with its much greater initial cost and operating complexity—and FM, with its present audience limitations.

FM is the less expensive choice for those applicants patient enough to develop its long-range potential. Recent applications reflect the increasing trend toward FM-only stations. Whether FM or AM, or both, the commercial radio station is a business and the business attitudes of its management will determine its degree of success.

THE PREVALENCE OF THE SHORT-TERM VIEW AMONG BROADCASTERS

Relying mainly upon entertainment to attract listeners and solely upon advertising to garner profits, radio broadcasting represents a sort of forced marriage between show business and commercial enterprise. Consequently, it has attracted an element composed of those who, a century earlier, would have fleeced the unwary through medicine shows or candy concessions accompanying traveling tent shows. The vast reach of radio has offered golden opportunities for promoters to turn a quick dollar at the expense of the listeners or the advertisers.

Missing in radio, however, is the one ingredient vital to the continued success of the medicine man: Mobility. Before radio, the unethical huckster closed his wagon and moved to new territory before his victims discovered the consequences of their gullibility. Radio stations are required to remain in one place, and the broadcaster who fails to give full value for the dollar must find new areas within his fixed reach to exploit.

It is impossible to derive statistics for the prevalence of the "grab-the-dollar-now" philosophy that drives radio management to neglect the future; few who follow it would admit as much to a pollster. However, in the various manifestations of that philosophy, every veteran radio man will recognize practices which historically have been far too widely followed.

THE LONG-RANGE VIEW IS ESSENTIAL IN THE SMALL MARKET

Prolonged success for the short-view operator has existed principally in metropolitan areas, where the lack of an operation's mobility usually is offset by the sheer quantity of prospects. If a station alienates its share of listeners through deceptive advertising, there is always another segment within the metropolitan audience to aim for. And the same is true of advertisers; if ten cancel because a station's practices don't meet its promises, there are ten more somewhere in the city who haven't yet learned this and are ripe for exploitation. While it may get by in the cities, the short-range view will not work in the small market. The broadcaster in a town of perhaps 5,000 people cannot afford to antagonize either his listeners or his advertisers—he needs them all. If he drives them away, he is left with no sponsors to support his broadcasts to nobody!

There was a time when experienced radio entrepreneurs selected a promising market, applied for a station, and constructed it with one intention: to sell it within a year or so for a neat profit. The economics of radio stations being what they are, a successful operation can sell for at least twice the actual investment in the plant. Then for an outlay of, say, $25,000 plus a year's intensive effort to make business show favorably on the books, an operator might receive a sale price of $65,000. In addition to living during the interim on his salary from the station, he has pocketed a generous profit.

On the surface, there seems nothing wrong with turning economic factors to one's benefit in this way. However, the practice almost inevitably led to sharp, corner-cutting practices and questionable ethics to hypo the financial figures into a highly favorable appearance within a year or so. Even a small market can be exploited that long, and the "build and sell" operator wasn't really concerned with the station's long-range stability and the problems left to his successor.

The Federal Communications Commission (FCC), charged with keeping use of the airwaves within the public interest, finally concluded that stations guided by such a short-term philosophy were not operated in the public interest. As a result, the law today restricts the builder or buyer of a radio station from selling it for a period of three years, except in cases of certain extenuating circumstances. This means that the erstwhile quick-buck operator must live with his operation long enough to reap what he sows. In a small market he will exhaust the exploitative potential before he can "unload" the property, and such markets no longer are attractive to him.

There is an obvious alternative: to operate a radio station just like any other long-range business, never engaging in any practice that will degrade its future stature in the eyes of either the public or the business community. It is with this long-range philosophy that this book is written. It is a philosophy that avers this principle: the broadcaster's private interest is best served by his devotion to the public interest.

PROGRAMMING MUST BE IN THE PUBLIC INTEREST

It is my contention that the man on the air is in the seemingly difficult position of working for three bosses: he must please his listeners; he must please the sponsoring advertisers; and he must please his management.

The difficulty evaporates, though, when priority is assigned to those various bosses. First and foremost is the listener. It is he—and more often she—who must be pleased enough to remain a listener and, hopefully, to urge acquaintances to listen, too. Given enough interested listeners, the response to good advertising will be reflected in the sponsors' swelling tills—the only way to please that group of bosses; and happily renewed advertisers are _guaranteed_ to please station management.

The first rule for continued success, then, is: _please the listener_. In other words, _interest_ the _public_. It is vital for the small market broadcaster to recognize that he must interest as much of his public as much of the time as possible. He's in the difficult position of striving for the impossible: to please all of the people all of the time! The metropolitan station can specialize its programming in an effort to acquire the intensive following of a fractional segment of those within range, but the operator in the smaller town is eternally challenged by the need for every local listener he can attract. He meets it by keeping that one ingredient—local public interest—uppermost in his plans.

Virtually every town today is served by strong signals from metropolitan stations, and it is with these that the small station must vie for listeners. Most local stations rely heavily on records for their programming, records also available to the city operations, and frequently accompanied by more professional and polished station voices. Only strong <u>local</u> interest can attract the steady listenership of the local public.

Turning to a deeper meaning of public interest, every broadcaster needs to arrive at a workable answer to this philosophical question: Is the function of our mass media merely to reflect our culture, or is it to supply an element of leadership? Is the mere mirroring of the status quo really "in the public interest," or does the addition of a circumspect degree of cultural leadership truly serve best in the long haul?

It's a chicken-and-egg question that each broadcaster must decide for himself. If modern teen music represents degraded musical professionalism, who's at fault? Is it the disc jockeys, perpetually jaded by their intimate association with music, who promoted change just for its own sake without regard for merit? Did they <u>lead</u> their listeners by making the grotesquely different familiar? Or are they playing the music today only as a reflection of their listeners' independently derived tastes? For me, the inescapable fact that the jockeys receive advance records and give them their initial exposures—and that some record companies offered big sub-rosa inducements to those jockeys to create a demand for those records—suggests the answer.

Where does this power of leadership lead? When my children hear mild profanity on television—words which in my boyhood usually were uttered by other boys and <u>never</u> by ladies and gentlemen in the presence of children—they assimilate the language into their vocabulary. After all, the words have been given the stamp of approval by a public medium, even though much of the public may feel they are detrimental to good usage. When I consider that tomorrow television will enter our homes using the stronger language that motion pictures have borrowed from the stage, all in the guise of realism and freedom of expression, I doubt that the medium is exercising its power of leadership in the right direction.

A culture does not progress by keeping its formative eye on its lowest common denominator. It grows by its awareness of what can be, not by what is; and since nothing is static, the only alternative to growth is decay. Mass media cannot serve the future by showing nothing better than today.

I am not suggesting that every station become a propaganda tool for its ownership's private views on morality. Actually, it can't, because the FCC's "fairness doctrine" requires the exposure of a variety of viewpoints. I merely suggest that ownership not abdicate all selective responsibility to the statistical mediocrity of "average" tastes. Indeed, the small market broadcaster cannot undertake a strongly cultural posture, even if he so inclined. He still must retain those listeners! But he can exercise a degree of judgment over the material his facility exposes to the public. A policy of restraint toward the culturally inimical and the gentle encouragement of the converse can effect an uplift subtle enough that it won't alienate the audience. And while one station cannot lead a society, its effort is like going to the polls: every vote counts. Voting, as everybody knows, is in the public interest.

The FCC is increasingly interested in the manner in which licensees program to serve the public interest, and a station applicant now is required to research the community's needs and outline in some detail to the Commission the programming proposed to fill them. Some of the specific programming approaches that successful small stations have used are included in Chapter 10. Each of them can be attuned to local interest.

Chapter 2
Audiences and Profits In The Small Market

For a number of years metropolitan stations and large advertisers have been obsessed with numbers; numbers which evolve from the statistical machinations of various survey organizations that undertake to measure radio and television listenership. To a time buyer on Madison Avenue, the surveys have offered the most convenient guide for advertising campaigns principally concerned with the yardstick of "cost per thousand"—the cost to the advertiser of each thousand listeners exposed to his sales message. In the absence of more detailed information pertaining to age, economic level, and tastes of listeners, advertisers have made do with the numbers. And broadcasters, dependent upon the support of the advertisers, have guided selection of their programming by the numbers, too, as every television viewer must know.

MEASURING SMALL STATION AUDIENCES

There are those who not only feel that numbers don't tell the whole story but that the story they do tell may be erroneous. The validity of extrapolation from small statistical samples is subject to attack, and accusations that surveys intentionally favor the stations paying for them continue to be heard. Added to these doubts, the small market broadcaster also is confronted with the substantial cost (relative to small station economics) of reliable professional surveys and the local businessman's unfamiliarity with their significance. How is he to ascertain his station's listenership?

There is one reliable guide; one which is highly valid and which the local businessman will readily understand. It is simply this: results for the advertiser. If a station is sending potential customers to the sponsors' doors, consistently and repeatedly, there can be no doubt about listenership? Even better than surveys, the measure of results is indicative not only of listenership, but of station effectiveness—which is all the advertiser really wants to know. It is the local advertisers' overall satisfaction with results that has kept some metropolitan stations prosperous despite chronically low numbers allotted to them by the rating services. If such audiences really are so small in number, they make up for it by exceptional listener loyalty and strong confidence in the veracity of those stations. Every station should try to cultivate those audience traits.

Welcome as it is, advertiser satisfaction may not tell station management all it would like to know. An accurate listener survey can be instrumental in pinpointing specific deficiencies and strengths in programming. Broken down into quarter-hour segments of the broadcast day, the survey immediately identifies those programming concepts which either are inadequate or exceptionally effective, so that hit-or-miss groping for improvement is minimized. How one small-market station managed a comprehensive survey at reasonable cost is outlined in Chapter 11.

PERSONNEL IN THE SMALL MARKET

Be it large or small, prosperous or insolvent, every radio station represents people. Listeners tune in to hear the sounds of people—the music they make, the opinions they express, the jokes they attempt, and the news they report. I venture to guess that when radio becomes totally synthetic, with electronically-composed and generated music interspersed with the flawless but disembodied product of speech-generating computers, people will stop listening to radio—if they have a choice by then.

Until that time arrives, then, a station's people are important. An announcer is not a flesh-and-blood speaking machine that rents its services to management; he is the station every instant he is on the air. In time he will take on a personality, for better or for worse, in the minds of steady listeners. If the station is to keep all those small-town listeners its prosperity demands, that personality had better be an attractive one. It doesn't necessarily have to be that of a Jim Ameche or a Dick Clark, but it must be one which is welcomed into their homes, businesses, and autos by the regular audience.

Other station personnel also play emissary roles. The contact with the business community inherent to the duties of management and salesmen also reflects upon the station's image for a significant portion of the potential audience. The office girl's phone courtesy may in time please a large percentage of the town's telephone users. And the engineer isn't always closeted in the back room; he represents the station to the utility companies, area radio "hams," and those sons of listeners who are interested in pursuing electronics. For all of these personal extensions of the station, a good measure of personable sincerity must be added to their professional requisites.

All of these personnel relationships with the public hold true in some degree for stations anywhere. However, there is one vitally important characteristic of a small town that is not encountered in the big city: the individual's personal life is public knowledge. Unjust as it is, guilt by association prevails in a small town, so that one employee's less-than-exemplary conduct can endanger the carefully nurtured image a station has built in its home town. This is a hazard in personnel selection: Because it is difficult to discharge a man for off-duty breach of conduct, which theoretically is none of his employer's business so long as it doesn't impair his professional performance, exceptional insight is needed at the time of hiring.

It is a fact of life that broadcasting, being on the fringe of show business, attracts certain individuals whose temperament clashes with small-town mores. Such individuals often are uncommonly expert in their professional specialties and would be valuable staff members if one somehow could conceal their proclivities for passing bad checks, over-imbibing, seducing others' wives, or whatever. In the small market, though, such concealment for any length of time is impossible, and a station is well advised to forego those individuals' talents. In short, then, personnel in a small-market station need to reflect the same integrity in their personal lives that the station practices in its professional life.

One other aspect of temperament needs consideration: the ability of the employee to be content with small-town life. There is little point and less economy to breaking in a new employee to a particular operation if he will tire in a few weeks of the limited public recreational facilities afforded by most towns. He'll be resigning shortly to return to the city's bright lights, leaving the station to go through the whole process again. Fortunately, though, there is a temperament that prefers the less hectic small-town pace; that derives the greatest satisfaction socially from small groups in private homes; that takes a direct interest in community affairs through active participation in local civic organizations. The small station that actively seeks those professionally qualified who are of this general temperament will be well staffed and will enjoy minimum turnover, thereby hewing in another way to the long-range view. The specific duties of small station personnel are considered in Chapter 9.

SALES IN THE SMALL MARKET

The principal source of revenue for the small-market station is the local retailer; local in this instance referring to the station's entire primary service area. In rural markets, this usually includes a scattering of outlying small towns in addition to the station's "home" town.

Local businessmen are addicted to the same drive as their metropolitan brethren—profit. However, a particular business may be the only one of its type in a small town, or one of but two, so that the edge of competition is not so sharply honed among local proprietors, and advertising as a competitive weapon is not so highly appreciated. The exception is the small town within a few minutes' drive of a metropolitan center with its encompassing newspaper, radio, and TV coverage. The battle cry of local businessmen so situated is, "Patronize your local stores." They are well aware of the value of advertising, if only as an "enemy weapon."

But the biggest problem for the radio operation opening in an area that has not had a local radio outlet is the advertisers' total unfamiliarity with the medium. Small-market advertising traditionally is almost totally newspaper-oriented, and the small-town retailer is prone to conservative thinking that may take considerable effort for the radio time salesman to update. That salesman does have one important factor working for him: even though this is the television age, a small town finds its own radio station to be a novel and somewhat exciting addition that may help to "put the town on the map."

This fascination and potential civic pride, when actively encouraged by the station, can be instrumental in enticing local retailers into wetting their advertising feet in radio. Whether or not they take the plunge later rests upon the results radio brings them—and the competitive counter-measures employed by the local newspaper(s).

A characteristic peculiar to the small town may contribute to the station's success or failure. Like its general population, the local business community has few secrets. If one retailer enjoys phenomenal success from using radio, his fellow businessmen soon will know it, just as they will if his radio experiment turns a dismal failure. Obviously, it is in the station's selfish best interest to exert every effort to avoid any dismal failures.

In general, the radio salesman will have to explain radio's advantages (and admit its limitations), earn the retailer's confidence and whet his curiosity. He'll have to weaken the tradition equating advertising with newspaper space, and he'll have to become a fellow member of the community. Active and sincere participation in one or more local civic clubs, an expressed interest in the town's local problems, becoming in fact a part of the community—all these help to remove the "outsider" stigma for the salesman, just as it does for all the other staff members.

Again, a reminder about small towns: There aren't many potential advertisers. It is vital that a station salesman leaves every retail establishment with a relationship that insures his welcome return. Browbeating, overbearing high-pressure tactics have no place in the small town, as indeed they really don't in the big one.

Local advertising is the major source of revenue for the life of the small-market operation, and it is essentially the only one for a new station. The minor markets are unknown quantities to national time buyers, and regional accounts and their advertising agencies prefer established stations that have proved their value to local advertisers.

There is one other source for rural stations with large blocks of unsold time: the PI, or "Per Inquiry" deal. The PI is a scheme that seems to offer minimal risk for station and advertiser alike, whereby a mail-order dealer contracts to pay a fixed fee for every mail response the broadcaster can entice through unpaid commercial announcements. The advertiser pays only for actual orders received, and the station garners a few dollars from otherwise unproductive time. As with any sure thing, of course, somebody pays. In my opinion, it's usually the listener, who then turns his wrath upon the perpetrating station.

A case several years ago illustrates the point. A station undertook a PI deal involving "talking" toys that sold by mail for a few dollars. The copy supplied by the agency was couched in glowing terms and an accompanying transcription purported to reproduce the sounds the toys made. A few weeks and many orders later, the station finally received samples of the products it had been advertising. The staff, who had believed their own words, were indignant to find the toys far inferior to the picture created by the advertising, at most worth 98¢ in any variety store. There was near-mutiny when a directive came down from management to continue the campaign!

In this instance, the station grossed perhaps a thousand dollars (well below the rate card value of the time involved) and, I'm sure, as many disgruntled listeners. Their dissatisfaction reflected on the operation because, as is the case with most PI deals, orders were addressed to the station to facilitate a mail count.

While certain powerhouses with large rural coverage have made a virtual science of mail-order advertising, many stations won't touch PI deals for several good reasons. PI advertising represents drastic deviations from established rate cards; there is the question of whether such merchandising puts a station in the category of a retail business, subject to all its legal ramifications; a broadcaster should not undertake to collect his advertisers' revenue; and—most important in the minds of many—the merchandise often fails to give commensurate value to the buying listener.

The last point is self-evident when one considers that an item retailing for $1.98 may net the station fifty cents, or one selling for $3.98 may be worth a dollar per inquiry. It seems obvious that a product priced to include so high a percentage for advertising, in addition to handling and postage in unit quantities and a probably high rate of returns, simply cannot represent a fair value to the buyer. The station operating with the long-range view, then, is well advised to avoid "per inquiry" business. It will do better to concentrate on the local retailer, who has a direct stake in satisfied customers.

HOW ARE "RATES" DETERMINED

Considering a daytime operation, a rock-bottom operating cost for any but the most marginal station is about $8.00 an hour, while more satisfactory staffing and programming will push the figure nearer to $12.00. If the broadcaster arbitrarily chooses the break-even point as that where 50% of available time is sold, the cost for those commercial hours becomes $24.00 to support the unsold time.

The National Association of Broadcasters (NAB) voluntary code stipulates a maximum of 18 minutes of commercial time per program hour, which breaks down to an operational cost of about $1.35 per minute. This is the average revenue per commercial minute needed to break even when half the station's available hours are sold to saturation. On this basis, the usual rate card listing rather high one-time rates which taper down as frequency of usage increases could reduce to a minimum 30-second announcement rate of $1.00 and a minimum 60-second figure of $1.65. These prices might be reasonable for a new station that has yet to develop its audience and prove its value and thereby justify higher rates.

As Fig. 2-1 shows, broadcast frequency discounts usually are graduated in multiples of 13. This arose because radio program schedules repeat weekly, and 13 weeks comprise a quarter-year. A program time contract, however, rarely will exceed these maxima:

one hour	once weekly for a year	= 52 times;
a half-hour	thrice weekly, a year	= 156 times;
a quarter hour	five times weekly, a year	= 260 times;

so the rate card does not taper beyond those frequencies. The corresponding minimum rates are adjusted to marginally exceed the commercial clock-minute operational cost of 40¢, which arises from the assumed $24.00 commercial program hour.

While this may appear to be shaving prices closer to costs than good business dictates, there are two redeeming factors. A firm contract for 52 hours is comfortable money in the bank, and there are at least two commercial announcement spots within each clock hour that are saleable, too.

KWZZ

Rate Card   1

Total Times	Programs			Announcements			
	1 hour (58 min)	½ hour (29 min)	¼ hour (14 min)	9½ min	4½ min	1 min	½ min or less
1	$30.00	$18.50	$10.80	$8.40	$6.00	$4.00	$2.65
13	28.50	17.60	10.35	8.10	5.75	3.75	2.45
26	27.30	16.50	9.90	7.80	5.50	3.50	2.05
39	26.15	15.80	9.45	7.50	5.25	3.25	1.85
52	25.00	14.90	9.00	7.20	5.00	3.00	1.65
104		14.00	8.55	6.90	4.75	2.75	1.45
156		13.10	8.10	6.60	4.55	2.50	1.30
260			7.65	6.30	4.40	2.25	1.15
500 & over				6.00	4.25	2.00	1.00

Fig. 2-1. Typical starting rates for a new small market radio station.

One aspect of "program time" should be made clear to all prospective clients: a radio hour is not an hour long! The local businessman, in the innocent belief that he has bought a 60-minute hour, or 30-minute half-hour, etc., may put a stop-watch on his program and become indignant. After all, he's expected to sell a 16-ounce pound or 2000-pound ton! After the fact is a poor time to convince him that the rate card doesn't mean what it says. The radio tradition of program time segments that are shortened for chain breaks should be explained at the time of sale. Fig. 2-1 suggests longer break announcement times, a trend arising from TV network practices.

RATE CUTTING

It is worth mentioning that probably few radio stations consistently saturate 50% of their total air time. Based on 18 minutes of commercial time for six hours of a twelve-hour day, with nine minutes of each hour devoted to 60-second announcements and nine to 30-second ones (a more-or-less typical ratio), the day's schedule will include 162 announcements. Numerous profitable daytime operations consistently log less.

At the minimum rates suggested here, revenue from the daily 162 announcements averages nearly $16.50 for every operating hour, which costs $12.00 to produce. Further, many sales will be for short campaigns at correspondingly higher rates, and some program time will be sold, with the result that the break-even point is met by sales of considerably less than 50% saturation. In actual practice, commercial schedules are spread over more of the day's operating hours with fewer announcements per hour, so that prosperity is achieved without excessive commercialization becoming an irritant to the listeners.

Having arrived at a trial rate structure, it must be evaluated next in relation to the rates that competitive media are charging. Some revision of the tentative rates may be necessary, but a need for drastic reductions is unlikely. Any competing radio station in the market also must meet its operational costs, and a prosperous newspaper likewise has its overhead. True, a very small-circulation paper may exist on peanuts, but the higher relative cost of radio in that case is justified by the deeper penetration into the retailers' trade area.

Once a competitive and profitable rate card is adopted, the first rule of business-like radio operation is to stick to the rates! Unfortunately, this is the first rule broken in the face of competition. Time after time, radio has reduced its stature to the level of the corner filling station in multi-station markets by indiscriminate rate cutting. It's another symptom of the short-range view. An operator of a station deficient in sales looks at the unproductive operating hours and thinks, "It's better that they bring even a little than nothing at all."

Then he proceeds to offer those accounts on competing stations announcements on his at perhaps 50¢ (in fact, 30-second announcements have been offered as low as 25¢—in major markets!)

To the unwary client the offer seems a bargain, and the distressed station will pick up a little immediate revenue, perhaps at the expense of its competitors. What the rate-cutting operator seems to overlook is the ultimate cost to all radio in the market, including his own operation. For the advertiser soon learns that he gets only what he pays for; no station can afford to develop and produce effective advertising for $9.00 per commercial hour, nor can it long jam more announcements into each hour, because the audience—not to mention the FCC—won't put up with gross over-commercialization. The deplorable result is destruction of the advertisers' faith in all radio at any price, and it takes a long time for reputable stations to rebuild that faith.

It may be most difficult, but the station confronted with cut-rate competition is well advised to counter with the proposition that "the other fellow must know the worth of his own product," and stick by the rate card. It will pay off in the long run from the advertisers' increased respect for the station's stature and expertise.

Most stations add variations to their basic rate card. Time often is divided into Class A and Class B (or, in the case of those who don't care to imply that any radio time is inferior, Class AA and Class A), in the theory that there are more listeners available during specific time segments. For commuting neighborhoods, the "drive" hours of 7:00 to 9:00 AM and 4:30 to 6:00 PM are considered choice, while for rural areas the "chore" and meal hours are preferred. Many an agricultural advertiser's early morning message is heard on barn radios by more cows than people. The rate card may reflect premium costs for prime time that are 25% above mid-morning and mid-afternoon hours. If the audience really is greater during those times, the differential is justified.

There is yet another variation on the basic rates—the national rate card. Dating from the era when nearly every station was heard regularly well beyond its immediate "local" market, the national rate card was intended to reflect the fact that every listener was a prospect for a nationally distributed product, while among only the nearby audience were there prospects for the local advertiser. In other words, the station's service was worth more to the national advertiser. Further, most national advertising schedules are placed by advertising agencies, which skim 15% off the top before reimbursing the stations, while most local advertising is placed directly by the retailer. The national rate gave some cushion for agency commissions.

A higher national rate also facilitated an abuse once prevalent in radio known as double billing. Many national manufacturers, or their distributors, offer co-operative advertising funds to local retailers. The national firm will pay a proportion, usually 50%, of the advertising of its products undertaken by the retailer. To qualify, the local dealer submits a paid advertising bill and copies of the ads, and he is reimbursed by the national firm to the extent agreed upon.

The abuse arose when the paid bill submitted to the national firm reflected national rates, while the local retailer actually paid only the local rates. The participating station's culpability lay in its affirmation of payment at rates different from those actually charged. Obviously, advertisng is easier to sell when the prospective local client pays but half the cost. Despite this legitimate advantage, certain radio operators acted in collusion with local retailers to defraud their co-operating national advertisers through double billing. Carried to its extreme, the practice enabled the local business to eliminate all cost if the station's national rate was pegged at twice the local!

Not all broadcasters have condoned double billing, although at least one group station owner provided his managers with a two-page rationalization justifying the practice. Some have engaged in it willingly, while others have felt forced into it by competitive pressures. A few have firmly refused even at the cost of lost sales. As eventually happens when abuse becomes widespread, government authority took cognizance of the situation. As a result, the FCC has outlawed fraudulent billing practices among broadcasters.

Within the limitations set forth by the Federal Trade Commission, co-operative advertising is a perfectly legal arrangement, beneficial to all concerned. It is only the unethical practice of disparate billing that has been outlawed, but it is mentioned in detail here because the broadcaster still may encounter it as a competitive weapon. Double billing has been a newspaper practice, too, probably having started even before there was radio. Since newspapers don't fall under the FCC's jurisdiction, there still may be an occasional unenlightened competitor offering it as a sales inducement. In this particular situation, the radio broadcaster now is required by law to follow the ethical course. No longer does the differential between local and national rates enable fraudulent practices. It is the national rate card that is published in the rate directories, thereby becoming the "published" rates upon which the costs of certain program services are based.

While some radio stations have gone to the extent of developing a third rate card, with prices intermediate between local and national—a "regional" schedule—the industry trend today is toward simplification. Many stations now boast a single rate card for all advertisers, often with relatively few gradations for frequency of usage, thereby reducing the chances of confusion and simplifying sales presentations. Some have reduced everything to a single rate for each unit of time, without exception. (While it costs a station proportionately more to sell and prepare a single announcement than it does for a dozen, practically nobody buys a single one, although they may buy one <u>program</u>. Nor should they; radio's secret is repetition and a single commercial usually is totally ineffective.)

Probably most local radio stations today should content themselves with a single rate card that is competitive, profitable, and frequency-discounted just enough to encourage relatively long-term contracts. The time saved by simplicity will offset any small advantage gained by more complex schedules.

NEW STATION, OR AN ESTABLISHED ONE?

With the increasing difficulty in locating markets where a new AM frequency is available without the complications of directional antennas, coupled with the limited FM audience immediately available in many rural areas, the prospective broadcaster may cast an eye toward acquisition of an established station. What are the advantages and drawbacks to this approach?

An existing station may be sold for one of three reasons:

—to turn a profit,

—to unload a liability,

—to retire, or to settle an estate.

The eminently successful operation, established in the community with substantial goodwill and committed advertisers, will command a figure greatly above its initial investment, offering a comfortable profit for its ownership. It is worth just what it can bring in the market. A good round figure for a small-market AM station comfortably in the black is $100,000, give or take maybe $20,000 depending on physical assets and projected potential. In all likelihood, its equipment would be worth a maximum of $30,000 new, barring unusual antenna tower requirements. For the $60,000 difference, the prospective buyer eliminates the multitude of details involved in application for and construction of a new operation, the months or years of delay while applications are in process and construction is under way, and the difficult first years of building toward consistent solvency. Avoiding these evolutionary details is worth a great deal, provided the erstwhile buyer has the price.

He also <u>may</u> buy a first-rate staff, modern equipment, and established programming policies in accord with his own, or he may acquire any or all of the opposites. In the latter case, the prospective buyer is cautioned that it is hazardous to take on a profitable operation with the intention of changing it completely.

Prices are considerably lower in the case of the second cause above for good reasons. Typically, this is an operation that chronically has lost money, perhaps through several shifts in management and programming policy; it is overburdened with substantial liabilities, and it probably suffers a negative image in the eyes of the public and the business community. Even this station, if liabilities are not to be assumed by the purchaser, may command a sale price of $40,000 or $50,000. Is it a bargain for the buyer who is sure he can reverse its dismal performance?

Extreme caution is in order in this instance. In general, it is much harder to overcome an established negative image than it is to build a positive one from scratch. By the time the operation is re-staffed and its new management is heavily promoted, along with the requisite follow-through in actual performance, the financial outlay is likely to approach the figures mentioned for the first cause. Further, the time required to attain prosperity will approach that of a well-run new station, including its application and construction time.

The purchase of a distressed property offers a full-sized challenge, which many have assumed successfully but which perhaps is best left to the widely experienced entrepreneurs.

A station selling under the conditions of the third cause, that is for retirement or estate settlement, may range in its financial position anywhere between the first two categories. If astute management simply has decided to retire, the property may be well-run and successful. If settlement of an estate is the reason for selling, temporary management may have contributed either positively or negatively. Only investigation of the particular property will reveal which. In either event, the pressure of time in the matter of settlement may induce the seller to accept less than the property could bring if given more time to consider offers. (The retiring ownership can wait for the best offer, perhaps for several years.) In any case, exceptional "bargains" in established stations are unusual, and the prospective broadcaster of modest means may realize success sooner by way of a new station.

INVESTMENTS AND PROFITS IN THE SMALL MARKET

Time was when any citizen with $25,000 available and a modicum of radio know-how could construct a 250-watt station. The liquid finances required were neatly tabulated by the FCC as a function of station power, and the figures bore little resemblance to variations in such realities as operating costs, potential revenue, and a host of related factors. Now the FCC tries to ascertain that station grantees are in a position to meet expenses for at least the first year after construction. Some general investment figures were mentioned in the previous section, and only generalities are possible here.

A 1000-watt daytime AM station can be quite well equipped today for a maximum new-equipment cost under $30,000, probably including the initial consulting engineer's fees. Land for the transmitter site and one or more buildings will represent another substantial sum, but these items sometimes are obtained through a favorable long-term lease arrangement that doesn't tie up construction capital. The major additional investment is a substantial bank deposit to cover operating costs, which begin well ahead of air time. There may be temporary office quarters, lawyers' fees, deposits for utilities, and at least a manager, an engineer, and an office girl on the payroll. There are office equipment items and other non-technical furnishings to secure, although some of these may be set up on an advertising exchange basis (such "trade-outs" must be properly entered on the books and the program logs), and the countless unforeseen drains on petty (and not-so-petty) cash.

Of course, not all this initial investment must be in cash. Equipment is readily available on various time-payment terms, and certain other obligations can be deferred until revenue begins coming in. The out-of-pocket initial investment can be much less than the FCC requirements for first-year operation, and with luck and ability, the new operation may operate in the black from its first day. Many have done so.

First-year operating costs estimated for FCC purposes by applicants for new stations in small markets range from a meager $3,000 a month to a more realistic $1,000 a week. Estimated revenues for that first year vary more widely and are less meaningful. In any event, the investment in a new operation can be a substantial figure. What are the potential returns and profits?

Statistically, they are not astronomical. In recent years, official financial reports to the FCC indicates that a given year may see from 30% to 40% of U.S. commercial radio stations reporting a net <u>loss</u>. On paper, the industry appears risky! Yet most stations continue on the air, and more are built every day. Evidently optimism is inherent to a broadcaster's nature.

On the average, a radio station realizes a net before taxes of less than 10% of gross revenues, which suggests a target for the new station operator. If he strives for a 10% profit, he's committed to a reasonable goal in terms of the industry, although many prosperous operations ultimately approach the 20% figure. This 20% figure gives a lead to revenues to be expected, as a function of operating costs. With reference to the daytime station for which rates were derived, the cost of $12.00 per operating hour amounts to a little over $52,000 yearly. To show a profit of 10% (before taxes), then, revenue must approach $58,000. This is not an unreasonable figure, as this case history (in approximate figures) of a 1000-watt daytimer in a town of 5,000 illustrates:

Initial cost of new equipment:
(land & building leased) $17,000
First year gross revenue: 49,000
First year operating cost: 51,000

This was a station that attempted to program better than the area competition, incurring operating costs greater than those typical at the time. Further, the sales department, though excellent, was undermanned; yet the first year gross in a very small market was nearly $50,000, and this was in 1954! In terms of present dollars, then, a small-market station is not aiming too high for that $58,000 gross. In fact, its sights should be set on building toward $100,000 in a few short years.

A hypothetical small-market station, excellently equipped and staffed, might stack up something like this today:

Total investment: $50,000 maximum
1st year operating cost: 50,000
1st year revenue: 50,000
Profit: 0.0
Investment return: 0.0

As revenue is increased the higher costs of increased service are justified, so that the second or third year of operation might approach these figures:

Yearly revenue: $72,000
Operating cost: 60,000
Profit: 12,000 or 16.7%
Year's return on initial
  investment: 24.0%

Of course, this is over-simplified and idealized. There will be those who scoffingly retort that many stations have been operated on far less overhead and managed greater profit margins, which undeniably is true. However, the underlying philosophy of this book is my contention that radio broadcasting worthy of the name must be capitalized and staffed well enough to provide genuine service to the business community and the public, while earning a reasonable profit therefrom.

Chapter 3

Choosing A Market and Selecting A Facility

Obviously, it would be foolhardy to build a station in a market incapable of producing the revenues required to operate it properly. In view of this, how is an area's potential determined? If there were a sure-fire formula to answer that question, radio would be unique among American businesses.

EVALUATING MARKET POTENTIAL

Because mass advertising is intended to promote business at the retail level, there is one general yardstick by which to measure its potential—total retail sales. A conservative figure for estimating the advertising cake available to all media competing for a slice is around one percent of a market's retail sales, which turns out to be a substantial figure even in surprisingly small markets.

Remembering that this one-percent "cake" must be divided among all media, including long-established newspapers, the prospective broadcaster must subdivide the figure accordingly, but not necessarily one-for-one. When the comparison is between newspapers (long commonplace in the experience of the small-town local retailer) and radio (which is not) the established medium has the edge. Offsetting that somewhat is the likelihood that a single radio outlet will cover the circulation areas of several small papers, so that a small inroad made into each one's share of advertising dollars adds to a respectable gross for radio. Also, hopefully, radio advertising will enhance the total retail volume and thereby justify the station's existence, perhaps even to the ultimate benefit of the newspapers!

In a typical rural market a new station might plan to secure 10% of total advertising revenue available, suggesting a first-year potential of 0.1% of the total retail sales as a satisfactory goal. How this applies in practice is best shown by a case history, a 1000-watt daytime operation assigned to a town of about 5,000. While the primary signal extended into parts of four states, including a metropolitan area approaching 100,000 population about 25 miles distant*. Sales and programming were directed principally to two counties that were served by no other station. These were midwestern counties situated in the heart of the country's most productive agricultural area. Yet family incomes in terms of those in many industrial areas were not high. The 1962 edition of the U.S. Department of Commerce's County and City Data Book gives these figures for the station's "home" county:

Population:	23,906
Median family income:	$4,164
Under $3,000:	34%
Over $10,000:	7 1/2%

The second county is remarkably similar in its statistical makeup.

Retail sales for the two counties during the station's inaugural year totaled $57,644,000, suggesting (by the 0.1% factor) a first-year potential radio revenue of more than $57,000. That the particular operation in this case fell short of that figure by about 15% can perhaps be attributed in part to the lack of the station's intensive cultivation of the second county. An undue turnover in "outside" salesmen led to diminished effectiveness in the outlying territory. Had both counties been as well sold as was the hometown, there seems little doubt that the 0.1% figure would have been realized during that initial year.

Radio operators in other markets have relied on various interpretations of total retail sales figures, and, of course, each market is unique. Probably 1% of retail sales is a conservative estimate for total advertising expenditure (although small-town business advertising percentages are modest); the figure is used here in the belief that it's better to underes-

---

* The broadcaster undertaking a suburban operation in anticipation of substantial revenue from the metropolitan market should be advised that those having succeeded in so doing are notable by their exception.

timate probable revenue than to be too optimistic. The results of miscalculation then are much easier to live with! Edward Whitney, of the Radio Advertising Bureau (RAB), has indicated that many stations have settled on 0.34% of county retail sales as the total available for all local stations; a figure that may be high in some geographical areas. It does, however, suggest a goal for which stations might aim after two or three years' growth.

Referring again to the station in the case history above, the total retail sales in its home county amounted to $28,834,000. As the only station in the county (the adjacent county eventually obtained its own station, thereby reducing the earlier station's area of dominance), all of that 0.34% represents possible revenue. In this instance, it amounts to just over $99,000— satisfactorily close to the $100,000 suggested in Chapter 2 as a desirable long-range potential.

While the station considered here stands an excellent chance of success, despite the competitive inroads made by another radio outlet in its original coverage area, the market evaluation figures indicate that a second station in its home county would seriously jeopardize its prosperity. With less than $100,000 in potential revenue to share between the two stations, at least one must suffer. Divided equally, the income would cover nominal overhead costs at most, stultifying growth in services and plants for both stations and denying the public the quality of radio service it has every right to expect.

It appears that in the past there has been a strong tendency among broadcasters to eye the smaller single-station markets as modest gold mines ripe for competitive invasion. Many small towns capable of supporting one station prosperously today are hosts to two which are struggling to survive. Like automotive service stations on every corner, they may change ownerships, managements, and business policies—but unlike those filling stations radio operations rarely close down. At least one, then, is going to suffer economically, and it's a poorly managed established radio station that is overtaken by a competitive newcomer!

Although the Commission is not directly charged with protection of a station's economic position, it is concerned with service to the public. This requires sufficient revenue to afford good service and to provide an incentive to the station's ownership, so that economic jeopardy to an established operation does receive the FCC's attention. (Economic injury cases are dubbed "Carroll" proceedings by Commission staffers, after the precedent-setting instance several years ago involving Carrollton, in Carroll County, Georgia, a town with a 1950 population of 7,753. It still has but one AM station, now with its FM affiliate.)

By no means is the hopeful broadcaster advised to write off all markets with established stations; there must be many that have grown with the economy and population boom to the point where another station may be entirely feasible. The admonition here simply is to examine such markets in the light of prosperity for all, and to bear in mind that an established station enjoys a considerable competitive head start.

An ability to foresee the future would be an invaluable asset to the potential broadcaster evaluating a market. Lacking that talent, he must make the most informed guess possible. Information takes many aspects. Certainly the past economic history indicates several trends. Is the population increasing, or is the market one of many that are losing people to the urban centers? Is personal income rising at the national average—or better? Are principal industries adding to their plants and payrolls? Or are they on the verge of moving elsewhere? If the economy is agricultural, what is the crop history, and the long-range weather trend? Is a new interstate highway going to bypass the town, or is rail service to be curtailed? Are stores being remodeled and modernized? Are officials of the local government and civic clubs predominately young, progressive men? Are inducements offered to the young generation to settle locally? Is the economy sufficiently diversified to withstand prolonged distress of a single industry? And are present advertising media prosperous?

There are a few basic questions to which the prospective radio operator should seek answers in his efforts to chart the future. At best, his conclusion must be an educated guess.

AM CHANNEL TYPES AND CLASSES

The standard AM broadcast band is divided into 107 distinct channels. They are identified by their center frequencies, which range from 540 to 1600 kiloHertz. Confined to these few channels are more than 4,100 stations, with additions appearing almost daily.

Several techniques are used to keep those signals in their home territories. Almost half of the nation's AM stations are licensed to operate only during daylight hours, when a given signal's range is much less than it may be at night. Limitations in transmitted power keep a station's reach within bounds, and directional antennas protect established stations by reducing radiation in appropriate directions.

In addition to protecting established stations on its channel, a new AM station also must protect (to a lesser degree) those that are one, two, and three channels removed on either side, (adjacent channels) so that potential interference must be investigated for seven channels in all. (This is due to the nature of radio receivers, which ordinarily are not selective enough to reject a very strong interferring signal close in frequency to the one they're tuned to.) With over 4,000 stations already filling the AM band, it is understandable that each additional prospect faces a tighter squeeze for all concerned, and the problem of locating an acceptable frequency (channel) can be pretty sticky. In an attempt to minimize further crowding, the Commission has tightened the standards on permissible signal overlaps.

The 107 standard broadcast channels are divided into four types:

—24 foreign clear and shared U.S. —foreign clear
—36 U.S. clear
—41 regional
—6 local

Channel designations by frequencies are listed in Fig. 3-1. Stations of Classes I through IV are assigned to appropriate groups of channels, with their powers, operating hours, and overlap limitations chosen in accordance with their intended coverage. The 60 clear channels are divided among the United States, Canada, Mexico, Cuba, and the Bahamas, with 36 of them exclusive in the United States. They are intended for high-power dominant stations of from 10,000 to 50,000 watts (with most of them opting for the maximum that can serve vast areas, especially at night. There may be a single dominant station, which is Class IA, or widely separated directionals, Class IB, which protect each other.

There is another "variety" assigned to the clear channels—

AM CHANNELS BY FREQUENCIES

U.S. Clear:

640 kHz	710 kHz	810 kHz	880 kHz	1100 kHz	1200 kHz
650	720	820	890	1110	1210
660	750	830	1020	1120	1500
670	760	840	1030	1160	1510
680	770	850	1040	1170	1520
700	780	870	1080	1180	1530

Foreign Clear and U.S.-Foreign Clear:

540	800	990	1060	1140	1550
690	860	1000	1070	1190	1560
730	900	1010	1090	1220	1570
740	940	1050	1130	1540	1580

Regional:

550	620	960	1280	1360	1440
560	630	970	1290	1370	1460
570	790	980	1300	1380	1470
580	910	1150	1310	1390	1480
590	920	1250	1320	1410	1590
600	930	1260	1330	1420	1600
610	950	1270	1350	1430	

Local:

1230	1240	1340	1400	1450	1490

Fig. 3-1. AM Channels by Frequencies.

Class II operations, subdivided into Classes IIA, and IIB, and IID. Class IIA is a very select one, reserved for additions to certain U.S. clears that long have been closed to new stations. Their power ranges from 10,000 to 50,000 watts, with directional antennas and geographical locations that protect their co-channel dominant partners (see 73.21, Vol. III, FCC Rules). Class IIBs are unlimited-time stations assigned to those clear channels not reserved for IIAs. Power ranges from 250 to 50,000 watts, and directional requirements may be stringent. Daytime and limited-time stations on clear channels are Class IID, operating at power levels of from 250 to 50,000 watts. Pre-sunrise operation by Class IID stations on many of the clear channels is not permitted, and directional antenna systems are frequent among this class.

Class III stations are assigned to the regional channels. They are intended to serve a city or town and a substantial surrounding area with strong, interference-free signals at powers of from 500 to 5,000 watts. It is on the regionals that many of the "typical" 1,000 watt daytimers operate, while unlimited-time Class IIIs usually are further designated as IIIAs or IIIBs, the distinction being made according to minimum power and nighttime facilities.

The six local channels serve literally hundreds of Class IV stations, which are intended to cover only their immediate cities and towns and the very near environs; they are not protected from interference beyond those limits. Most Class IVs are nondirectional, and all are unlimited time operations. Minimum power for new Class IV stations is 250 watts, which is also the maximum nighttime limit, while those more than 62 miles from the Mexican border may justify the daytime maximum of 1,000 watts.

It is from the latter three classes that the prospective broadcaster must choose his new AM facility; about the only way to own a Class I station is to buy an existing one!

THE AM FREQUENCY SEARCH

Investigation of any tentatively open frequency requires a thorough study of the coverage areas (both day and night, in many cases) of any other stations on that channel that might receive interference from the proposed addition. Also, as was mentioned above, certain adjacent channels must be protected to a smaller degree. Conversely, it must be ascertained that the new station will not fall short of its intended service through interference it receives from the established stations. Further, AM applications pending at the Commission have to be checked for possible interference problems, assuming that they will be granted. It must be remembered that the Commission will not "find" a frequency for you. The frequency search is entirely incumbent on the applicant; the FCC can only check the final conclusions once they are incorporated within an application.

The complexity of making an AM frequency search to the Commission's satisfaction leads most applicants to the services of professional consulting engineers who are familiar with the requirements and procedures (and whose qualifications are known to the Commission; most station engineers commanding small-station incomes are too inexperienced in rigorous frequency searches to satisfy the FCC at face value.) They, in turn, recently have begun to use computers to aid in the laborious chore of computing (or checking from FCC records) the coverage areas of the many existing stations that must be protected from the proposed newcomer.

The consultant searching a potential frequency may find that a costly directional antenna would be necessary. This means at least two towers, and several licensed operating engineers on the staff (see Chapter 5), thereby increasing initial and operating costs considerably and perhaps rendering the channel economically unsound for the market under consideration.

It may develop that a directional antenna would be required only at night, with an effective daytime power permissible on a non-directional basis. On any but the local channels (which are unlimited time), this possibility brings the prospective applicant to a moment of decision: Will daytime operation be satisfactory? It has been for thousands of existing daytime operations, but the key issue in the question is one of the importance to the market of early morning programming.

The official definition of "daytime" operation is from local sunrise to local sunset, averaged to a uniform time over each month, either at the daytime station or at the principal unlimited time outlet it is to protect, as geographics dictate. The license for a daytimer stipulates sign-on and sign-off times, with sign-on as late as 8:00 AM in some locations. This is pretty late to be of service to early risers in the audience, and most stations have taken advantage of a permissive loophole incorporated into the regulations since 1941. Under this exception, stations on regional channels and many clears were not prohibited from operating with their daytime facilities prior to local sunrise, provided no interference complaints were lodged by co-channel unlimited-time stations. Thus, daytime stations, as well as unlimited-time stations with inferior night facilities, were able to serve their early morning audiences with full coverage.

That all changed in August, 1967, when a new pre-sunrise rule was adopted. Under this regulation most Class II and III stations are permitted to utilize their daytime facilities prior to local sunrise only after 6:00 AM local standard time, and then only with a maximum power of 500 watts. Even that power may be reduced if interference calculations indicate that it is excessive. For daytime-only stations, this means no pre-sunrise operation before 6:00 AM standard, or 7:00 AM daylight time—although during the summer months, when local sunrise precedes 6:00 AM, earlier full-power operation is permitted by the terms of the license. Class II stations operating on foreign clears still are prohibited from any pre-sunrise operation, as they always have been. It is important to know the Class distinctions and avoid the mistake one broadcaster, long accustomed to Class III regionals, made when he routinely operated his newest station in the usual pre-sunrise manner. After several years, the Commission finally caught up to him and advised that his frequency was a Canadian clear and that no pre-sunrise operation was permissible! The 8:00 AM winter-month sign-on enforced thereby put him at an unexpected disadvantage with his unlimited time local competition.

The operator considering a daytime operation must ascertain the specific early morning service his license will permit and weigh it against his market's needs. The new pre-sunrise rule was introduced as the solution to a quarter-century of "temporary" permissive rules, and it seems unlikely that it will undergo major amendments. If daytime-only service under these new early morning restrictions is not suitable, and if the added expense—construction and operating—of a directional antenna are not justified by the market, the prospective applicant is left with the local channels to investigate. There may be one available, enabling non-directional, unlimited-time operation at a power level that is modest but adequate for a small-area market.

With consultants' frequency searches running to four-figure sums, it would be advantageous to the prospective applicant if he were able to make his own preliminary search. He may be able to dismiss a market that has simply no economically feasible frequency available, without going to the expense of having a consultant tell him so, although there also is the risk of discarding a market where a consultant could have squeezed something in.

With the thought in mind of a preliminary search, the manager or station engineer who wants to tackle a frequency search is referred to the technical literature for more detailed procedures. He also is referred to Paragraphs 73.21 through 73.38 (Vol. III FCC Rules), which fill several pages pertaining to interference limitations; to 73.182 through 73.187 (21 pages of charts); and to 12 more pages of charts in paragraph 73.190. Upon digesting these, he will have an inkling of the job an AM frequency search can be.

HOW ABOUT FM?

After many years of uncertainty, FM radio seems finally to be on its way to prosperity. It has suffered from a switch in its allocated band of frequencies, inhibited growth during World War II, the post-war impact of television, inexpensive receivers of inferior design, plus the apathy of established AM broadcasters who added it for mere duplication.

From the engineer's viewpoint, FM's technical superiority should have justified its early adoption, and that persistent factor has kept FM barely alive in the major cities. That feeble breath gradually has brought a public awareness, resulting in a slow but steady growth in the number of FM listeners. Now that air space for new AM operations is becoming critical, the forces of expansion are being diverted more and more into this newer form of radio broadcasting. Recent grants—heavily FM-only—have numbered as many as 20 within a week.

Without doubt, FM will be the total radio service of tomorrow. Stereophonic broadcasting, possible but prohibited on AM, gives FM an exclusive dimension of technical performance that will become standard for all FM stations. FM's capability of multiplexing other services simultaneously with normal broadcasting affords additional sources of revenue not specifically limited to advertising. These include background music, paging services, facsimile transmission, network relay, and a variety of other services permissible under an FM Subsidiary Communications Authority, or SCA, discussed further in Chapter 6. In the larger cities this capability alone has helped many FM stations over the hump, and doubtless most operators' ingenuity will devise remunerative multiplex applications in the smaller markets. In the meantime, once an FM channel is secured, its potential nonbroadcast capacity is reserved until such time as the broadcaster is ready to expand into the SCA field.

All FM stations are licensed for unlimited time, usually without the complexity of directional antennas, day - night pattern changes, and audience depletions during thunderstorms. Antenna ground systems, relative to those for AM, are simple and inexpensive. The technical portions of the initial application are much less demanding than those for standard broadcast stations. But most important, FM is tomorrow's radio, available in limited channel assignments today. Many established AM operators ultimately will see a need to add FM—perhaps too late to obtain a channel. All of which should suggest to the potential broadcaster that he give FM serious consideration in the light of his prospective market. If it might support an FM-only station from the outset, it is good long-range planning to acquire an FM channel now.

The crucial factor in this modern form of radio is available listenership. There must be enough FM receivers in the market's homes to comprise a sufficient potential audience from the station's first day. With the recent surge of interest in stereo records, many modern homes have added FM-equipped stereo consoles, but a much smaller proportion have become habitual FM listeners, so that local sales statistics giving FM set counts may be misleading. It will take promotional campaigns in other media to get those idle sets tuned in!

Probably the best audience prospect for a new FM - only broadcaster is a market that has been served for several years by nearby metropolitan FM stations, in which case there has been time for set owners to have discovered FM and formed some listening patterns. Consequently they should be particularly receptive to good local FM service. And, of course, there's the market that already has local FM, in which event it must be large enough to support another. Recognizing this economic factor, the FCC has had to be sold—by exceptionally convincing argumentative showings—on assigning a second FM station, in rare cases, to cities of less than 10,000 population. In many areas of the country, FM set penetration will remain hazardously small for some time. The prospective broadcaster will have to consider the long-range FM view for those areas as a sort of long-range struggle, and decide for himself whether he's willing to chance it.

FM CHANNEL SELECTION

Channel selection for FM is vastly different from the AM procedures mentioned before. In fact, the FCC already has done the job and neatly tabulated more than 2,000 community assignments of the 80 commercial channels in the FM band (of the 100 channels between 88 and 108 megaHertz, 20 are reserved for educational FM). These are listed in Paragraph 73.202, Vol. III of the Rules and Regulations.

These assignments are rigid; the rules state that requests for channel re-assignment will not be accepted. The sole exception is for the minor instance where an unused channel is requested for an unlisted community within 25 miles of the assigned location, in which case it still must meet the mileage separation requirements in regard to other co-channel and adjacent-channel stations. If there is no open allocation either for the proposed market or another within 25 miles, present regulations put an FM station beyond further consideration.

FM stations, too, are divided into classes, and the United States is divided into FM zones. Zone I includes the most populous parts of the country—portions of 18 northeastern states and the District of Columbia (see Paragraph 73.205). Zone IA covers southern California, Puerto Rico, and the Virgin Islands, while the rest of the United States, Alaska, and Hawaii are designated Zone II.

FM station classes are determined by the coverage necessary to various types of intended service, which is dependent upon radiated power and antenna height. In the case of FM, however, power is rated in terms of effective radiated power (ERP), rather than actual transmitter power delivered to the antenna (as in AM). Because an FM antenna concentrates its energy toward the horizon to eliminate the waste of useless vertical radiation, it is said to have a gain—much as the lamp energy from a lighthouse is concentrated in horizontal directions by the Fresnel lens. The effective radiated power of an FM station is the actual transmitter power multiplied by the net "gain" of the antenna system.

The second factor in the coverage of an FM signal is the antenna's height above average terrain. With propagation at FM frequencies being principally line-of-sight, it follows that greater elevation of the originating point increases the distance to the signal's horizon. These two coverage parameters, then, determine the three classes of commercial FM stations.

Class A is intended to render service to a relatively small community and its immediate area. ERP is 100 watts minimum and 3,000 maximum. The greatest permissible antenna height above average terrain is 300 feet. Specific Class A channels for all zones are designated in the allocation table.

Class B stations are to serve a sizeable city or area in Zones I or IA. ERP ranges from 5,000 to 50,000 watts; maximum average antenna elevation is 500 feet.

Class C is a category designated for service to a city and a large surrounding area in the less populous Zone II. ERP limits are from 25,000 to 100,000 watts, and antenna height may reach 2,000 feet above average terrain.

For a given market, the available FM facility is determined by the Table of Assignments and the applicable FM zone. Most of the smaller towns are allotted only one station and an FM application for such a town automatically must be for that facility.

Interference calculations are not required for FM applications, except in certain instances where the distance to an established station may be less than the standard spacings upon which the Tables are based.

Paragraph 73.313, Vol. III, details the procedures for making the required contour predictions. Involving far less investigative and engineering expertise than does the AM frequency search, these predictions may be within the abilities of the experienced station engineer willing to follow the straightforward path set forth in the pertinent paragraph. If he can satisfy the Commission as to his qualifications—(which should include some academic training and considerable experience) his calculations may suffice. Or, if a consulting engineer is deemed necessary, his fee should reflect the substantially simpler requirements.

Chapter 4

Form 301 to the License

FCC Form 301 is not an application for a broadcast station; it is an application only for permission to <u>construct</u> one (or to make major changes in an existing one). The same form is used for AM, FM, and TV applications, with 11 of its 35 pages pertinent only to TV. The AM applicant is responsible for 22 of the remaining pages, while the FM aspirant is to use 21. The form is divided into five sections, all to be filed in triplicate, except for Section V-G which must be in quadruplicate. With many pages of additional supporting exhibits required, as well as a copy for the broadcaster's files, the total paperwork involved becomes considerable.

SECTION I

Concerned largely with instructions, Section I is the simplest part of Form 301. The exact name and address of the applicant, the purpose of the application and the specific facilities requested are all to be listed in this section, as is the certifying signature. Exhibits—the additional pages of information, graphs, contour maps, and tabulations—are to be indexed in this section by Exhibit number and pertinent Form 301 paragraph number.

Legal and engineering counsel, if used, are to be listed by name and address. If a consulting engineer was employed for an AM frequency search, directional antenna design, or FM coverage contours, this section is where he first is identified to the Commission. In this connection the engineering consultant ordinarily is not engaged on a retainer basis, but is called upon for specific projects as they arise. In addition to the pre-application AM frequency search, one usually is called in during construction of an AM station to measure the actual antenna resistance—a vital parameter in the determination of transmitted power and in the case of a directional AM installation, to adjust and confirm the radiation pattern. While it is not mandatory that antenna <u>resistance</u> be determined by the same engineer who made the frequency search, the directional antenna adjustment certainly should be performed by its initial designer.

The applicant considering a consulting engineer probably should look for one within a reasonable distance from the station. Members of the Association of Federal Communications Consulting Engineers are located strategically around the country, and many of them display their cards in the trade press. Wherever their locations, most of them are up-to-the-minute on FCC requirements and procedures, and their qualifications are well known to the Commission. With fees running in the broad vicinity of $150 a day plus all expenses, the advantage of a consultant's reasonable proximity to the station under construction is apparent.

The converse is true of legal counsel. The function of a Washington attorney is to serve as an on-the-scene representative of the station in its dealings with the Commission, as well as to advise his client of pertinent actions by that body. In the unhappy event of involvement in hearings, appeals, and similar complications, legal counsel that is experienced in broadcast matters becomes a virtual necessity.

The station operator whose outlet is within convenient traveling distance of the Commission's home office may prefer to discuss his official matters first-hand (Commission staffers are quite personable and cooperative), but one whose station is more remote may consider a Washington legal firm either on a per-case or regular retainer basis. Washington legal firms specializing in broadcast representation are listed in any edition of the <u>Broadcasting</u> <u>Yearbook</u>.

Of course, local attorneys are retained by the broadcaster for local legal matters like the lease or purchase of land and buildings, utility contracts, billing collections, and similar matters.

SECTION II

In this part of Form 301 the applicant's legal qualifications to operate a broadcast station are examined. The FCC is meticulous in its determination of the identity, character, and business interests of those who own broadcast facilities. Citizenship, moral integrity, and business honesty are attributes that the Commission must confirm to its satisfaction. It also requires the applicant's assurance that he will exercise complete control over programming, as the regulations require. The detailed questions in Section II are designed to show these legal qualifications.

If the ownership is to reside within a partnership, corporation, or an unincorporated association, copies of the organizational papers are required, properly certified and attested to, including proof that state laws are complied with. Names, addresses, positions within the organization, shares held and subscribed, and percentages of ownership or voting stock are to be tabulated for officers, directors, and major stockholders, or comparable details pertaining to partners and associates are to be listed.

Citizenship bases for all parties to the application are asked, as is disclosure of those who may be representatives of alien or foreign governments. In the case of a corporation, if more than 20% of the capital stock is owned or voted by foreign interests, an Exhibit must be drawn up listing the full details. The same is true for a subsidiary corporation if 25% of the parent corporation is alien-controlled.

Other questions in this section deal with previous revocation of station licenses, conviction under U.S. laws relating to unlawful restraint of trade, monopolies, and similar business abuses. Convictions for felony, moral turpitude, lotteries, or violation of state laws concerning monopolies, trade restraints, and similar competitive malpractices also must be divulged. Any history of bankruptcy or outstanding judgments against any principal requires detailed explanation.

All business and financial interests, present and for five preceding years, are examined in detail. In particular, any interests in or connections with other radio or television operations—direct or indirect—require full disclosure, as do family relationships among the applicants and between them and owners of other stations.

The actual control of the proposed station also comes in for close scrutiny. If the applicant will not have absolute control of the station, its day-to-day operation and its programming, the Commission wants a convincing explanation. Copies of any contracts or understandings relating to ownership or control must be attached. This matter of control is a sensitive one with the Commission, and an applicant should avoid any agreement that may raise official eyebrows!

SECTION III

In the eyes of the Commission, a station fighting imminent bankruptcy cannot operate in the public interest; therefore, in Section III it seeks to ascertain that an applicant represents sufficient financial substance to weather the period of establishment. Estimated construction costs are to be broken down into such categories as costs of the transmitter proper, antenna and ground system, frequency and modulation monitors, technical studio equipment, acquisition of land and buildings, and "other." Usually, an applicant who has progressed to the point of filing Form 301 already will have signed a contingent contract with one or more equipment manufacturers, will have an option agreement on land for the site, and some tentative arrangement concerning building needs. The necessary figures are gleaned from these negotiations. Copies of credit, time payment, and loan arrangements are to be included as appropriately numbered Exhibits.

Estimated first-year operating costs are asked in this section, also, as are predicted first-year revenues. The bases for these estimates are to be outlined in enough detail to show that they weren't extracted from thin air. If the figures are unusually optimistic, the Commission will want convincing documentation to support them.

At this point, enough information will have been entered on Form 301 to give an indication of the necessary reserves to insure that critical first year. While the regulations are vague on the details, the fact is that large liquid assets are not mandatory. Loan commitments, other holdings by the various individuals in an applying partnership or corporation, firm revenue agreements, and various other available means are taken into consideration. Insofar as other holdings are concerned—stocks and bonds, business ownership, real estate, etc. —the more readily they are convertible to usable funds in case the station falters, the better. Of course, assurance of availability to the corporation in case of need must be made by stockholders who list their private holdings as available capital.

Estimated station revenue during the first year does not, of itself, satisfy the Commission—even though it is aware that many stations operate in the black from the very beginning and that practically none reaches a first anniversary with a record of zero revenue. When that revenue estimate is made conservatively from an in-depth analysis of market potential and is backed by substantial contracted advertiser commitments, however, it will carry more weight in Washington. (There may be a touchy question of timing when it comes to advance selling of advertising on a station not yet applied for!)

To weigh all these financial elements, Form 301 requires detailed divulgence of the personal and business finances of the applicant, including members, partners, or stockholders contributing one percent or more of the total "things of value" toward the establishment and operation of the station.

SECTION IV -A

Concerning programming, Section IV-A consumes nine pages of Form 301 (IV-B is the TV programming counterpart). While portions of it refer to past programming and do not apply to new stations, the section's length is indicative of the emphasis placed by the FCC on a station's programming proposals.

The Commission has found itself treading a narrow, disputed line in the area of programming. It leans one way to avoid accusations of censorship in violation of our Constitutional freedom of the press, but it peers over a broadcaster's shoulder to ascertain how well he is discharging the mandate to serve the public interest.

The lack of specific guidelines has resulted in inconsistent views on proper programming balances as Commission membership has changed, leaving some broadcasters with the feeling that rule in this area is by whim. Recently, however, a method of judging program performance by comparison with the licensee's own proposals has been adopted, reducing the uncertainty to just the question of what proposed programming practices will meet approval. At least, this method invites the Commission's displeasure before three years of disputed balances have gone by!

The official FCC position is set forth clearly on page nine of Section IV-A, which states in part:

"Pursuant to the Communications Act of 1934, as amended, the Commission cannot grant, renew, or modify a broadcast authorization unless it makes an affirmative finding that the operation of the station, as proposed, will serve the public interest, convenience, and necessity. Programming is the essence of broadcasting.

"A broadcast station's use of a channel for the period authorized is premised on its serving the public. Thus, the public has a legitimate and continuing interest in the program service offered by the station, and it is the duty of all broadcast permittees and licensees to serve as trustees for the public in the operation of their stations. Broadcasters must make diligent and continuing efforts to provide a program schedule designed to serve the needs and interests of the public in the areas to which they transmit an acceptable signal.

"Thus we do not intend to guide the licensee along the path of programming; on the contrary, the licensee must find his own path with the guidance of those whom his signal is to serve. We will thus steer clear of the bans of censorship without disregarding the public's vital interest."

Since the program proposals set forth in the station application become the reference by which actual performance will be judged at renewal time three years later, the applicant must plan a lineup that he actually can deliver. The FCC sees the fundamental requirements in this light:

"The major elements usually necessary to meet the public interest, needs, and desires of the community in which the station is located as developed by the industry, and recognized by the Commission, have included: (1) Opportunity for Local Self-Expression, (2) The Development and Use of Local Talent, (3) Programs for Children, (4) Religious Programs, (5) Educational Programs, (6) Public Affairs Programs, (7) Editorialization by Licensees, (8) Political Broadcasts, (9) Agricultural Programs, (10) News Programs, (11) Weather and Market Reports, (12) Sports Programs, (13) Service to Minority Groups, (14) Entertainment Programming." (It may be just coincidental that the major fare of most stations—records—falls into the last category!)

Many metropolitan stations completely avoid several of these 14 program elements, perhaps even specializing heavily in a relative few. Providing that other stations are filling the programming voids, such specialization may be justifiable and even desirable. In the smaller markets, though—especially single - station markets—some diversity of programming will be expected, at least in Washington.

The station applicant is expected to research the actual programming needs of the community. The Commission doesn't presume to know a particular market better than does the operator on the scene, but it does expect him to avail himself of the knowledge and opinions of others in the community, and to submit a description of the methods by which that information was obtained and incorporated into the proposed programming. Again, from page nine, Section IV-A:

"What we propose will not be served by pre-planned program format submissions accompanied by complimentary references from local citizens. What we propose is documented program submissions prepared as the result of assiduous planning and consultation covering two main areas: first, a canvass of the listening public who will receive the signal and who constitute a definite public interest figure; second, consultation with leaders in community life—public officials, educators, religious (groups), the entertainment media—agriculture, business, labor, professional and eleemosynary organizations, and others who bespeak the interests which make up the community."

This official paragraph suggests that documentation of the community's program needs can be only a little less demanding than is an AM frequency search! Consultation with the officials of the assorted groups and organizations isn't difficult; polling the listening public may be another matter.

In the case of the former, individual appointments or attending meetings as a guest is readily arranged, with confirming letters summarizing the accords reached available on request. With the permission of the parties concerned, tape recordings of discussions with community leaders may afford a variety of usable, quotable statements—and recorded confirmation, if need be, that the required exploratory consultations were held. Canvassing the public—to the extent necessary for statistically useful samples—may be approached in any of several ways. Advertising in the local newspaper, offering a modest prize for the best community interest programming idea, is an obvious method if the potential broadcaster cares to spend money with a future competitor.

If the timing of Form 301 preparation happens to coincide with a county fair, opinion sampling of fairgoers should be relatively easy to arrange. Or civic clubs, PTAs, church auxiliaries, and similar organizations represent segments of the public susceptible to polling as individuals, as distinguished from official comments made by spokesmen for such groups. Sometimes an appropriate member of a local high school or junior college faculty will cooperate in making a class project of a survey, either telephone or door-to-door, similar to the listener-survey method described in Chapter 11.

Probably the most expensive to prepare and execute is the comprehensive direct mail questionnaire, and the returns percentage may be disappointing. The FCC requirement of "assiduous planning" ordinarily does not demand that every individual in the market be directly queried. Of course, community leaders and organization members are not professional radio programmers. Yet simply asking, "What type of program do you think would serve the local public?" places the burden of creative programming on their shoulders, and the response is certain to embody many of the first trite reactions that come to their minds. The composite result may look just like the "pre-conceived" format so abhorred by the Commission.

On the other hand, the broadcaster who applies his professional touch to creating or adapting a variety of program concepts to his prospective market in advance accomplishes three desirable results: he impresses his audiences with his thoughtful planning; he plants seeds of anticipation of the day when some of the proposed programs will be available; and he creates the concepts, so that his hearers need do nothing more demanding than to rate the suggestions in order of preference. This is not to suggest that the field of choice be limited, leading-question fashion, to a run-of-the-mill format. A dedicated development of the manner in which each of the various program ingredients mentioned in the FCC quotation above is in order. Other required Exhibits include statements of the proportions of time to be devoted to regional and local news; policy and procedures concerning discussion of public issues; the nature of planned entertainment programming; and the manner in which the applicant proposes to contribute to the diversity of program services available in the market area. Any proposed network affiliation is to be described, including a copy of the network contract. (The FCC is closely concerned with network affiliation because such contracts customarily contain clauses reserving "option time" periods in which the station is to carry network programming. This treads close to relinquishment of programming control by the licensee, and any such contract must contain satisfactory safeguards vesting the local broadcaster with the final over-riding authority.)

The minimum number of public service announcements proposed per week is asked, and the figure entered will serve as the reference by which actual performance is checked at renewal time three years later.

For FM stations, duplication of the programming of any AM station must be indicated. In this instance, duplication means the simultaneous broadcast, or delayed broadcast within 24 hours, of an AM station's programs. Present regulations require that FM stations in markets of 100,000 or more population duplicate not more than 50% of an AM station's programming. It remains permissible—if not desirable—to duplicate 100% in smaller markets, but the AM-FM operator in such a market must anticipate the day when some separation will be required.

Section IV-A's Part IV applies only to existing stations. Part V, however, investigates proposed commercial practices; that is, the percentages of time expected to be devoted to commercial matter for various segments of the broadcast day and the maximum number of commercial minutes per hour to be normally permitted. Actual performance will be checked against these proposed commercial practices at renewal time, just as with the program proposals.

The NAB Radio Code, which the FCC does not impose but tacitly advocates, sets 18 minutes of commercial time as the maximum permissible in any hour. This would seem sufficient; it allows 36 thirty-second commercials—an average of one every 1 2/3s minutes! If a station's rate structure is at all reasonable the prosperity point should be reached at a considerably smaller commercial-time percentage.

Conversely, if an applicant genuinely feels that a greater commercial proportion is necessary, the lack of specific FCC limits permits him to propose accordingly. If the Commission then questions the alleged need for what it may consider over-commercialization, action on his application will be delayed while he is queried for further justification. At this point, the applicant may submit additional documentation, or back down to a less commercial proposal. Tangling with the FCC on this issue at proposal time is far preferable to explaining actual performance beyond that proposed when renewal rolls around.

While the Commission's deference to freedom of speech has precluded absolute commercial limits, a general statement on page nine, Section IV-A, expresses that body's guiding policy:

"..... With respect to advertising material the licensee has the additional responsibility to take all reasonable measures to eliminate any false, misleading, or deceptive matter and to avoid abuses with respect to the total amount of time devoted to advertising continuity as well as the frequency with which regular programs are interrupted for advertising messages. This duty is personal to the licensee and may not be delegated."

Part VI, still in Section IV-a, deals with general station policies and procedures. Established program and advertising standards are to be summarized, unless they are to be exclusively those published by a "national organization or trade association," in which a mere statement to that effect is adequate. As things presently stand, the broadcaster stipulating the NAB Code (published in the Broadcasting Yearbook) probably will satisfy the Commission on this score, although there is nothing to prevent formulation of his own code, be it either more or less restrictive than that of the NAB.

The FCC also wants the names and employment status of those who will make the day-to-day decisions in programming and operation of the station. The total number of employees is required, and if there are to be ten or more, an Exhibit listing their duties and employment status (full- or part-time) is to be submitted. If, after answering all these questions, the applicant feels that his policies require further

elaboration, he is invited to attach additional Exhibits out-
lining them in depth.

SECTION V

This final Section is concerned with the engineering aspects
of the proposed facility. AM applicants are to fill in Section
V-A, while FM applicants are to complete V-B. If an engineering consultant has performed the AM frequency check,
he probably will supply enough completed copies of Section
V-A in his report; if not, all the necessary information will
be available somewhere in its text. The same is true of Section V-B if the application is for FM. The required information for this section essentially is that required by the FM
Technical Standards, so that (lacking the services of a consultant) the station engineer who has made the necessary
computations has the appropriate answers at hand*.

All applicants must complete Section V-G, the one that requires submission of one extra copy. It is concerned with the
mechanical and geographic details of the antenna tower (s),
and no doubt the extra copy is forwarded to the Federal Aviation Agency (FAA), which is the final authority on air navi-
gational hazards. An application may be perfectly acceptable
to the FCC in all other respects, but if the FAA will not approve the particular structure at its proposed location, the
application will be denied until suitable changes are made to
that body's satisfaction. In extreme cases, it has been necessary to search out an entirely different site. The information required in Section V-G also will be available from the
consulting engineer's report, or from the station engineer's
computations, as the case may be, and the results of sur-
veyors' measurements. Pertinent rules for the painting and
lightning of towers are found in Vol. I, Part 17, and Vol. III
Part 73, FCC Rules and Regulations.

The final line of Section V-G completes Form 301. However, there is one further requirement to applications for
new stations which are to be situated within an area surrounding the radio-telescope installation near Green Bank,

---

* There are minor exceptions, such as Item 13, Section V -B, which asks,
"Will the studios, microphones, and other equipment proposed for trans-
mission of programs be designed for compliance with the FM Technical
Standards?"

West Virginia. This is because possible new sources of interference to the sensitive receivers located there (they probe celestial radio mysteries) must be evaluated and approved. The specific requirements are found in paragraphs 73.21 and 73.215, Vol. III, with notification to be sent to the Director, National Radio Astronomical Observatory, Green Bank, West Virginia.

IMMEDIATE POST-APPLICATION PROCEDURES

Once Form 301 is on its way to the Commission, it is necessary to alert the local community to the applicant's intentions. Regulations require that local newspaper notice be given, setting forth the pertinent details. If the community publishes a daily paper, the notice is to be published at least twice a week for two consecutive weeks within the 3-week period immediately following the tendering of the application for filing. If there is no daily, but there is at least one weekly, the notice must be published in it for three consecutive weeks within the first four post-application weeks.

In the unlikely case where there is not even a local weekly, the out-of-town daily enjoying the largest circulation within the local community is to be used. In this instance, the notice is to be published at least twice a week for two consecutive weeks within the first three weeks following the application. (For major changes in ownership or facilities of an existing station, notice also is to be aired over it. In some instances, concurrent newspaper notice is not required. (See paragraph 1.580, Vol. I.)

The information required in the public notice of a CP application includes the following:

- Name or names of the individual owner, partners, or officers, directors and holders of 10% or more of the stock, as the case may be.
- The purpose of the application—in this case, a construction permit.
- The date when the application was tendered for filing.
- The frequency or channel applied for.
- The type and class of station, power, studio location, transmitter site, and antenna height.
- A statement of the effect that a copy of the application and

pertinent material is available for public inspection at a given address in the local community.

Within seven days of the last day of publication of the required notice, full details are to be filed with the Commission (in triplicate, of course) giving the dates of publication, the newspaper utilized, and the text of the notice. In those cases where the notice is broadcast over existing facilities, similar pertinent information is to be submitted. The purpose behind the public notice requirements is to give interested parties an opportunity to file objecting petitions before action is taken on the application.

The FCC also makes public notices; one when the application is first received, and another when it is accepted for filing. Then there is a minimum of 30 days before any action is taken, during which objecting petitions will be entertained from parties who feel that a grant would not be within the technical, legal, and financial requirements of the Commission. (This is the interval during which an economic injury objection may arise.) Competing applications for the same facility may be developed and submitted during the FCC's inaction. A specific cut-off date is stipulated for competing AM applications; in the case of FM (and TV), competing applications may be filed up to the day the initial application is ready for actual Commission action.

HEARINGS

When a competing application for the same facility is made, or an objecting petition raises serious questions regarding the propriety or feasibility of a grant, a hearing usually is required to resolve the conflict. In the case of an application for a new facility, any necessary hearing is held in Washington, where an FCC examiner hears arguments and considers evidence from the litigants concerned. The FCC hearing is not a court process, but an attempt to arrive at a satisfactory solution of the conflicts. The hearing examiner reports his findings and recommendations to the Commission, which—after due deliberation—reports an initial decision. The parties to the hearing then have an opportunity to contest the decision, carrying the dispute to a higher echelon within the FCC. If the subsequent final decision still is not acceptable to the concerned parties, recourse to courts of law is available. Commission action on its decision is stayed, pending the court's determination.

While it sometimes is possible to resolve the precipitating objections short of a hearing, even after one has been designated, the wise applicant for a new station will do all he can to avoid those objections at the outset. The legal costs and undue delay occasioned by hearings can strike a crippling blow to an infant radio enterprise.

Aside from bona fide competing applications for the same facility (as distinguished from those intended only to discourage new competition, which the FCC will not knowingly condone), the best insurance against involvement in hearings is to be absolutely certain that there is nothing in the applicant's technical, legal, and financial qualifications that can be attacked. Again, the exercise of unassailable integrity and high professionalism will stand the prospective broadcaster in good stead.

THE CONSTRUCTION PERMIT

With the hopeful assumption that the applicant's request is in good order and is uncontested, it is finally granted when its chronological turn arrives, and he receives a Construction Permit (CP). Even so, he's still not completely in the clear; objecting petitions can be filed within 30 days after the CP is issued. In this event, however, the burden is on the objector to show excellent reasons why he failed to make his stand known during the appropriate pre-grant period.

The CP customarily does not assign call letters. The permittee may request specific call letter sequences of his choice once the CP is received, and if the call is available and in conformance with FCC requirements, it will be assigned. (A call must begin with W for locations east of the Mississippi and with K west of it. Also, a call must be readily distinguishable in sound from other calls in its area.)

It is important for the applicant—now the permittee—to observe the necessity of filing an Ownership Report (FCC Form 323) within 30 days after the grant of the CP. In general, the Report is a reiteration of the ownership information submitted with the initial application, but final action on the subsequent license application will not be taken by the Commission without it. With fines now imposed for the late filing of various reports, the permittee must keep an eye on the calendar during the press of construction (see Chapter 5 for particulars on ownership changes).

EQUIPMENT TESTS

Once construction has progressed to the point where equipment tests are necessary to the final adjustments, notice to that effect is given to the FCC and to the FCC Engineer in Charge of the radio district in which the station is located. The notice is to be given at least two days prior to the anticipated start of the tests, so that—if there is good reason—the Commission can return notice to withhold them. For the FCC to do so is unusual, but the authority to deny equipment tests is protected by the notice requirements. Unless the permittee is specifically prohibited by return notice from the Commission, the equipment tests may be conducted following the 2-day interval without further authority.

Equipment tests consist of those transmissions necessary to the final adjustment of the station facilities, normally conducted during the experimental period. For AM the experimental period is between 12:00 midnight local standard time and sunrise, and AM equipment tests must be conducted only during those hours—except in certain cases, for which prior FCC approval must be obtained. The FM experimental period comprises the hours between 1:00 AM and 6:00 AM local standard time. The FM regulations do not specifically state that equipment tests must be conducted during the experimental period, but that is the customary and logical time to do so.

PROGRAM TESTS AND THE LICENSE APPLICATION

Once the installation is determined to be fully operable in conformance with all stipulations and requirements expressed and implied in the grant, the permittee is ready to apply for program test authority. This request usually accompanies the license application; it cannot be made before.

From 302 is the license application form, which calls for showings that all requirements have been met, including engineering data supporting compliance with the terms and conditions of the CP. In the case of a directional AM antenna, a detailed proof of its performance is required. Since a consultant almost certainly will have been employed for its design and adjustment, the directional antenna proof may be completed under his direction. The permittee who has coped successfully with Form 301 should have no great difficulty with Form 302, and most of the further FCC Forms he will encounter in the course of year-to-year operation.

The application for program tests is made informally to the FCC in Washington and also to the regional Engineer in Charge. When granted, it is the authorization to inaugurate regular programming, effectively marking the station's public debut. Because this date often is planned with considerable promotion, it is very important that the request be made at least 10 days before the planned date. Specific authority is required before program tests can begin, and the station that arrives at the publicly-announced day without that authority will find itself a bit embarrassed!

An inspection of the installation by a representative of the Field Engineer's office ordinarily is required, with a favorable report to Washington from him, before program test authority will be given. Thus, it is most important to meeting the planned debut date for the installation to pass the inspection in all respects. It may be that the chronic scarcity of FCC personnel will make it impractical for the initial inspection to be made within a reasonable time, in which case the Commission customarily authorizes program tests without it—if the CP application reflects enough experience and expertise to give reasonable assurance that the operation will be in full compliance.

Once Program Test Authority is granted and an FCC inspector has given the installation a clean bill of health, the operation is in business at long last. Operation under program test continues as long as is necessary for the Commission to act upon the license application, which may take months, and the test authority automatically terminates with the issuance of the license. Once that is received, the sailing through the sea of regulations should be pretty smooth until the first Annual Financial Report is due.

Chapter 5
The FCC

The Federal Communications Commission was established in 1934, superseding the Federal Radio Commission, to administer the then brand new Communications Act of the same year. It is charged with the regulation of all interstate and foreign communications by wire and radio, including all U.S. broadcast services.

Being a governmental agency, the FCC's administration is rife with rules, regulations and paperwork to the point where it sometimes seems to the broadcaster that he is overwhelmed by bureaucracy. The fact that much of the federal regulation imposed on broadcasters has resulted from their own past abuses is of little solace to the neophyte, who may feel—with some justification—that he is paying for the sins of others. There is little point, though, in adopting an antagonistic attitude toward the Commission. A philosophy of conscientious compliance all the way down to the least among the welter of rules will serve the broadcaster best in the long run, for the FCC, now with the power to levy fines for infractions, is cognizant of the difference between willful or negligent violation and inadvertent breach. The station that shows its intention to abide by the letter and the spirit of imposed regulation will accumulate a favorable dossier in Washington.

The power to fine is a relatively recent enforcement tool given to the FCC; violation of the laws embodied within the Communications Act always has been punishable by the usual $10,000 fine and/or prison term penalty. Fines are imposed through "broadcast forfeiture orders," which exceeded a total of $39,000 in 1966. This emphasis on compliance is not intended to discourage the exercise of the right to dissent. The broadcaster who sincerely feels that a Commission order, rule, or decision is unjust or improper is given every opportunity to appeal, through the courts if necessary. However, the onerous restriction is best attacked through organization with other broadcasters sharing the same view; there is little constructive point to defiant violation.

The first rule of legal conformity is to <u>know</u> the rules. This Chapter touches upon certain general rules of preliminary interest to the prospective station applicant, and others are related to their specific applications throughout this book, but the official publications should be referred to for comprehensive interpretations. Those regulations pertinent to the broadcast services are included in <u>FCC</u> <u>Rules</u> <u>and</u> <u>Regulations</u>*, Volumes I and III, both of which should be within fingertip reach at every station.

THE ANNUAL FINANCIAL REPORT

Every broadcast station is required to file an annual financial report on or before April 1 of each year. Unlike the CP application (Form 301) and the subsequent license application (Form 302), to which interested members of the public have access both in Washington and via the station's public inspection file, the financial report is held confidential

FCC Form 324 is the appropriate schedule, which should offer no particular difficulty to the broadcaster whose bookkeeping is orderly and accurate. In essence, the required information reflects the station's profit or loss for the fiscal year, with revenue, expenses, capital improvements, and depreciation totals broken down into some detail. The licensee filling out an FCC financial report will find it quite similar to making an income tax return. The information required on Form 324 is combined with that from other stations to develop the general statistical analysis of the industry included in the Commission's public Annual Report.

OWNERSHIP CHANGES AND REPORTS

As was mentioned previously, the FCC endeavors at all times to know exactly who owns and controls a broadcast station. The report filed within 30 days of the CP's issuance will suffice until license renewal time, or until such

---

*Available on a subscription basis, which includes updated amendments as they are adopted. Currently, Vol. I is $2.50; Vol. III is $4.50. Address: Superintendent of Documents, U.S. Government Printing Office, Washington, D.C. 20402.

time as any change in ownership or control is contemplated. In the latter case, <u>FCC</u> <u>approval</u> <u>must</u> <u>be</u> <u>obtained</u> <u>before</u> <u>the</u> <u>change</u> <u>is</u> <u>consummated</u>.

Besides outright sale or change of controlling interest, Paragraph 1.540 (Vol. I) sets forth those instances of technical organization changes that also require Commission approval:

- Incorporation by individuals or partners where there is no substantial change in their respective interests;
- Assignment from a corporation to its individual stockholders without effecting any substantial change in the disposition of their interests;
- Assignment or transfer by which certain stockholders retire and the interest transferred is not a controlling one;
- Corporate reorganization which involves no substantial change in the beneficial ownership of the corporation;
- Assignment or transfer from a corporation to a wholly-owned subsidiary thereof or vice versa, or where there is an assignment from a corporation to a corporation owned or controlled by the assignor stockholders without substantial change in their interests; or
- Assignment of less than a controlling interest in a partnership.

For any of these technical cases, a short form (316) suffices. It also is applicable to involuntary assignment of control, resulting from the death or legal disability of a person directly or indirectly in control of a broadcasting entity.

Outright sale to new interests requires the filing of Form 314, Assignment of License, while Form 315—Transfer of Control—is used for corporate changes short of outright sale. In any change of ownership, application should be made to the Commission at least 45 days before the date of the comtemplated change.

MODIFICATION OF LICENSE

If a broadcast licensee desires to change its name, where no change in ownership is involved; or to change the station location where the transmitter site remains unchanged, a modification of the license is necessary. This is true also of certain studio location changes for FM (and TV) stations, and changes in the operating hours for AM stations. Form 301 is used to apply for such modifications, as it is for major technical changes like an increase in power, modification of an antenna system, and changes in certain items of equipment. However, having developed the necessary Form 301 information for the initial CP application, subsequent filing is greatly simplified because much of the information already is on file with the Commission and need not be repeated.

LICENSE RENEWAL

Station licenses presently are issued for a period of three years. At least 90 days before the expiration date, a renewal application (Form 303) must be filed with the FCC. Through this application the FCC undertakes to determine whether any changes have occurred in the ownership, control, and technical facilities of the station; it asks for a current financial statement; and it examines minutely the past programming and commercial practices.

For this last concern, the composite week (seven weekdays of non-consecutive dates selected by the FCC from the two years prior to renewal time) must be broken down into the various categories according to the performance as logged by the station for that week. This performance will be compared by the Commission to the proposals made in the original application (or in the last renewal period), and serious discrepancies will be questioned.

Proposed programming and commercial practices for the next three years are to be listed, and a re-statement of station policy in their regard is asked.

LOGS

In addition to the principal reports and applications encountered in the normal course of radio operation, also required are daily-operating forms called logs. In general, all broadcast logs are to be maintained by those station personnel who are in possession of the pertinent facts. Further, the technical logs—transmitter and maintenance—must be kept by persons suitably licensed by the FCC. All logs are to be signed by the responsible individual when he begins and again when he concludes, and all become a part of station records, which must be kept on file at least two years.

A program log reflects the minute-by-minute program and commercial content broadcast. It must be kept in sufficient detail that the program type and commercial content of any moment of the broadcast day may be accurately reconstructed (see Chapter 2). Various methods of automatic program logging are acceptable to the FCC, but the old manual method, whereby the announcer or control operator enters the pertinent information on a paper form, is still used in most radio operations today. An individual does not need an FCC license to keep a program log; it can be maintained by any employee with a knowledge of the necessary information.

An operating log—customarily referred to as the transmitter log—is a record of the transmitter's operation. In it are entered the time the "carrier" is turned on and off and modulation (programming) begins and ends, plus the adjustments necessary to maintain proper signal conditions and half-hourly entries of significant electrical parameters. An engineer or technician holding an appropriate FCC license must make the entries in this log; unlicensed personnel may not operate a broadcast transmitter (See Chapter 9). Under certain conditions, automatic logging of transmitter functions is permissible; it is simpler than is automatic program logging and may be considered in planning a new station.

A maintenance log is another technical record in which are entered notations of repairs, maintenance procedures, trouble reports and remedial actions, outside frequency checks, and daily inspection of the transmitting equipment, which is required at least five days a week. The maintenance log is kept only by a station engineer or "contract" engineer (see below) holding a First Class Radiotelephone Operator's License. (See Chapter 18.)

OPERATORS

Thus far, the word "operator" has been broadly used in reference to the proprietorship of a radio station. However, in FCC parlance an operator is a technician qualified to engage in the technical operation of various types of radio (and TV) transmitting equipment—the individual customarily called an "engineer" within the broadcast industry.

Less than 20 years ago, every broadcast transmitter required the direct supervision of a licensed First Class Radiotelephone Operator at all operating times. Because a fairly comprehensive technical understanding is necessary to pass the examination for this license, many announcers who might utilize one are defeated by their fundamental disinterest in things mechanical and electronic.

Because personnel is the largest single expense category in radio operations, small stations in particular sought ways to alleviate what they saw as a form of government-decreed featherbedding. Eventually, over the objections of the technical unions, the Commission capitulated and permitted routine operation of smaller transmitters by holders of the very least license level, that of Restricted Radiotelephone Operator Permit, available without examination or technical knowledge. Under this relaxed rule, one full-time First Class Phone license holder was required on the staff; it was he who was responsible for the maintenance and non-routine transmitter adjustment.

After 15-odd years under this dispensation, the Commission finally concluded that the unions may have had a point after all when they contended that lesser-grade operators would degrade compliance with broadcast operating standards. The number of detected violations rose sharply, and the FCC reverted to somewhat more rigid operator requirements. Presently, AM and FM broadcast transmitters may be routinely operated by anyone holding at least a Third Class Radiotelephone Operator's License with a Broadcast Endorsement, IF the AM transmitter is one of 10 kilowatts or less, or the FM transmitter is 25 kilowatts or less, and IF the AM antenna is non-directional (or, if directional part of the time, only during its non-directional operation). Also qualified is the holder of a Second Class Radiotelephone Operator's License, which in broadcasting is a relatively uncommon, intermediate-level certificate. (Second phone licenses are required for transmitter maintenance in other communication fields.)

It now is common practice for those announcers who also must be transmitter operators to be schooled—usually by the station chief engineer, if they haven't attended a trade school for the purpose—in the regulations and technical knowledge necessary to pass the Third Class examination, including the special element necessary to obtain the requisite broadcast endorsement. Examinations are given periodically in various locations by the FCC; a test grade of 75% is necessary to earn the license.

Many stations today are maintained on a contract basis, although there are obvious drawbacks. The local First Phone engineer almost certainly is employed elsewhere—perhaps by a competing station—and his availability in a crisis may be subject to previous and higher-priority commitments. In many cases, he may be the only such man in a small community and subject to transfer on short notice; and he certainly can't be on top of impending failure to the extent that the full-time staff engineer is.

Since an established station that has settled into a comfortable post-construction routine does not ordinarily require an employee's full time for engineering duties, there is nothing wrong in a chief engineer's doubling in brass, taking on other duties. It is the general rule for him to do so in smaller operations. This is sanctioned by the FCC in these words: "... operator may be given other duties, provided, however, that such duties shall in nowise interfere with the proper operation of the transmitter" (FCC emphasis).

It is important to realize that this requirement applies to all operators, including Third-Class-licensed announcers. The sometimes hectic pace of modern radio requires so much of the man on the air—manipulating controls, selecting copy and records, keeping program logs, and even answering the phone —that he may feel justified in neglecting the half-hourly entries in the transmitter (operating) log until some convenient but tardy moment. The FCC inspector will not condone such neglect; log entries are the official record of requisite transmitter supervision. However, the frantic announcer caught in tardy log entries may be able to make a pretty good argument to the effect that "other duties" have interfered with the proper discharge of his operator's responsibilities. A bit of preliminary planning on management's part will wisely avoid the genuine overburdening of the announcer-operator.

The United States is practically the last remaining country in the world to require attended broadcast transmitter operation. Unattended, automatically-corrected-and-logged transmitter operation is standard elsewhere, as it is for many nonbroadcast services in this country. Modern broadcast transmitters are highly stable and reliable, being evolutionary descendants of the world's pioneer broadcasting installations. Perhaps the American technical unions have been effective in delaying official sanction of unattended operatic..., but its eventual adoption seems inevitable.

THE PUBLIC INSPECTION FILE

In keeping with the Commission's policy of enabling public inspection of public-interest enterprises, most of the forms and correspondence submitted to the FCC by applicants, permittees, and licensees are available to members of the public at its Washington offices. However, each station is required to maintain a similar open file at its main studio location, as is stipulated in Paragraph 1.526, Vol. I. Included are all applications that require public notice, as well as all exhibits, documents, and letters tendered with them or in response to FCC queries. Copies of Initial and Final Decisions in hearing cases, Ownership Reports, such contracts as are required to be submitted to the FCC (except network contracts), and virtually all other official interchanges with the Commission are to be available in the file. Excepted are the Annual Financial Reports, which are considered to be tendered in confidence. As part of the Public Inspection File, certain records pertaining to political broadcasts also must be available to the public.

POLITICAL BROADCASTS

In recent years, charges and counter-charges of political favoritism and discrimination in broadcasting have forced the Commission to attempt a definitive guide for this specialized area of programming.

A radio station is not required to air any broadcasts by or on behalf of political candidates, but if it does, then it must make available similar facilities for all legally qualified candidates for any specific office. The rates charged must be equitable; if one candidate is allowed free time (which is permissible), then all must be accorded comparable free time. Further, political candidates may not be charged time rates that exceed those charged to commercial advertisers for similar quantities and classes of time (in the past, some stations have received premium rates for political broadcasts). The definition of a "legally qualified" candidate appears in the political broadcast rules, Paragraph 73.120, Vol. III.

In the event of question of qualification, the burden of proof of legality rests with the candidate.

A specific exception to the general control a broadcaster exercises over his programming content is made for political candidates; he is not permitted to review, approve, or censor a political broadcast in any manner! The obvious intent of this prohibition is to avoid suppression of political views contrary to those of the broadcaster, in keeping with the general admonition to shun political discrimination in any manner.

The actual broadcasts by political candidates fall under the general FCC Sponsorship Identification Rules, which are discussed, generally, later in this Chapter. Announcements are required at the beginning and at the end of a political program or a program related to public controversial issues— one of five minutes or less needs but one such announcement —disclosing the source of talent, scripts, transcriptions, or other services, if they were offered as inducements to the station to carry it. Further, as is specifically stated in Paragraph 73.119, Vol. I:

"In the case of any program, other than a program advertising commercial products or services, which is sponsored, paid for, furnished, either in whole or in part, or for which material or services...are furnished by a corporation, committee, association, or other unincorporated group, the announcement required by this section shall disclose the name of such corporation, committee, association, or other unincorporated group. In each such case the station shall require that a list of the chief executive officers or members of the executive committee or of the board of directors of the corporation, committee, association or unincorporated group shall be made available for public inspection at the studios or general offices..."

Thus the venerable tag announcement that "this was a paid political broadcast" does not of itself fill the sponsorship identification rule.

The FCC regulation quoted above specifies certain information that must be available in the Public Inspection File at the station. Other records pertaining to political broadcasts also must be made publicly available. They include all requests for time made by, or on behalf of, qualified candidates for any public office, accompanied by information showing the station's disposition of such requests. Charges imposed for those granted are to be shown, and scripts, transcripts, or actual recordings of all political broadcasts are a vital part of station files, too.

EDITORIALS AND THE FAIRNESS DOCTRINE

Once strictly forbidden, station editorializing is now not only permitted but encouraged by the Commission. The broadcaster who chooses to exercise this privilege needs to familiarize himself with the broad guidelines of the FCC's "Fairness Doctrine," which in essence requires a broadcaster to present the various sides of controversial matters in a reasonable balance. Thus, if an editorial viewpoint is expressed, reasonable time (not equal time, as is the case for political programs) must be made available—free, if necessary—to qualified proponents of opposing views. In fact, it is not enough to allow rebuttal time passively; it is necessary for the broadcaster to actively seek out those qualified opponents.

When the path of editorializing approaches election campaign time, a recent ruling requires that candidates to be discussed editorially within 72 hours of an election must be notified in advance and given a timely opportunity to respond. This requirement may be broadened on occasion to include critical programs other than those that are strictly editorial, to the extend of giving advance notice to any individual to be subjected to personal attack on the air, without regard as to political campaigns.

To clarify the somewhat cloudy issues involved in the Fairness Doctrine, the Commission has distributed reprints of the pertinent part of the Federal Register of July 25, 1964, in a pamphlet titled, "Applicability of the Fairness Doctrine in the Handling of Controversial Issues of Public Importance." However, the Fairness Doctrine, like the political broadcast rules, is subject to continuing fresh interpretations; the editorializing licensee must keep abreast of the latest on the subject from Washington.

The licensee contemplating a step into editorializing, once armed with a knowledge of the Fairness Doctrine, should be prepared to devote the time and research necessary to the expression of a reasoned and well-documented statement of his position. Certainly a responsible stance by a public medium on controversial issues is an asset to any community, if only because it forces others to think a matter through in order to justify an opposing viewpoint. The long-range effect must be a better-informed public. However, hasty and ill-formed broadcast opinions can only reflect unfavorably on the station.

Radio editorials need not be regularly scheduled. Without the press of regular airing, they can be dispensed with until a worthy issue arises and preparation time is available. In this respect, as a relatively new editorial outlet radio has an edge on the traditional newspaper page, which must be filled with something by press deadline for every issue. On the other hand, the newspaper is not bound by any fairness regulation.

Most recently, FCC considerations of fairness have invaded the domain of commercial matter. Specifically, the Commission has ruled that those stations carrying advertising for cigarettes (which only recently have become controversial, although we've all strongly suspected since childhood that their regular use is injurious to health) must make time available for expression by anti-cigarette interests. At the moment, it has firmly restricted this invasion of the commercial domain by the Fairness Doctrine specifically to cigarettes, but many broadcasters are apprehensive that the precedent may entitle the W.C.T.U., or auto-safety critic Nader, or nearly anyone in opposition to some commercial product to their "reasonable" time—free!

SPONSORSHIP IDENTIFICATION

In addition to the rule quoted in the above section on political sponsorship, general identification requirements are that no paid (or otherwise substantially compensated) commercial inducement be aired without an on-air identification of the underlying interest. Thus a commercial product—or its manufacturer—is to be identified by name; a program sponsor is to be revealed as such; and product mentions in return for substantial favors must be so identified.

This rules out the "teaser" ad, which usually takes the form of a very short announcement hinting at a forthcoming product or commercial event without specifically naming it, hoping to build suspense and curiosity among the audience. Such teasers, when paid as commercials or included as an inducement when selling commercials to be used subsequently, are prohibited. So, too, is "payola" or "plugola," where the broadcaster or his employee receives sub-rosa cash or consideration in return for mentioning a record or other product prominently on the air. Again, the Commission believes that the public interest is best served when it knows who is paying for the enticements propagated along the airwaves.

A detailed exposition of sponsorship identification rules is made by the FCC's Public Notice pamphlet titled "Applicability of Sponsorship Identification Rules," which bears the FCC number 63-409. It, too, pre-dates subsequent additional interpretations. For instance, certain stations recently have undertaken the broadcasting of paid classified ads for individual members of the public (many stations have provided similar service through "swap shop" and "trading post" programs on a no-charge basis). They have sought permission to eliminate the broadcast identification of the sponsoring individuals on the basis that it serves no useful purpose. In some cases, the Commission has agreed and waived the identification requirements, with the condition that:

"The licensee shall maintain a list showing the name, address, and (where available) telephone number of each advertiser and attach it to the program log for each day's operation; and the licensee shall make this list available to members of the public with a legitimate interest in the information therein contained."

OFFICIAL INSPECTION

The initial pre-license inspection by an FCC field representative is only the first—and the most predictable. The regulations state that a radio station is to be available for inspection "at any reasonable hour." Strictly interpreted, any reasonable hour is any time that the station is on the air; 24-hour operations have had visits by FCC inspectors at hours such as 2 AM. However, inspection today includes perusal of the Public Inspection and Political Files and past program logs, all of which often are kept within offices that are locked outside of normal business hours. Further, FCC field men don't enjoy working a 24-hour day any more than anyone else does, and unless specific violations are suspected during the wee small hours, official visits are most likely during usual office hours. Nevertheless, a well-run radio station will be kept shipshape at all times.

In addition to a check of the Public Inspection and Political Files, an FCC inspection includes a careful examination of the technical operation for compliance in all respects and ascertainment that logging procedures are up-to-date. Also, the following items are to be available to the inspector:

- Maintenance logs;
- Last proof of equipment performance;
- For AM, the last antenna resistance measurement; and
- For directional AM stations, the last antenna proof.

The unexpected arrival of an FCC representative always creates some consternation among the station staff present, because the quantity of regulations is so great that a determined and tenacious inspector probably can find some small infraction in the best of stations. Fortunately, broadcast operations represent a numerically small percentage of the FCC's total inspection domain, and most of them are operated by individuals who are better informed and more conscientious about the rules and regulations than are many nonbroadcast licensees. For those reasons (presumably), broadcast inspection is relatively infrequent; those required for license application and periodic renewal may be all that a station experiences—unless the Commission has received complaints of technical violations from the public or its own monitoring stations.

THE EMERGENCY BROADCASTING SYSTEM

On millions of radio receivers the familiar encircled triangle symbol of Civil Defense appears at 640 kHz and 1240 kHz. They are so marked because the old Conelrad system of maintaining broadcast contact with the public during national emergencies utilized the indicated frequencies exclusively, in a complicated scheme of sequential switching of active transmitters. The objective was to render broadcasting stations useless as homing beacons for enemy aircraft. Fortunately, Conelrad never had to be employed for its purpose, and with the sophistication of warfare techniques and the advent of missiles, its awkward complexity was deemed no longer necessary. The simplified successor to Conelrad is the Emergency Broadcast System (EBS).

Under the EBS, in the event of enemy attack (or certain other national emergencies), participating radio stations continue on the air, unidentified. The principal distinction from the old Conelrad system lies in the continued operation by EBS stations on their regular frequencies instead of shifting to 640 kHz or 1240 kHz—a considerable simplification. Stations not participating in the EBS are to leave the air upon receipt of an alerting message, which is disseminated by certain "key" EBS stations upon authorization by appropriate government officials.

All stations are required to monitor continuously their respective key EBS stations during every operating hour. While it is permissible to employ "human watch" aural monitoring, it's highly impractical. No employee can devote uninterrupted attention to a radio on the slight chance of a genuine EBS alert. The practical solution lies in automatic receivers that are silent until the key station initiates the technical sequence preceding an official alerting message. Once the alert is sent, the automatic receiver sounds an alarm, or becomes audible, or in some suitable manner announces initiation of the alert. Such a receiver is practically mandatory equipment in every station.

The two major news wire service also are geared to send EBS alerts. A given sequence of teletype bells is intended to sound the alarm, which may be effective in those large stations where news personnel are in more or less constant newprinter attendance. However, small stations ordinarily isolate their news machines in some remote corner (to remove the noise as far as possible from open microphones), where they operate unattended except for periodic clearing of accumulated material. Under these conditions the signal bell is inaudible, rendering the news wire alerts useless for timely attack warnings. Attachments designed to respond to the particular EBS alert bell sequence and trigger any suitable auxiliary alarm circuit are available, but as yet they are neither supplied by the news services or required by the Commission. A station desiring an effective EBS alarm facility for its news teletype will have to foot the expense.

Tests of the EBS alerting systems are made weekly, with all stations responsible for logging receipt of those from key stations and wire services in their transmitter (operating) logs, and in specific cases they are required to make periodic reports of those EBS tests received to an appropriate Civil Defense office. These weekly tests serve as a check on any automatic alarm equipment and the staff's alertness to such alarms. Further, every station is required to conduct its own EBS test procedure once weekly.

Active participation in the Emergency Broadcast System is not mandatory, although it is likely that the broadcaster is a single-station market will be urged to serve as an EBS outlet for his community. To be eligible for participation, a station must apply for a National Defense Emergency Authorization (NDEA), which amounts to a license to operate within the EBS requirements during an alert. The qualifying requirements are not burdensome. The participating station is expected to conduct radiological monitoring (checking levels of radioactivity) with equipment and staff training supplied by the Office of Civil Defense. The OCD also may make available emergency power generators and austere fallout protection facilities sufficient for a minimal operating staff during active EBS operations.

OPERATING HOURS

All commercial radio stations are required to maintain regular operating schedules consisting of at least two thirds of the authorized hours between 6:00 AM and 6:00 PM, local standard time, and two thirds of those authorized between 6:00 PM and midnight, also local standard time. (Daytime stations are exempted from the post-6:00 PM requirement.) There is but one exception to the requisite minimum operating hours: they do not apply to Sundays, although commercial stations that are silent on Sundays are extremely rare. Notice that holidays falling within the week are not excepted; the minimum schedule must be maintained, although some stations do sign on an hour or two later than their regular schedule on certain major holidays.

Incidentally, it's not permissible to discontinue a station's operation without Commission approval. Even in cases of impending bankruptcy, the FCC endeavors to keep an established operation in service until alleviating measures (refinancing, sale, etc.) can be attempted.

Chapter 6
Land and Building Requirements

Nowhere is the long-range view more beneficial than in the planning of a station's physical facilities. A neatly wrapped package efficiently using every square foot of space for the station's initial needs is <u>not</u> enough; it soon will become inadequate, crowded, and operationally makeshift.

In general, it is more economical in the long run to plan for future expansion in the initial construction. It's cheaper to add an extra 100 square feet of control room or transmitter room space during the blueprint stage than to build it on later as an afterthought, and it minimizes disruption of the functioning operation when the time for growth arrives.

Of course there must be a limit to built-in growth room, because every square foot of commercial floor space represents investment and overhead (even in heat and air conditioning), and holding initial construction costs to reasonable values is of fundamental importance to most applicants. Compromise is the word, then. A balance should be sought between lavish, visionary dreams and austere, immediate-need limitations; a balance that may accommodate foreseeable technical, programming, and staff growth for five years or so with a minimum of inconvenience and expense.

THE SITE

The instrument that makes a public address system into a radio station is the transmitter, with its associated antenna. The transmitter/antenna site must serve the technical requirements with regard to geographical location, elevation, soil conductivity, air traffic patterns, and convenience of access and utilities.

Unfortunately, the optimum requirements for AM and FM

antenna locations are conflicting in some fundamental aspects. FM propagation is best effected from hilltop elevations, while AM sites preferably are selected for soil conditions more commonly found at lower levels. For substantial economic reasons it is desirable to operate an AM-FM outlet via a common tower and transmitter plant, which obviously requires some compromise. The new FM-only station probably won't be concerned with the subsequent addition of AM (although a few AM-FM outlets did start with FM only), but the new AM installations almost surely will add FM at such time as additional allocations and station finances make it possible to do so. Nevertheless, the new AM builder will select the best site available for that medium, unless expansion to FM within two or three years is an unusually firm prospect, in which case some degree of site compromise may be in order at the outset.

GROUND SYSTEM

A vital component of an AM radiating system that is never seen once the installation is completed is the ground system, which is composed of a large number of wires buried radially from the tower base. The longer wires are at least as long as the tower is high, and they may approach half of the electrical wavelength.* While it may be permissible to shorten some of the wires a few feet if property boundaries so dictate, it is preferable to have enough clear land to install an unobstructed ground system.

The ground system is at least as important to an AM station as is the tower; for a given power and frequency, ground conductivity is the principal determining factor in signal strength. It is for this reason that several miles of costly copper wire are systematically buried a few inches deep in soil of the highest conductivity available. Because moisture content bears heavily on conductivity, AM transmitter sites usually are found in valleys and lowlands, where natural drainage maintains the moisture consistently higher than that of hilltop soil. Some installations tolerate the inconvenience of swamps, bogs, or river islands purely for the excellent ground conditions they afford. In very hilly terrain some

---

*Approximate electrical wavelength in feet can be obtained by dividing 984,000 by the frequency in kHz. For 1000 kHz, one wavelength is about 984 feet.

compromise may be necessary to avoid a shadow effect caused by peaks intervening between the site and the market to be served, although shadowing is a much smaller problem with AM than it is with FM (and TV).

In an earlier era, many small radio stations erected towers on downtown buildings and used counterpoises—substitute ground systems, of sorts. Modern practice avoids the "downtown" approach to AM sites because adequate radiation efficiency atop a building is difficult to achieve, possibly delivering a weaker signal to the desired area than would a comparable rural installation where a proper ground system could be installed. There also is the matter of the "blanket" area, which is that area near the antenna where the signal is so strong that it interferes excessively with normal reception of other stations. Arbitrarily defined as that area where the signal strength is one volt per meter (the actual radio voltage induced in a receiving wire one meter long) or more, the circular blanket area contour may have a radius of nearly 0.2 mile for a kilowatt station. If that blanket area incloses more than one percent of the population residing within the 0.25 millivolt (milli = 1/1000) the site is unsatisfactory, except for the case where the total population within the blanket area is less than 300. The blanket area limitation alone requires most AM transmitters to be located beyond their concentrated population centers, as do the open-land requirements for efficient ground systems.

Paragraph 73.188, Volume I, also indicates the desirability —and often the necessity—of conducting field intensity surveys to determine the AM signal characteristics of potential sites, particularly for stations of higher powers. Such surveys must be made by engineers equipped and qualified to make the measurements.

Site considerations for FM are in some ways less demanding. Because ground-system requirements are minimal, an in-town antenna location may be feasible and preferable if it affords the highest available elevation relative to the principal population. Except for nulls, which may occur at locations very close to the tower, shadow effects caused by buildings will be minimized and the maximum signal strength will be centered in the desired area. A simple mast supporting the antenna on a downtown building may serve well, particularly for Class A FM stations which must cover a single community

Fig. 6-1. A typical guyed, uniform cross-section tower, part of a multi-tower directional AM installation. (Photo courtesy of **RCA**)

with relatively low power. Class B or C stations may achieve their intended greater-area coverage more readily from an out-of-town promontory, even though <u>maximum</u> signal strength falls short of the principal market.

Without the need for an AM-type radial ground system, land requirements for an FM tower are a little less imposing. Assuming a conventional triangular guyed tower of uniform cross section, for which the outermost guy anchors are spaced at 80% of the tower's height from the base (see Fig. 6-1), the minimum rectangular land area necessary to accommodate the guy anchors has dimensions of 120% X 139% of the tower's height.* This minimal requirement does not, however, permit orientation of the tower and guy anchors to the best advantage, while a plot that is 139% of the height in both dimensions gives complete freedom as to guy placement. Thus, a 300-foot tower requires a plot 418 x 418 feet for optimum land utilization, or a circle 480 feet in diameter. In contrast, the ground system for a 300-foot AM tower would encompass a circle of at least 600 feet.

An alternative approach, often necessary in a city where the above dimensions may represent more than a square block, is the self-supporting tower (see Fig. 6-2). Guyless, wide at the base and tapering toward the top, the self-supporting tower has grown increasingly unpopular for new construction because of its considerably higher cost, which is justified only for those major FM or TV installations where space is at a premium.

In addition to the tower, the site also must accommodate a building that is adequate for housing at least the transmitter equipment. If the station is to employ remote control, permitting unattended transmitter operation, the building needs only to protect the equipment from weather and temperature extremes and provide ample maintenance room. In this case, it is preferable to locate the building very close to the tower's base, which then does not increase land requirements. The cost and maintenance of transmission lines, tower lighting circuits, and metering facilities is reduced materially when the building is adjacent to the tower, and since it will be unattended most of the time, certain risks inherent to the tower's close proximity are of no great concern.

Many stations, though, operate from a single combined plant that houses studios and offices in addition to the transmitter. While some have been built so close to their associated towers that it is possible to reach through the windows and practically touch them, there are three potential hazards that must be weighed—physical failure of the tower, falling ice, and lightning danger. Admittedly it is rare for a broadcasting tower to fall, and it is a technical calamity when wind, aircraft, negligent maintenance, or even sabotage causes one to do so. However, it is a catastrophe far worse for a toppling tower to maim or kill personnel, and even the

---

*Based on Tables prepared by the Ft. Worth Tower Co., Inc., P.O. Box 8597, Ft. Worth, Texas 76112.

Fig. 6-2. Guyless, self-supporting tower typical of those used for in-city TV or FM transmitter sites. (Photo by permission of WTVR)

slight risk is worthy of avoidance if at all possible. For this reason, a combined-plant building should be located at least a tower's height from its base. The same holds true, of course, for a transmitter-only building in directional AM stations where engineers will be on duty for considerable times.

Optimum building locations for FM and AM also conflict in other ways. A building some distance from its associated tower is no great problem with AM; transmission lines to transfer energy from the transmitter to the antenna are relatively inexpensive (for modest station power), and line losses at AM frequencies are small. For FM, however, suitable transmission line may come as high as $10 a foot and introduce enough loss to reduce overall efficiency considerably, added as it is to the necessary line running the height of the tower before the energy is delivered to the antenna (the tower is not an active element of the FM radiation system; it merely supports the antenna proper at the desired elevation). Technically speaking, then, the FM transmitter should be close to its associated tower.

In a plant with studios at the transmitter site, it may be sensible to locate the main building apart from the tower and house the FM transmitter in its own minimal building near the base. The transmission line investment saved and efficiency gained may offset the cost of the small building and the inconvenience of operating the transmitter by remote control for just a few hundred feet. This approach has several advantages over a conventional remote control installation with in-town studios feeding an out-of-town transmitter. First is the economic advantage of maintaining a single property location; second is the economic and technical freedom from relatively long telephone lines between studios and transmitter for program and remote control functions; and another is the proximity of station personnel to the actual "remote" transmitter so that attention is but two minutes away when it fails. In the case of an AM-FM installation, the AM transmitter well could be housed in the main building, with its attendant advantages, and the FM unit located near the tower.

Alternatively, a split studio-transmitter operation that is both AM and FM might best have the FM transmitter at the downtown studios and the AM remotely controlled at its rural location, in which case the AM transmitter house may be adjacent to the tower. The possible combinations are numerous; the best depends upon individual circumstances.

UTILITIES

In addition to matters of soil conductivity and moisture, elevation, and available land area, there are other factors to consider in site selection. Ready availability of utilities, for instance, will assure the necessary power and telephone line facilities. Sometimes an otherwise ideal site requires an extension of these utilities beyond their present limits, a situation which is handled differently by various utility companies. The station applicant may have to tender a substantial deposit to be forfeited in the event that anticipated use fails to justify the costs of extension, or that he simply can't meet his bills. (Such deposits usually are recoverable after one year of satisfactory patronage, and the applicant making one should insist that it draw interest in the interim. It may be, however, that just a signature on a power-usage contract, for example, will suffice. If an applicant is fortunate enough to make this arrangement with both principal utilities for a given site, he is fortunate indeed.

ACCESS

Another important consideration in selecting a site is one that often is overlooked, it seems: Convenient access. Even an unattended plant requires a daily inspection regardless of weather conditions, and a site with difficult access should be tolerated only when there is absolutely no otherwise suitable alternative. For a combined studio-transmitter plant, ready access is a necessity. There will be many visitors on both business and pleasure: staff personnel must make numerous daily trips, and lady employees in particular should not be expected to negotiate tortuous unpaved paths on their way to work.

Convenience of access for the general public suggests proximity to town. A mile or two is about as far as non-employees should be expected to go beyond the outskirts of the residential area—and that preferably by a main highway. Of course, a heavily traveled highway offers a disadvantage, too. Many small station studios insulate well against most rural noises but fail miserably when speeding trucks roll past on a highway not 50 feet distant. If at all possible, studios should be set well back from—but convenient to—a passing highway.

A vital requirement of the studio-transmitter plant, or the directional AM transmitter plant, is water. Ordinarily, commercial water and sewer services do not extend to rural transmitter locations, which means that either a reliable well be drilled, or that copious quantities of water be hauled in. Toilet and washroom facilities, served by a septic tank, and perhaps water-cooled air conditioning, require many gallons daily. These can be supplied by any adequate well without regard for its purity; if necessary, bottled drinking water can be brought in.

OTHER CONSIDERATIONS

Potential air hazards will be carefully checked by the FCC. Distance of the site from the nearest airport and tower protrusion into local landing patterns may rule out an otherwise suitable site. Paragraph 17.15, Volume I, outlines the restrictions.

The considerable open area surrounding a broadcast tower needs some attention. It should not be abandoned to uncontrolled weed and brush growth, especially if it is an AM installation. Such excessive growth interferes to an extent with proper operation of the antenna system, since it is part of the dielectric path between antenna and ground and therefore introduces some unnecessary loss. The land can be kept in grass or pasture and grazed; it can be sowed and harvested for hay; or put to almost any other similar use where planting and harvesting machinery will not penetrate the soil and disrupt the ground system. While these precautions are less applicable to FM- only installations, it still is good housekeeping to keep the antenna field manicured.

REMOTE CONTROL

As it is used here, remote control refers to the operation of a broadcast transmitter without direct personal supervision. The required supervision is effected through instruments that remotely indicate and control the transmitter's operation, usually located in the studio control room and monitored by the announcer - operator on duty. All stations with studios separate from the transmitter site must utilize remote control in the absence of an operator at the transmitter proper. Therefore, the applicant for any station that is to use separate locations must—as a simple matter of economics—plan for remote control facilities.

An FM or non-directional AM station may apply for remote control authorization as part of the license application, but an AM directional operation must prove that the antenna system is properly adjusted and stable. The Commission may not be satisfied as to stability until the new station has been in operation for some time, suggesting that the transmitter building for such a station should be designed to accommodate an operating staff for the first year of operation.

It also is important to note that directional operation by remote control does not relieve the requirement that only First Class Phone operators be in attendance during directional hours. Further, all antenna readings (currents and phase relationships) normally monitored by remote control must be logged at the transmitter at least once daily—seven days a week—within two hours after directional operation begins. Thus, in a split operation that goes directional at sunset, a First Phone man must be on duty at the studio end of the remote control equipment from sunset to sign-off and another must check the readings at the transmitter within two hours following sunset every day. It is virtually certain that the demands placed on a directional operation will be relaxed somewhat in the future. Pending this, the AM station going directional should plan accommodations in its transmitter building for an operating staff and its total plant for the ready adoption of remote control facilities, even though they may not be economically advantageous at the outset.

THE BUILDING(S)

The simplest building, of course, is a transmitter house for unattended operation. It must protect the transmitter from the weather, unauthorized tampering and vandalism, and it must accommodate the associated audio and monitoring equipment and provide maintenance access. It should be designed for expansion to FM, or to higher AM power, or for the inclusion of a studio-transmitter program link. The transmitter building may be of any conventional construction, unless it falls under zoning restrictions with which it must comply. It must be capable of supporting the equipment's weight and reasonably fireproof. Frame, cinder block, and quonset - hut buildings are commonly used for transmitter houses. See Fig. 6-3.

The heating and ventilation needs of an unattended transmitter often are overlooked; yet the lack of direct supervision does not alter or obviate the need for certain environmental control to achieve the maximum reliability so vital to uninterrupted operation. Manufacturers' recommendations for maximum ambient temperatures (for transmitters) range from about 113 to 122 degrees Fahrenheit (at sea level); the minimum temperature may be as high as +41 degrees if mercury-vapor rectifiers are used. Modern equipment using solid-state rectifiers may withstand a few degrees below zero, but temperature extremes also adversely affect other circuit components, thereby disturbing frequency stability, power output, and other functions.

Heat is the greatest single enemy of electronic equipment, as some have learned the hard way! In one small transmitter room (part of a combined operation) where the ceiling was about 18 inches above the transmitter's top, summertime temperatures of 135 degrees occurred at head level—despite an open window and a large open door. The subsequent failure of several components in the transmitter and its associated equipment, which happened in rapid succession, was blamed—at least in part—on the excessive heat resulting from poor ventilation.

A one-kilowatt AM transmitter converts about three kilowatts of its electrical consumption into heat, which amounts to a round-figure value of 10,000 BTU, and an FM transmitter produces only a little less. In a small building, particularly one with a low ceiling, the hot air tends to accumulate about the equipment unless excellent circulation and exhaust-

Fig. 6-3. A small building is all that's necessary for an unattended transmitter. (Photo by permission of WFMV)

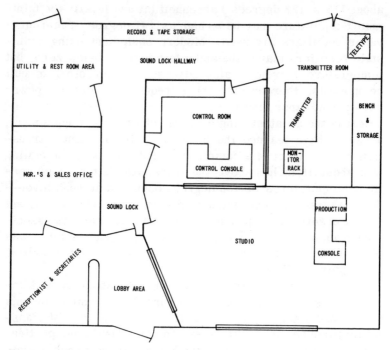

Fig. 6-4. A studio 12 by 15 or 18 feet will handle most of the needs of a small station, if a second microphone position (in addition to the board operator's) is available in the control room. (Not to scale)

ing are provided. Suitable filtered air-intake vents located near floor level, coupled with a high plenum-chamber-like ceiling and husky thermostatically-controlled fans exhausting through the roof or upper walls are necessary for adequate heat removal in a small transmitter house.

The problem of excessive heat notwithstanding, auxiliary heating is required in most climates. This is particularly true if mercury-vapor tubes are used and wintertime lows less than 40 degrees or so are commonplace. Provided that the transmitter house is built with insulation techniques appropriate for a residence, thermostatically-operated electric heaters of a few kilowatts are adequate in many areas to hold overnight temperatures within the designated limits. Power costs for modest electric heat usually are a small part of the total for transmitter operation. In many climates there are long periods of the year when the heaters will operate at night and the exhaust fans for most of the operating day, but in a very small building there seems no economical way to store the day's surplus heat to offset the night's deficiency.

Typical modern transmitters in the kilowatt range occupy about eight square feet of floor space, which should be tripled to allow plenty of maintenance access room. Even the smallest transmitter installation needs one standard 19-inch equipment rack, taking another 10 feet or so including access space. A workbench with tools and test equipment may consume another 12 feet, while some clear wall space is necessary for power distribution, telephone line termination, tower light monitoring, and assorted needs. So in light of these minimal requirements, the building for an unattended transmitter in the least elaborate installation cannot reasonably be smaller than 8 X 10 feet—preferably with a 12-foot ceiling or roof height—and this size allows virtually no satisfactory room for future growth. Of course, a larger building incurs greater construction expense, and greater heating costs, unless it can be partitioned so that the unused area remains unheated until additional equipment is added. The final decision as to size has to be made on the basis of the actual equipment to be used and the broadcaster's projection of future needs.

An unattended building can be located very close to the base of the tower and enclosed within the required fence surrounding it. If the structure is of metal, metal frame, or reinforced concrete, all metal components must be thoroughly and permanently bonded to the station ground system.

THE STUDIOS

Among the fundamental considerations in the planning of a combined operation is the FCC requirement that the "transmitter shall be readily accessible and clearly visible to the operator at his normal operating position." For most installations, this means that the control room is to be located adjacent to the transmitter room, with a window providing a view of the strategically located transmitter and its associated antenna current, frequency, and modulation meters, since they give as much vital information as does the transmitter proper.

In the single-transmitter station (AM or FM only) this requirement is met simply. It can become more difficult when two transmitters must be observed, particularly when initial planning failed to include the subsequent addition of another

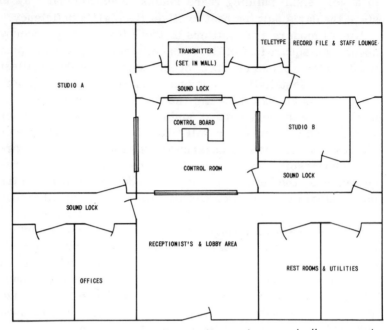

Fig. 6-5. The station contemplating substantial news and talk programming will find two studios highly useful. (Not to scale)

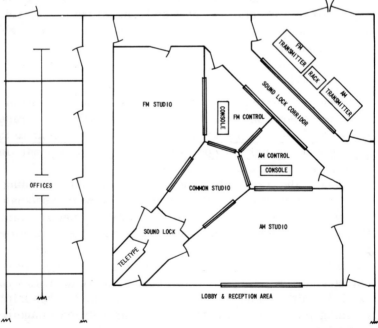

Fig. 6-6. This unusual AM-FM arrangement incorporates irregularly-shaped studios. (Not to scale)

transmitter. There reputedly have been past instances where a station had to seek remote control authorization for a transmitter that was in the same building with the studios.

Figs. 6-4 through 6-8 suggest several possible floor plans. In some, the transmitter view is to the rear of the operator as he normally sits; the acceptability of this arrangement is dependent upon the Commission's interpretation of "normal" operating position. Perhaps the customary use of a swivel chair in the operating position makes a view to the rear satisfactory. For a more complex station with two complete control rooms, either of which may feed either or both of two transmitters and either of which may be used by a sole operator, the regulations indicate that transmitter supervision must be provided for both. While it is relatively easy to duplicate the important meters within the building and to provide access to the transmitter room, it still appears that—strictly speaking—remote control authorization may be required for at least one control position, if it lacks an unobstructed view of the transmitter(s).

The requirements are slightly less difficult for a separate operation utilizing unattended transmitters; the studio terminal of the remote control equipment, with its metering and adjustment facilities, is to be visible and accessible to the operator. Being much smaller and quieter than a transmitter, the remote control terminal usually is mounted in a rack in the control room. If there are two transmitters, both must be monitorable at the operator's position. Some remote control units are sufficiently flexible to accommodate two complete transmitters and thereby serve in a dual capacity. For two control rooms it is possible to duplicate the studio end of the remote control equipment. In any case, the separate studio-transmitter operation requires only enough control room space for the remote control terminals, permitting greater flexibility in studio planning than does the combined operation with its requirement of transmitter visibility.

In addition to overall space requirements and studio configuration, the station applicant should recognize those peculiar studio requirements that are beyond the experience of local contractors in smaller towns. Most of them have negligible experience in building structures with special acoustic needs. Acoustic treatment for intra-studio requirements is susceptible to some modification, if necessary, after the building is completed; this is less true of those problems of inter-studio sound transmission or leakage, which are closely related to internal construction.

Masonry construction—poured concrete floors and cinderblock partition walls—provides fundamentally satisfactory isolation for speech levels. Most leakage problems in such construction can be traced to openings like doors, windows, ventilation ducts, and conduit passages. In buildings of frame construction there are two sound leakage problems: vibration transmission, and wall transmission. The worst offender in vibration transmission is the common floor joist, which carries the sound of footsteps and other vibrations from one floor area to an adjacent one. Additional support piers under floor centers and divided joist techniques that eliminate the sharing of any joist by two rooms helps to reduce the transmission of those vibrations.

The popular frame-building wall construction—wallboard sheets nailed to 2 X 4 studding—is fairly transparent to sound. Short of building two separate walls, probably the most effective improvement is the use of separate studs for the two sides, so spaced that the wallboard on one side does not contact the studs supporting the opposite side. This method reduces the mechanical coupling between the two sides, which solves part of the problem.

Additionally, the diaphragm action of a large area of wallboard under impinging sound is coupled by the captive air within the wall to the opposite panel, causing it to vibrate similarly, if weakly. Sound thus transmitted can be reduced by "damping" the walls internally with curtains of thick rock wool or glass-fiber fabric, which should hang freely between the two rows of studding. This material absorbs some sound directly, but it also provides an acoustic "resistance" to minimize the transmission abilities of the captive air. Frame construction walls employing separate studding and absorbent curtains are much more opaque to sound than those of conventional design.

A very common source of sound leakage is found in studio doors. The average local contractor thinks of studio doors in terms of the ordinary home-type interior "flush" door; it has been my surprising experience to have worked in four widely assorted stations that used such doors—complete with conventional latches—for studios and control rooms!

The station already "stuck" with such doors can help matters somewhat by applying felt weatherstrip around the stops and floor-sweeps on the doors' lower edges to seal against the floor. Sometimes covering one or both sides of the doors with acoustic tile reduces sound transmission through them. A better approach is to use exterior residential doors, close-fitting to felt-stripped or rubber-stripped frames, with some means of sealing against the floor. All studio doors should contain small peep windows (to avoid collision between those approaching simultaneously from each side), push panels or plain pull handles, and hydraulic closers to supplant latches. Acoustic doors, especially designed for studio applications, are available; for instance, those made by the Overly Manufacturing Company (Greensburg, Penna. 15602).

The sound lock—an arrangement of two doors separated by a small illuminated vestibule—is the classic and best design, and of course the most expensive. The theory is that two substantial doors will seal out sound very effectively, and that only one at a time is open during an entry or exit, thereby minimizing the momentary admission of extraneous noise. The function of the sound lock may be obtained without doubling the number of doors necessary by planning the studios around hallways that are common to several doors and that themselves serve as sound locks. Some examples of sound-lock corridors are included in Figs. 6-4 through 6-8. Such corridors, while effective in insulating against sound leakage, may give less than ideal traffic flow patterns within the building. With sufficient care in planning a specific plant, it is possible to devise a sound lock corridor system that will not become a labyrinthine maze.

Another point of sound leakage is the ceiling. In multistoried buildings vibration noise from footsteps and machinery above can be most difficult. A suspended false ceiling, cushioned from the offending upper structure and well insulated, may be necessary. In single-story frame construction the attic space common to several rooms may provide an acoustic coupling between them. Again, generous insulation in all ceilings will be of considerable value in minimizing ceiling transmission, not to mention improved heating and air conditioning efficiency.

Which brings up an important matter: The air conditioning requirements in a radio station are much more demanding than for a residence. While some stations actually have resorted to window-type air conditioners for studio use (I've

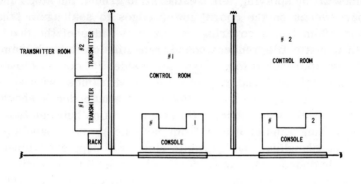

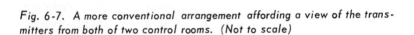

Fig. 6-7. A more conventional arrangement affording a view of the transmitters from both of two control rooms. (Not to scale)

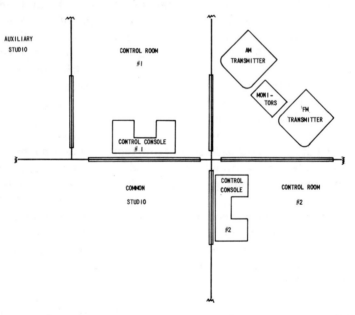

Fig. 6-8. An alternate arrangement of two control rooms, giving direct transmitter observation from each. (Not to scale)

worked in two that did), the noise they produce renders them entirely unsuitable in a professional installation. Yet, air conditioning is a necessity in nearly all U.S. climates. In sealing out extraneous noise, most studios and control rooms also seal out fresh air, and even moderate days will result in excessive interior heat. Control rooms are particularly difficult in this regard, being as they often are surrounded on all sides by other rooms and filled with heat-generating equipment. While modern transistorized gear reduces the heat buildup problem in control rooms, the average vacuum tube in audio equipment probably delivers about 15 British Thermal Units (BTU) into the ambient air. The usual non-transistorized control room may have 60 tubes in operation, delivering 900 BTUs of heat.

In terms of air conditioning engineers' rules of thumb, this amounts to the body heat of 1 1/2 people. Add to this the usual heightened tension when a man is on a live microphone—as though the room temperature rose five degrees whenever the mike is opened—and the need for an adequately cooled control room is evident. In fact, during certain seasons it is usual for office girls, thinly clad and seated in peripheral offices, to demand heat at the very times announcers are dialing more air conditioning! Further, enclosed control rooms and studios are prone to air stagnation, unless the atmosphere control system maintains good circulation throughout the building. This need for adequate ventilation poses an additional problem not usually considered in residential systems: the noise of rapidly moving air.

There are two ways to move large quantities of air. The cheapest and therefore most common is to increase the pressure and thereby the velocity; it is the resulting rapid air motion that produces noise at the grilles. The more expensive alternative is to provide large ductwork and numerous large-area outlets so that enough air can be moved quietly at low velocities. It is this method that should be used in radio studios, for both heating and air conditioning. The large ducts also must be acoustically designed to minimize inter-room sound transmission through them.

Adding but a little more to the premium cost of suitable heating and air conditioning, the combined studio-transmitter installation should have ducting and control dampers arranged so that warm air from the transmitter can be fed into the heating system in the winter. Recovery of electricity dissipated

Fig. 6-9. Studio window panes are set non-parallel (A). A closer view of window construction (B).

as transmitter heat in this manner will soon pay for the necessary sheet metal work. (In summer, of course, the transmitter is to be exhausted directly outdoors. It usually is not practical nor necessary to air condition the transmitter room.)

Perhaps the local building contractor will have heard somewhere that studio windows are double-paned with plate glass, but he may not know that the panes should not be parallel. There are various schools of thought on the particular configuration such non-parallel windows should take. Some acoustic builders insist that the panes should converge at the top of the window, theoretically reflecting the incident sound toward the ceilings, which in modern studios are more absorbent than are the floors. Others opt for the opposite, converging the panes at the window's bottom (as can be seen in Fig. 6-9).

In practical terms, since the slant is but half the wall's thickness and only a few degrees for large windows, and since the lower-frequency reflected sounds tend to propagate in all directions, the choice seems pretty academic. The elevation of the window relative to the anticipated microphone placement may be as satisfactory a guide as any; a window slanting downward may reflect more unwanted sound into a desk microphone near it; the pane slanted upward may do the same for a floor stand microphone.

A more effective configuration may be used for those windows of which but one side faces a studio. For the windows between transmitter and control room, or between studio and foyer or corridor, the outside pane can be set vertically, permitting the studio pane to slant the full depth of the frame and thereby double the slope's angle.

The important purpose of pane convergence is to minimize sound transmission through the window as a whole; the non-parallel internal surfaces minimize standing sound waves between the panes and dissipate the sound "leaking" through. While it often is neglected, the installation of a thick sound absorbent within the window frame opposite the convergence side will soak up the sound that "bounces" its zig-zag way between the panes to that point.

No matter how immaculate the panes of a double window may be at installation, and how well they are sealed (the glass should be set in felt, rubber, or other pliant material), it will become dirty in time. It is important, then, that the retaining stops of at least one pane be set with screws, to facilitate removing it for internal cleaning. (A couple of "plumber's helper" plunger cups are of great help in maneuvering a pane during removal and replacement.)

Even at their best, studio windows pose some acoustic problems because of their high sound reflectivity. In particular, control rooms—from which all studios and probably the transmitter room must be visible—are prone to have so much glass area that acoustics become difficult. The relatively small size and high noise levels of most control rooms compound the problem. Further, the control room is the main studio for most small stations; therefore, it should produce the best possible sound. These conflicting factors can be minimized through several approaches. Since it is a studio, the control room should conform to the rules-of-thumb that often are applied only to non-control-room studios.

To avoid reinforced single-frequency resonances, a studio should have a height X width X length ratio of about 3 X 4 X 5. For a conventional ceiling of eight feet, then, the minimum dimensions for width and length are of the order of 11 feet and 14 feet respectively. Many existing control rooms are much smaller, limiting their acoustic values. This probably is a carry-over from the era when a control room needed only enough area to house equipment and a non-announcing operator. As the heart of the entire operation, embracing announcing, operating, production, and transmitter control functions, the control room should be given prime consideration during the planning stage. The crammed, cramped cubbyhole found in so many of today's operations is not conducive to professional quality; there is no place in a modern radio station for the inordinately small control room.

Other problems peculiar to control rooms are decreased by generous room volume. Irreducible equipment noise is better dissipated as it traverses the longer distances between reflective walls and windows, so that less of it reaches the microphone. Also, the necessary expanse of control room window glass is a smaller proportion of the total wall area, permitting more satisfactory control of the acoustic environment; and the heat generated by electronic equipment results in a markedly reduced buildup problem in a larger room.

There is a simple addition that is rare in most control rooms, but which is surprisingly useful—a second microphone position. A small table with its own microphone, situated within convenient view of the control board operator, will find wide application in many operations for two-voice production or live commercials, interviews, short newscasts, etc.—there are many occasions when the additional microphone position will eliminate awkward switching between studio and control room, or requiring a guest to wear headphones, or tying up an extra man to operate the board for a studio interview program. It's almost as useful as the small announce booth so often incorporated into older stations. Which brings up another admonition: The conventional announce booth—a small room perhaps for or five feet square—is an excellent candidate for extinction. Its only merit lies in its suitability as a teletype machine closet!

The emphasis in modern "juke-box" radio on the control room as the main studio has led some station builders to exclude any other studios in the conventional sense of the word. The most compact of modern installations have but two rather small acoustic rooms, one for conventional control room application and the other for a "production" studio, used for the preparation of recorded commercials and similar effects. Neither could accommodate a live production more complex than a two-man interview program.

During the years of my budding interest in radio, I discovered that it was possible to identify many of the smaller stations in my area upon hearing a few words delivered by their local announcers. While it is true that the staff of a given station tends to develop a uniformity of sound (intentional or sub-conscious) through interemulation, and that local station voices become quite familar to regular listeners, my discerning ability was not attributable to either. It resulted from a more insidious sameness of sound caused by acoustic peculiarities of the studios, or control rooms, or whatever were used most frequently by the announcers. In other words, the acoustic environment in which an announcer worked colored the aired sound with the indelible stamp of his particular station, and even widely differing voice timbers seemed to acquire a remarkable similarity of tone.

As sound reproduction techniques developed in the direction of more "liveness," it was recognized that room reverberation should be reasonably uniform at all frequencies, without pronounced resonances. To minimize the buildup of back-and-forth reflections at certain frequencies (determined by room dimensions), the concept of non-parallel walls has been employed successfully. By directing reflected sound in a path diverging from that of the incident wave, it is better dispersed into the general room area before it builds up to resonant standing waves between opposite walls.

The room's longer walls preferably should be nonparallel, since the shorter distance between them offers less natural attenuation of the sound waves on each reflection, but—as a practical matter—it may be structurally more convenient to produce an irregular area by angling a shorter wall. Several of the sketches in Figs. 6-4 to 6-8 include non-parallel walls, even to the extreme of triangular shapes. In some cases, this may be too extreme and should be considered with care. Microphones do not work well in corners, and a triangle, being all corners, may prove difficult.

Non-parallel walls may be troublesome to achieve in those studios located in existing office buildings, but the station constructing its own combined plant at its transmitter site should plan irregular studios as a matter of course. It may be that a single angled wall can divide two studio areas effectively, or, alternatively, the entrance foyer or waiting area can be modernly irregular. There is an infinite variety of possible configurations that will enhance studio performance.

The actual acoustic treatment of studio interiors is highly variable and depends upon size, expected application, microphone types and working distances, and personal preference. Any library has references listing typical reverberation times, sound absorption coefficients, and dispersion techniques. A workable environment may result in a medium-sized studio if the ceiling is totally surfaced with conventional acoustic tile (to offset the hardness of the typical vinyl-tiled floor) and the walls contain spaced panels of acoustic tile about 4 X 4 or 5 X 5 feet square on three sides of the room. Some modification of acoustic properties can be made after the station is constructed, if experience proves it necessary. Absorption can be increased by adding more acoustic tile panels, or even heavy drapes across one end of the room; brightness can be increased with hard-finished reflective panels, which usually are semi-cylindrical to create dispersion of the reflected sound.

Microphones, to a degree, determine the permissible "liveness." Also, the closer the announcer is to his microphone, the stronger his voice in relation to the indirect sound level, and so the less the "liveness." When a local announcer follows a modern record with its exaggerated reverberation from studios with only optimum liveness, he may sound dull and liveless in contrast, so some stations have added artificial reverberation to their microphone circuits. Again, this is a matter of personal choice, but it suggests that a station builder might design his studios to be relatively "dead," and then enhance their sound as necessary electronically. In this way, undesired room resonances are minimized by the substantial acoustic deadening, and the subsequent injection of artificial reverberation can be controlled to a fine degree.

All the unusual construction features of the studios—once the specific requirements are decided upon—need to be brought clearly to the attention of the local contractor(s) before any bids are drawn up. It'll be cheaper than tearing out and redoing later. The contractor also should be given to understand that all wiring within the control room-studio-transmitter room complex—in fact, throughout the entire building in a combined operation—is to run in well-grounded conduit, if at all possible. It is permissible to use unshielded AC power wiring, if local codes permit, and loudspeaker and other high-level audio runs can be made without conduit, but it's a good engineering "must" for microphone and other low-level circuits to be suitably enclosed. Since conduit best can be installed during the early stages of construction, it is important to foresee all future needs with the greatest possible prescience; this is especially so for poured concrete floors!

AUTOMATION AND SUBSIDIARY COMMUNICATIONS AUTHORIZATION

The increasing use of automation was mentioned previously. The broadcaster planning a new station—even if no initial automation is contemplated—will wisely allow ample space in his blueprints for all foreseeable automation equipment needs, including generous tape storage space.

True, it seems logical that the next major breakthrough in sound recording will be information storage methods that eliminate such mechanisms as tape transports and turntables. Just as magnetic tape revolutionized aural broadcasting, a new all-electronic data storage and retrieval system—perhaps along the lines of magnetic memories or electron-beam storage tubes now used in some sophisticated nonbroadcast equipment—that eliminates mechanical apparatus will result in vastly superior automation handling and record storage techniques. Perhaps a small wafer the size of a business card will contain an hour's worth of program recording, for example, requiring simple insertion into the slot of a "reader" to reproduce on the air. (The recently-developed technique of holographic photography permits an astronomical amount of information to be optically recorded on a single frame of ordinary film.) Obviously, the storage requirements and mechanical handling equipment for an all-electronic recording system will be drastically smaller and more reliable than present tape methods. However, it will be a matter of years before such advanced methods attain practical application, so that the station being planned today should be conceived in terms of present equipment requirements.

Presently, a total automation system—complex enough to program a station entirely—may occupy five standard racks (about 21" X 21" X 72"). Much of it is mechanical, tape transports and cartridge players, which may not be susceptible to marked miniaturization, although the electronic circuitry undoubtedly will continue to shrink. An appropriately located 20 or 30 square feet of floor space should be included in the planning for an automated station for this gear, and wiring plans to accommodate audio, control, and power needs incorporated.

Installations that ultimately are to be AM-FM should include about twice the space for automation equipment, in anticipation of required separate programming. And the same is true for FM stations contemplating the addition of Subsidiary Communications Authorizations, most of which today are used to transmit background music for commercial and industrial use by reception on special leased receivers.

An SCA also may require additional space for associated switching and signal facilities, as well as SCA generating and monitoring equipment at the transmitter end of the operation. In fact, future uses for SCA facilities no doubt will include functions that as yet are unconceived, so that it is most difficult to predict the space requirements that may occur. Again, it is preferable to err on the generous side. The SCA is available to the FM broadcaster virtually for the asking, and it would be unfortunate if space limitations were to preclude a future profitable application of the facility.

OTHER PLANT REQUIREMENTS

Little has been said about office space, but obviously some is necessary. However, radio station offices differ in no important respect from other business facilities, and they offer nothing outside the experience of the local contractor. Their number and size are entirely a matter of individual preference. Some stations manage with a single office, which may serve the manager and any additional salesmen, and a rather large reception area with enough room for the receptionist, traffic, and continuity activities. Others may include four or five individual offices and a receptionist's area or foyer, so that the various activities are confined to specific domains.

The announcer's lounge, once a standard adjunct to the studio complex, has pretty well been squeezed out of modern installations—partly because fewer announcers are tied more closely to their microphones than was true when much programming was simply carried from a network, and most voice changes were live instead of recorded. In the small station, the announcer off air duty for, say, an hour very likely has other station chores to attend to.

The chief engineer rarely has his own office in a small operation. His corner may well be one end of the workbench in the transmitter room, which may force him to borrow an office for telephoning or corresponding, unless his alter responsibility in the station includes duties that require an office. Storage space for spare parts and remote broadcast equipment usually can be incorporated into the transmitter room, although separate storage closets are not uncommon.

The "news room" in smaller installations is the euphemistic name for the corner or cubbyhole housing the wire service teletype, although the ideal coverage of local and other non-wire news requires an office or area affording typewriter and telephone facilities, and perhaps monitoring terminals for local police and fire department radio calls.

There is one space conservation approach that may interest the frugal builder—the combined office-studio. When only a limited need for a studio (other than the control room) is anticipated, and when the manager, as chief or only sales-man, will be out of his office most of the day, a single room can double for both. For a short time each morning and after-noon, it is a rather large office with unusual acoustic treat-ment; the rest of the day and night it is a studio with a busi-ness desk and perhaps a file cabinet or two in one corner. This combination may appeal particularly to those who are planning an initial combined studio-transmitter operation,

Fig. 6-10. A combined operation housed in what could pass for a resi-dential building. This one was built in 1954 by a local contractor who planned to convert it to a residential property when the station failed! (1968 Photo courtesy of KLEM)

with the hope of adding an intown office and studio complex when business justifies it.

When station planning has progressed far enough that the particular operation's needs can be stated specifically, it is time to approach one or more local contractors capable of constructing a transmitter-studio building. Practically every town has several of varied talents. Probably one can be found who is willing to build to specifications on a long-term lease basis, which may require pre-payment of the ninth and tenth years and then settle out at something about $200 a month in a rural location. It may help to allow the contractor a "safety factor," seen in some radio stations that look externally much like nearby residential homes. This resemblance often is a simple matter of matching neighborhood decor; it makes of the studios a property readily converted to residential use if the station defaults! (See Fig. 6-10.)

For in-town studios, which usually are installed in an existing office building, the necessary modifications are so dependent upon the particular situation that little generalization is possible. Inter-studio leakage probably will be less severe, while inappropriate room dimensions and acoustic "hollowness" may be substantial problems. Often heating and wiring conduits and trenches will be in short supply. One successful approach to this latter problem has been to elevate the control room with a false floor high enough to provide a crawl space beneath, so that most of the inter-equipment wiring can be run between floors. Microphone, intercom, and monitor speaker wiring to the surrounding studios is passed through the control room walls below the false floor level. The same method is applicable to a transmitter room installation, requiring, of course, sufficient strength in the false floor to support the hundreds or thousands of pounds a transmitter weighs. The sometimes extensive modifications necessary to adapt conventional offices to studio use usually are undertaken by the building's management when suitable lease terms are firm.

Chapter 7

The Transmitter Plant

There are four avenues open to stations acquiring equipment: to purchase it new*; to buy it used; to lease it from firms specializing in that service; and to construct their own. Of the four, the last is the least practical today. Even if an applicant had the necessary shop facilities, engineering talent, and time to build every electronic item from scratch, the hurdle of obtaining FCC approval of key units would remain. For example, the composite transmitter—a highly modified or elaborated version of a manufactured unit, or a combination of two or more—was a commonplace sight in radio stations thirty years ago. Today, the Commission requires type approval, which established manufacturers obtain through submission of their equipment to exhaustive and lengthy laboratory tests and detailed analysis of engineering accuracy. An individual builder can subject his product to approval tests, too, but the expense and time involved make it highly impractical for single-unit quantities. It is transmitters, along with frequency and modulation monitors, that require type approval for use in broadcast installations. Associated audio equipment does not require official approval, but it must pass audio proof-of-performance measurements, of course.

There is one practical avenue of do-it-yourself equipment construction open to permittees. Certain firms, such as Bauer Electronics Corporation, have developed broadcast equipment that is available in kit form. In addition to unfinished audio consoles, Bauer offers an AM transmitter kit (Model 707) for powers of 250, 500, and 1,000 watts on which

---

*New equipment manufacturers are indexed in such annual publications as Mactier Publishing Corporation's Broadcast Equipment Buyers Guide; Howard W. Sams' Broadcast Industry Buyers Guide; and the Broadcasting Yearbook.

type approval already has been obtained. With this technicality disposed of, assembly of such a kit-form unit becomes a straightforward electronic construction job. Since manufactured transmitters are produced in limited quantities and therefore are hand-wired in the factory, the substantial cost of labor is saved by purchasing the kit. Of course, the engineer wiring his first one will take even longer, so that his labor cost must be considered. However, there is an obscure but important benefit if the transmitter is assembled by the engineer who is to be responsible for its actual operation: he learns it literally inside-out, far better than most engineers know theirs until they have lived with them for several years. This knowledge can be instrumental in drastically reducing off-air time if trouble develops. The Bauer kit transmitter is checked out by a factory representative (in the continental U.S.) after assembly is completed, and his confirmation that all is well is the broadcaster's assurance of reliability comparable to that of a factory-assembled unit. (The 707, along with many other broadcast items, is available from Bauer factory-assembled if desired.)

The principal reason for purchasing used equipment is an economic one: it's cheaper. The lower cost may spread the available purchase capital over a greater abundance of technical apparatus, and—under favorable conditions—an excellent and highly flexible facility can result. However, the applicant looking at the attractive costs of used equipment must balance them against the reality that professional gear bought "as is" from previous owners almost always needs considerable overhaul, refurbishing, and adjustment to put it in shape for reliable continuous use. If he has the engineering personnel and the time and place to recondition a full complement of equipment before the rush of installation, then he may choose this route. As a matter of practical fact, though, many new installations wind up with studios full of boxed used equipment that must be worked over during the station's construction efforts, and the added delay in getting on the air offsets the savings effected by the purchase of used gear. There is enough pressure on the technical staff to meet a construction deadline and get the station productive, without the further burden of doctoring neglected equipment in the process.

An alternative to buying "as is" non-guaranteed equipment from an assortment of original owners is to check the several firms specializing in used broadcast gear. Some of them recondition their stock as it comes in and offer a guarantee of satisfactory performance upon its resale. The "penalty" for this servicing and assurance is considerably higher prices, bringing such used equipment close enough to the cost of new to encourage a hard second look. While several thousand dollars may be saved in filling a complete plant with such equipment, the broadcaster must consider the prospect of beginning his operation with technical apparatus that is practically obsolete. When one considers that the useful life of broadcast equipment seems to be decreasing because of rapid innovation, used gear of any age becomes less of a bargain. A broad rule for the industry used to be a ten-year write-off of equipment; now, with the rapid turnover in technology, the trend is to depreciate some items completely in only five or six.

For the added expense of new equipment, the station operator obtains the latest advances in the state of the art, thereby delaying obsolescence as far as possible. (In view of the fact that transistorized circuitry, late in coming to the broadcast field, already is in its third generation, obsolescence—

Fig. 7-1. **NEW EQUIPMENT COSTS FOR BASIC STATIONS**

Tower & ground system	$6000	Tower & transmission line	$5500
Antenna coupler	400	Six-bay antenna	3400
I kilowatt transmitter	6500	I kilowatt transmitter	6500
Frequency monitor	1000	Frequency monitor	600
Modulation monitor	700	Modulation monitor	1000
Limiter amplifier	500	FM limiter amplifier	600
Auto-gain amplifier	300	Auto-gain amplifier	300
Audio console	2100	Audio console	2100
Two turntables	1200	Two turntables	1200
Tape cartridge (play)	650	Tape cartridge (play)	650
Tape cart. (play-record)	1100	Tape cart. (play-record)	1100
One reel tape machine	650	One reel tape machine	650
Five microphones	325	Five microphones (for FM)	600
One control room speaker	175	One control room speaker	175
One two-channel remote ampli.	350	One two-channel remote ampli.	350
EBS receiver	150	EBS receiver	150
Test equipment	875	Test equipment	875
Miscellaneous	1500	Miscellaneous	1500
BASIC AM TOTAL	$24475	BASIC FM TOTAL	$27250

like old age—seems much too iminent.) He also obtains the manufacturers' guarantees; the possibility of obtaining the entire package from one source; and reasonably extended payment terms. At construction time, new equipment is ready for interconnection and routine adjustment, incurring minimum delay.

Fig. 7-1 suggests orders of magnitude for new equipment costs in combined studio-transmitter plants. The two stations listed are minimally equipped. They can manage with but two turntables, two cartridge tape machines, and possibly with a single reel-to-reel tape machine if economics demand, although a real need for more facilities will be felt from the first day's operation. In particular, a production recording center apart from the on-air control room is a virtual necessity in most modern stations. The prices shown do not represent a particular manufacturer's offerings. They are selected—and inflated a little in view of economic history and publication delays—only to give an inkling as to the range in cost. The careful shopper will locate certain items at appreciably lower figures; conversely, the most deluxe equipment sells much higher. Despite published prices, there often is some negotiation room in the figures quoted for major pieces such as transmitters and towers. If it is feasible to purchase the entire equipment complement for a new station from a single manufacturer (or supplier), there may be a package price available that will prove preferable to shopping for the lowest single-item prices at a number of sources.

The new station builder will want to postpone a firm decision on equipment acquisition until he has checked the terms for leasing it. Probably the greatest inducement to leasing is the substantial reduction of necessary initial cash outlay, perhaps enabling a station of limited means to be equipped more completely with new equipment than it would be otherwise. The operator exercising the long-range philosophy will examine those aspects of leasing relevant to equity buildup, options to apply payments toward the eventual purchase of the equipment, modification and adaptation restrictions, maintenance responsibility, and tax technicalities. Only by weighing all of the advantages and drawbacks can a business-like decision be reached.

The broadcaster who, after due consideration of the merits attendant to the various avenues of acquisition, opts for outright purchase of new basic equipment may justifiably obtain used professional gear for the desired additional flexibility that his production and engineering staff will desire. Once the plant is on the air and bidding for income, there will be time available for refurbishing used auxiliary equipment.

The reference to professional equipment, either new or used, is quite intentional. Nothing less should be considered for apparatus that is to be the technical backbone of the operation. While there is a confusing array of consumer-oriented high fidelity and stereo equipment available—much of it comparable in technical performance to the best broadcast equipment—it ordinarily will not stand up mechanically to professional applications.

I once walked into a position in a metropolitan radio station where I found all 45 RPM records played on $12.95 changers intended to be plugged into home radios, and all tape recordings (this was in the pre-cartridge era) handled by home-type machines in the $100 class. Although it could be justified as a stop-gap measure, this equipment had been in daily control room use for years! The turntables were audibly inferior to professional standards, and the tape machines, while of reasonably good sound quality according to the present state of the art, required extensive mechanical maintenance on an average of twice weekly. The inference is clear: If new broadcast equipment is beyond reach, good used professional gear is preferable to consumer-type apparatus, even at the expense of greater cost and rejuvenation labor. This is not to say that sub-professional equipment can't be used to advantage in appropriate applications. A suitable remote amplifier can be made from a good public address amplifier, or relatively inexpensive turntables may serve admirable for certain remote uses, where operating hours are few and the chances of theft or damage are great enough to deter the use of more costly equipment.

THE TOWER AND ANTENNA

It is difficult to list a tower cost figure that has any validity. Each tower installation is unique and priced accordingly. Tower height, load capacity, location, and accessibility all affect the erected cost. The beginning broadcaster will be wise to obtain bids from several reputable tower construction companies and, if possible, to inquire of other broadcasters who may have bought from them. The tower should be the most permanent and trouble-free part of the whole installation, and it will be if it is properly chosen and constructed. (The nature of their work attracts some workers who tend to a devil-may-care attitude, and the station should —in its own best interests—satisfy itself that the installation is made under responsible supervision. This is particularly true for concealed work, such as the AM ground system.)

The standard broadcast tower is designed for a wind load of 30 pounds per square foot, or just over 86 miles per hour, although many broadcasters prefer to pay a little more for the added security of a 100-mile-per-hour design. Stations in the hurricane belt use stronger towers as a matter of course. A higher load design also offers leeway for future additions. It used to be commonplace, for example, when adding FM to an existing AM tower, to add a slender mast on top to support the FM radiating elements, thereby adding perhaps 60 feet and 3,000 pounds to the load. It is simpler today, and usually satisfactory, to attach the FM antenna elements directly to a tower leg, eliminating the unguyed and considerable load of the mast. The weight of each element is small (see Fig. 7-2); the principal effect of their addition lies in increased wind loading. If the AM tower has been designed with a healthy reserve, adding FM ordinarily poses no problem, particularly with modern bolt-on-to-the-tower techniques.

The antenna element in Fig. 7-2A produces the horizontally polarized field conventional to FM broadcasting. Within recent years, however, the advantages of a vertically-polarized component have been investigated and found to improve FM reception in difficult areas and, in particular, for automobile receivers using ordinary whip antennas. To attain the improved service it affords, the FCC now permits an FM station to transmit a vertically-polarized component up to—but not exceeding—the power radiated with horizontal polarization. The practical result is an opportunity for FM stations to deliver twice their assigned ERP. Some installations use two transmitters, one for each polarization, providing the failsafe feature of equipment redundancy.

Older installations have found it expedient to add vertical radiators to their existing antenna system, using elements

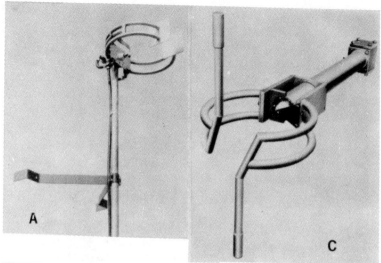

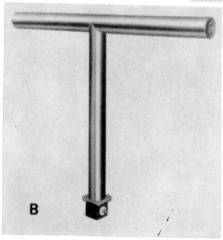

Fig. 7-2. A typical FM antenna element for horizontal polarization (A). Up to 16 elements may be stacked to provide the required antenna system "gain." "B" is a single section FM antenna suitable for mounting directly on a tower leg. Usually several such elements are "stacked" for improved ERP. The circularly polarized FM antenna element (C) combines the functions of A and B. Up to 16 may be stacked for "gain." (Photo courtesy Gates Radio)

like those shown in Fig. 7-2B. The broadcaster making a new installation may, however, take advantage of recent antenna developments that produce radiation in both planes (in this case, <u>circular</u> polarization) with elements like that shown in Fig. 7-2C, which may be stacked to produce suitable "gain" figures. While official sanction of double power may not continue indefinitely, it appears that circular polarization will become the standard for FM broadcasting, warranting its serious consideration at the outset of a new operation.

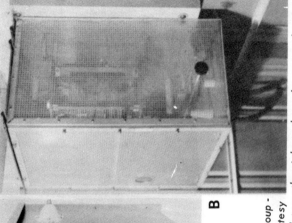

Fig. 7-3. A factory-made antenna coupling unit, or tuning unit (Photo courtesy Collins Radio). It is designed to be weathertight and can be mounted on a simple post near the tower's base. "B" is a "homemade" antenna coupling unit, mounted in a metal building of the sort popularly used for backyard storage. The interior of the unit shown in "C," showing typical component arrangement.

The FM installation (whether or not there is AM) requires a transmission line scaling the tower, which ranges from $1.65 to $10 a foot, as power capacity and efficiency requirements may dictate. The antenna and transmission line costs add to the basic tower expense in an FM installation. These extra FM costs are countered to some extent in the AM-only installation, where the tower itself is the radiating element and the signal connection usually is made simply near its base. The AM system must include an extensive network of buried ground wires, and essential insulators which support the tower and divide the guy cables. Because the electrical parameters of an AM tower rarely match those of transmitters and transmission lines, a coupling unit (Fig. 7-3) is used to bridge the incompatibility. (FM antennas, transmission lines, and transmitters all are designed around common electrical characteristics, but AM antennas do not lend themselves to such uniformity.) The differences in AM-only and FM-only tower-antenna requirements tend to balance out to roughly similar costs for a given tower height. The AM-FM station sharing a common tower obviously must meet the combined requirements.

THE TRANSMITTER

The lowest power for which a new AM station will be licensed is 250 watts. A typical transmitter capable of that power is illustrated in Fig. 7-4. Most 250-watt transmitters are convection cooled, eliminating the noise of blowers and permitting installation within the control room if desired. Virtually all transmitters of 1,000 watts and up incorporate cooling blowers, necessitating their enclosure in rooms apart from live microphones. Typical one-kilowatt transmitters are shown in Fig. 7-5; units similar to these are found in "typical" 1000-watt stations everywhere.

Conventional AM transmitters in the 1000-watt class measure about 6 1/2 feet high, three feet wide, and 30 inches deep, with weights of approximately 1000 pounds. When planning an installation, it is important to allow room for the transmitter doors to be opened and its panels to be removed for normal maintenance and repair. The one-tube AM transmitter illustrated in Fig. 7-6 typifies the trend toward smaller physical size in transistorized equipment. It is several inches

Fig. 7-4. A modern 250-watt transmitter. (Photo courtesy of Gates Radio)

Fig. 7-5. A popular Gates 1000-watt transmitter (left), and an RCA "kilo-watt."

narrower than its tube-type predecessors, and a few hundred pounds lighter. Not all of this miniaturization is directly attributable to the use of transistors; this particular model eliminates certain large and heavy components by utilizing "low-level" modulation, which by no means is unique to transistorized transmitters.

A transmitter that is modulated at a low-level point requires subsequent power amplifying circuits that inherently are less efficient (in terms of electrical power consumption) than are those in conventional "high-level" modulated transmitters, so that the unit in Fig. 7-6 draws a few hundred watts more from the power lines. In practical terms, it might cost as much as two or three cents an hour more to operate than would its conventional counterpart. However, most specifications for the transistorized model exceed those for the great majority of tube-type units, remarkably good as they are, and the broadcaster interested in the highest possible AM sound fidelity, coupled with ultra-modern electronic design, reduced maintenance requirements, and lower tube replacement costs, may choose to pay the somewhat higher purchase price it commands.

Transistors have come into use for FM transmitters, too, reducing tube needs to but one for a 1000-watt unit, and just two are necessary for powers up to 7,500 watts (Fig. 7-7). Because FM is a completely different method of modulation, the variance in size and weight between transistorized and

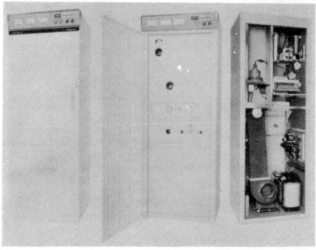

Fig. 7-6. This Gates 1000-watt AM transmitter uses only tube.

conventional transmitters is negligible. In fact, some tube-type FM units are physically smaller than the particular one-tube model shown in Fig. 7-7. The required performance capabilities of all type-approved FM transmitters are more demanding than those for AM, and it is unlikely that even the trained ear could detect any aural superiority in the transistorized unit's signal. The principal advantages in equipping a new station with a transistorized FM transmitter lie in cooler operation, greater operational reliability, reduced maintenance, lower tube replacement costs, and of course delayed obsolescence.

It is well to bear in mind that a 1000-watt AM transmitter is necessary to power a 1000-watt station, but the factor of FM antenna "gain" makes it possible for a 1000-watt FM transmitter to supply an ERP of several times that figure, with 12,000 to 14,000 watts ERP being commonplace. Thus,

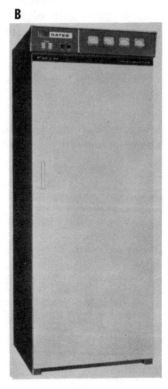

Fig. 7-7 This Gates 1000-watt FM transmitter (left) also uses just one tube, and the 5-kilowatter (right) uses only two.

really impressive ERPs are possible with higher powered FM transmitters, such as those in Fig. 7-8.

SPECIAL FM TRANSMITTERS

A specialized FM application not heretofore mentioned is that of educational radio. The FCC has reserved twenty of the lowest-frequency FM channels for use by bona fide educational organizations and institutions, which may elect to use very limited power.

In general, Classes A, B, and C educational FM stations must conform to all technical and operational requirements applicable to commercial FM outlets (except that no commercial matter or announcements are permitted), but an additional category, Class D, may be employed exclusively for educational purposes. Class D FM stations are limited to transmitter powers (not ERPs) of 50 watts or less, and certain technical and operating rules are less stringent for this class. Major manufacturers offer low-powered transmitters for Class D stations, an example of which is shown in Fig. 7-9. This particular 10-watt model is used as the "exciter" in its maker's higher-powered transmitters, so its technical performance meets the more demanding requirements for stations of higher classes, and it should provide completely professional quality in Class D service.

MONITORS

Frequency and modulation monitors, which measure the transmitter's performance, rank high on the FCC's list of stringent performance requirements, quite understandably. In accuracy and reliability they must resemble laboratory instruments, and the exhaustive tests monitors have to pass for type approval discourage any attempt to device "home-brewed" substitutes.

The relatively small number of monitors sold means that the considerable cost of research, development, and type approval is reflected in premium prices, with little competitive pressure to shave them. Since they are required, the broadcaster has little choice but to pay the prices. An exception may be made for AM frequency and modulation monitors, which are separate units. They have been highly refined, stable

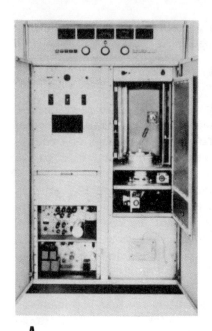

A

B

Fig. 7-8. This RCA transmitter (left) produces ten thousand watts of FM power. The 10-KW package on the right is a Collins unit.

Fig. 7-9. This RCA 10-watt FM transmitter may be used for a Class D Educational Radio outlet.

devices for many years, and well maintained used ones may serve long and well. However, FM monitors, which often combine frequency and modulation indicators in one unit, still are in the process of evolution. Operating at higher frequencies and measuring a different type of modulation, they have been, in many instances, a little less reliable than their AM counterparts. Used FM monitors should be selected with care; they may be victims of inept repair and modification.

The FM monitor situation has been further clouded by the relatively recent addition of stereo standards accepted by the FCC for monitor type approval. A totally modern FM monitor must be able to measure a number of parameters relative to the main channel, subchannel(s), pilot carrier, and SCA functions. At the moment, the choice of comprehensive single-unit monitors is very limited; yet it seems unrealistic for a new FM station to invest in a monaural monitor—even a used one—because of the virtual certainty that adoption of stereo at an early date will render it obsolete before its investment value is realized. Some FM monitors are available in "building block" form, enabling the broadcaster to buy only those functions he needs at the moment, leaving the option of adding complementary facilities as the need arises. This is an alternative solution to the problem of long-range requirements, although the single, comprehensive monitor seems to me to represent a better engineering approach.

LIMITERS AND AUTOMATIC GAIN AMPLIFIERS: SPEECH PROCESSORS

The fundamental sound signal "processor" for AM is the limiter (Fig. 7-10), a device which can be set to abruptly curtail sound volume excursions beyond, say, 98% modulation. While the regulations do not stipulate that a limiter be employed, they do insist that <u>negative</u> audio peaks not exceed 100% modulation (negative peaks, because <u>they</u> produce the inter-channel splatter). Sound signals, being very complex and irregular, cannot entirely be anticipated by the operator, but a properly adjusted limiter amplifier will remove most errant audio peaks before they reach the transmitter. The 100% level for frequency modulation is not set by the inherent nature of the modulation process; it is pegged arbitrarily at plus or minus 75 kHz for FM radio, and 25 kHz for TV audio. Most FM transmitters will deliver 133% modulation without difficulty, and some receivers will take it in stride. Thus an occasional peak excursion beyond 100% does not create transmitted distortion and splatter as it does with AM, although inferior receivers may generate some in the reproduced sound. Nevertheless, the FCC requires that modulation not exceed 100% for FM, and the limiter is now pretty much standard equipment in FM installations.

Fig. 7-11 illustrates a limiter designed for FM service. At first glance, it would seem that what serves AM would serve FM as well, but many broadcasters have learned that the latter has some special characteristics. These arise from pre-emphasis, which is an exaggeration within the FM transmitter of the higher audio frequencies. Complementary de-emphasis in FM receivers reverses the process, so that the final sound is heard in proper balance. In the meantime, natural noise acquired along the way also is de-emphasized, so that the overall result is an improved signal-to-noise ratio. This is possible because the high-frequency content of average program material is of considerably lower intensity than are the mid-range components, so that the exaggeration in the transmitter still does not result in over-modulation. However, modern sound enhancement techniques effectively have raised

Fig. 7-10. A modern limiter amplifier intended for AM use (Photo courtesy of Gates Radio).

Fig. 7-11. A limiter designed expressly for FM service. This one is dual channel, suitable for stereo (Photo courtesy of Gates Radio Co.).

the high-frequency content of some material, and transmitter over-modulation can result if a conventional AM limiter—which makes no frequency discrimination—is installed in the circuit prior to the pre-emphasis action.

It is important to note that stereo FM requires two distinct limiters, one for each channel, but they must be inter-connected so that both limit to the same extent simultaneously, regardless as to which channel is excessively loud. The unit shown in Fig. 7-11 contains the dual facilities necessary for stereo; most monaural limiters can be connected in tandem for similar concerted action.

This technique of dependent coupling between units also is necessary for the second type of amplifier common to trans-mitter installations when stereo is involved. This is variously known as the "compressor," or "automatic gain control" (AGC) amplifier. It, too, tends to limit the maximum excursions of the sound signal, but in a different manner than does the limiter. The AGC device does not simply remove sporadic peaks; it reduces the entire sound signal when its average in-tensity becomes excessive. Conversely, the AGC amplifier increases the total signal when its average falls too low. It tends to compensate for inadvertent errors on the part of the operator exercising manual control. Further, it can react faster than the human operator in reducing excesses, although its time constants usually are set for a fairly gradual re-covery once the excess has passed. Fig. 7-12 shows two AGC amplifiers as they might be mounted in a stereo in-stallation.

An ordinary AGC amplifier can introduce an undesirable effect when a momentary lull occurs in an audio signal con-taining appreciable background noise. In its blind igno-rance, the amplifier attempts to correct for what seems to be an inadequate incoming level, thereby boosting the back-ground noise perceptibly. This effect is particularly trouble-some with control room microphone signals, in which room noise is excessive at best, and (in TV) with old film sound-tracks. Modern "machine-gun" radio minimizes the noisy lull problem for the control room by virtually eliminating moments of silence, but feature films contain many sound track passages where excessive AGC action brings the noise to the fore. There are highly sophisticated amplifiers de-signed to distinguish between those desired signals that are only modestly deficient in level and mere residual noise. Such amplifiers are reasonably successful in correcting audio level variations without giving undue emphasis to background noise. An amplifier designed to do this automatically is illustrated in Fig. 7–13.

Fig. 7-12. *A pair of automatic gain control amplifiers, as they might be used for stereo FM* (Photo courtesy of Gates Radio Co.).

Fig. 7-13. *A sophisticated automatic amplifier designed to distinguish between desired signal and noise levels* (Photo courtesy of Gates Radio Co.).

Other audio signal processors to be found in many stations include Kahn Research's Symmetra-Peak, a sealed circuit that tends to correct for the imbalance between positive and negative excursions characteristic of many complex sound signals, a condition particularly common in speech wave-forms. This dis-symmetry creates difficulties for AGC amplifiers, limiters, and especially transmitters. Redistributing the relative instantaneous energies in the complex wave, the Symmetra-Peak tends to equalize the peak excursions inaudibly, thus improving the performance of the succeeding equipment.

Some broadcasters also use RCA's Power-Max immediately prior to the transmitter to introduce an intentional dis-symmetry (or asymmetry) to the audio signal. This may be done even when that signal has previously been squeezed through a Symmetra-Peak! While this may seem self-defeating, there is a sound principle behind it: FCC regulations stipulate that AM modulation be limited to 100% on negative peaks, while positive ones are not specifically restricted. The Power-Max can be adjusted to produce positive peaks in excess of 100% without exceeding the legal maximum for the negative, the degree of unbalance being limited by transmitter capability, permissible distortion, and acceptable carrier shift. In this manner, the AM signal is given a slightly better "push" into the fringe areas. Unlike the random asymmetry of the original audio signal, the product of the Power-Max is a controlled imbalance, and its use following a Symmetra-Peak is a logical, if sometimes controversial, procedure.

While it is not a part of the program chain, an Emergency Broadcasting System alerting receiver is a requisite part of the broadcasting plant. Commercially made models are available, although many broadcasters simply modify an ordinary inexpensive home radio, adapting it to alarm actuation when the key EBS station interrupts its carrier. This method has been satisfactory for the present EBS method, as well as Conelrad before it, but more sophisticated alerting receivers will be required under a proposed new signalling system. In view of the impending change, an investment of $150 or so in a commercial EBS receiver may not be justified.

Chapter 8

Control Room and Studio Equipment

Commonly dubbed simply the "board" by broadcasters, the audio control panel or console is the station's programming nerve center. In that capacity it must provide a maximum of operational flexibility with a minimum of confusion.

The variety of consoles available from a relatively large number of manufacturers represents all shades of operating philosophies, yet the array of stock models often fails to contain one that <u>exactly</u> conforms to the planned needs of a specific radio operation. Many engineers would prefer to custom-build their own versions, and some do. Starting from scratch, however, entails inordinate construction time and probably greater overall cost than does a suitable stock model when engineering labor is considered.

Some operators find a satisfactory compromise to the custom console dilemma by purchasing professional components— amplifiers, mounting cabinets, etc.—and assembling them into a custom configuration. The Altec Corporation, among others, has made a specialty of supplying compatible building-block audio components for custom consoles. With these, the engineering is already done, and only mechanical assembly and interwiring is necessary in the field. There probably is no particular economy in this approach, in comparison to a ready-made stock unit of comparable flexibility, but the result is a professional console tailored to the specific operation.

A check of the equipment list (Fig. 7-1) suggests that a console should accommodate, at the minimum, two turntables, two cartridge and one reel-to-reel tape machine, three control room and studio microphones, at least one incoming remote line, and a beeper telephone. This seems the barest minimum for a beginning station, and it amounts to ten signal sources which must be switched, controlled, and faded.

A highly flexible consolette (also available in a stereo model) that can handle 20 sources through its four mixing channels is shown in Fig. 8-1. 14 of those 20 are divided between two "pots," with the remaining six routed to the remaining pair. Apparently any two sources assigned to a single mixer channel cannot be cross-faded, unless they also are duplicated on the corresponding alternate "pot." Carried to its extreme, this means that total flexibility is achieved at the expense of halving the input source capacity to a scant 10. Since there are many source combinations that rarely are cross-faded, such as beeper phone and remote lines, this consolette should be applicable to a beginning small station's needs. It subsequently would make an excellent production recording control facility.

Gates Radio, which probably manufactures a greater variety of stock consoles than any other one firm, has recognized the now universal need for a production facility apart from the main control board. The unit in Fig. 8-2 is not intended to serve the usual control room function, and would leave much to be desired in that capacity. Conversely, almost any standard control room console will serve production facility needs quite well. Fig. 8-3 depicts a more traditional approach to inexpensive small station master control facilities. It is a

Fig. 8-1. This RCA consolette is capable of handling 20 inputs through four mixing controls.

reasonably compact unit that affords only 13 inputs, but they are spread among eight mixing channels so that fading and blending arrangements are more flexible than is true of the consolettes. For studio productions involving three microphones in simultaneous use, a board of this configuration becomes a virtual necessity.

The advent of stereo, with its requirement of two independent program circuits, has brought its own problems to the area of control consoles. Many monophonic boards incorporate two complete program channels, theoretically enabling them to handle stereo material after a fashion by assigning half the mixing facilities to one main channel and the remaining half to the other. Many stereo operations began with some similar arrangement, because the equipment manufacturers seemed to be tardy in bringing out consoles designed for stereo. (Some current models are "semi-stereo," with several of their mixing channels being limited to monaural use.) While operating a 2-channel monophonic console in stereo is feasible, there are difficulties encountered in fading a stereo channel because two knobs must be operated simultaneously at exactly similar rates; two switches have to open or close at the same instant, too. A board designed for stereo is far preferable, and the station anticipating stereo at the outset will do well to invest in a suitable console.

For the station that can afford to anticipate all possible future needs, a console similar to the one shown in Fig. 8-4 may be in order. This one can accommodate separate program-

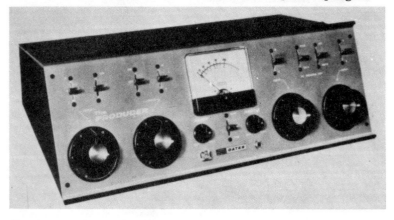

Fig. 8-2. Here is a consolette specifically designed for a production recording facility. (Courtesy of Gates Radio Co.)

Fig. 8-3. A compact Gates tube-type console offering eight mixing channels at relatively low cost.

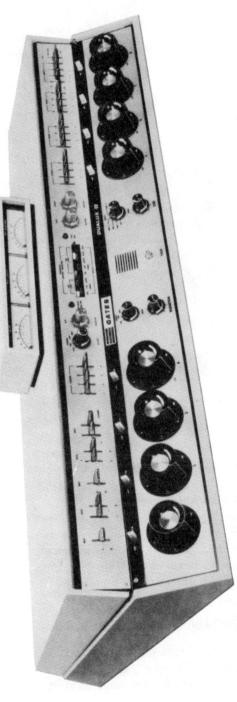

Fig. 8-4. One of the most comprehensive stock consoles available, this Gates model is suitable for simultaneous AM, FM stereo and SCA programming.

Fig. 8-5. A typical 16-inch, three-speed turntable, mounted in a cabinet such as is used in many broadcast installations. (Courtesy of Gates Radio Co.)

ming for AM (monaural, of course) and FM stereo, with complete cross-switching for duplication of either program on both channels. Control provisions for an SCA channel also are incorporated. A stock console with all of these features costs upwards of $3,500; therefore, the broadcaster will have to weigh its cost in terms of long-range utility.

TURNTABLES

For the great majority today, recorded fare is the principal program offering, and nothing requires more rugged reliability than an independent station's main turntables. Most radio stations today are equipped with 16-inch three-speed turntables (Fig. 8-5) and accompanying stylii for both the "standard" grooves, used by the old 78s and the earlier transcriptions, and the microgroove 45s and LPs. They thus can play almost any record to be found in their extensive accumulated files, perhaps including those recorded with the vertical process, like those old Edison platters. However, the new station, starting its record library from scratch, will find the microgroove stylus is its "standard"; that a 16-inch turntable is unnecessarily large for playing 7- and 12-inch discs; and that 78 RPM is an unused speed. Unless there is an acquired library of old records among the station's complement, or the use of someone's personal collection is anticipated, there will be no occasions to use the obsolete speed and stylus. Notice, though, that the pickup arms used should clear a 16-inch disc, since some commercial and syndicated material still is circulated on that size, but microgroove cuts are now universally used. The long arms not only assure that large discs can be accommodated, but they also minimize certain inherent tracking errors. As for the 12-inch table, the occasional 16-inch disc can overhang its edge with no discernible ill effects.

The new station, then, can begin with 12-inch turntables, providing more compactness in the busy control room. Microgroove stylii and but two speeds—33 1/3 and 45—will suffice. Fig. 8-6 illustrates a modern two-speed, 12-inch turntable mechanism. If a new station begins with a pair of tables, when it comes time to add a third, and perhaps a fourth, it will add to general flexibility if it is equipped with

Fig. 8-6. A basic turntable mechanism incorporating the two modern speeds and convenient 12-inch size. (Courtesy of Collins Radio Co.)

the third speed and a choice of stylii. Perhaps a good used table with these features can be acquired, giving the station the necessary facilities for those unusual occasions when a 78 RPM record or old transcription comes to hand, meanwhile freeing the most-used tables from unnecessary complexity.

It should be noted that the record industry is "phasing out" the monaural LP, planning to eliminate duplication of effort by simply packaging everything in stereo. To the monaural broadcaster this means that his turntable cartridges must play stereo discs with good quality and minimum wear. The stylus dimensions commonly employed for microgroove stereo are slightly different from those for monaural, but more important is the matter of vertical compliance in the pickup cartridge itself. Most monaural cartridges don't offer enough freedom of vertical needle motion (inherent to stereo recording) to avoid undue record wear and sound distortion with stereo discs. Therefore, the monaural-only broadcaster should equip his new tables to meet the mechanical demands of stereo records anyway, since his library will in time include them.

CARTRIDGE TAPE EQUIPMENT

Much radio production that is commonplace today was impossible ten years ago. The item of technical magic that transformed production procedures is a plastic cartridge enclosing a reel of endless magnetic tape. Any self-respecting mechanic, seeing one for the first time, would be justified in dismissing the whole concept as an unworkable Rube Goldberg concoction. The tape never could slip freely from the reel hub, all the while rewinding at a greater linear velocity near the rim—at least not with the uniformity of motion required for broadcast sound reproduction! Despite appearances, though, its proponents stuck doggedly to their convictions and made it work. To be sure, it was just a few years ago that the splice was audible; that the tape began to bind and falter after relatively short service; and that the lubricant used fouled the playing heads rapidly and sometimes suddenly. During this evolutionary era of professional use, the degradation resulting from less-than-perfect tape cartridge recording led certain advertising agencies to prohibit the dubbing of their disc transcriptions to cartridges. With its maturity at hand, I have been expecting the agencies themselves to adopt the cartridge in lieu of the seemingly roundabout process of cutting master discs and pressing a short run of transcriptions. Evidently economics still dictate the old approach, although many now do submit their material on reel tape, expressly for dubbing to cartridge.

For convenient use of production material, the cartridge has no equal today. It is readily selected from a rack, inserted in the playback machine, and put on the air instantaneously by the touch of a button. It then is self-cueing, ready to go at the next occasion for use.

Most cartridge machines today provide for an additional "auxiliary cue," recorded at the end of a tape insert, so that other steps in the operation may be triggered in close sequence. This auxiliary cue may start the next tape machine, a turntable, a time tone, or any of a variety of devices. If nothing else, it can release an automatic audio switcher, thereby taking the tape signal off the air. Such a switcher, used with two, three or more cartridge machines, selects the one in use to feed the console, and switches audio as the different machines are called upon. Since the need for cross-fading between cartridge sources is uncommon, a single input channel on the board can accommodate the whole string of machines with an audio switcher. In fact, the switcher can be bridged (through a volume "pot") directly across the console output, making the whole cartridge facility independent of the console. With either method, the cartridge channel can be left "open" at all times, reducing operator manipulations to simply one of pressing the start buttons as needed. The switcher puts the tape on the air and subsequently removes it on command of the "cue" tone, leaving the operator free to attend to his other duties. With a little care in recording, the levels of the various tapes will be uniform enough that playback volume adjustments are unnecessary.

Cartridge machines are available in stereo models, which understandably are more costly than are their monaural counterparts. The broadcaster planning stereo later on must evaluate for himself the wisdom of investing in stereo now. Cartridge tape machines now are in their third generation in less than ten years. The trend now seems to be toward multiple mechanisms in single, compact units, consuming less space and costing less than the earlier pattern of using several complete, single machines. Fig. 8-7 illustrates one manufacturer's 4-cartridge model.

REEL-TO-REEL TAPE EQUIPMENT

Revolutionizing the broadcast industry immediately after World War II, the reel-to-reel tape recorder today is an indispensable part of any radio station. Not quite so indispensable as it was in the pre-cartridge era, perhaps, but vital, nevertheless. Fig. 8-8 shows a reel-to-reel machine suitable for any studio application. However, the beginning station may find greater versatility in a portable model, available in professional quality at prices beginning near $600. One will serve studio needs well, and also be available for on-location use.

The principal need for a reel-to-reel machine in many operations is for the original recording of production material (it's simpler to do "takes" on reel-to-reel tape until satisfaction is attained, and then "dub" to cartridge), any delayed programming, and airing of tapes from outside sources. Unless tape programming is done back-to-back—successively—a single machine may suffice at first for a small operation. As prosperity permits, more machines inevitably will be added.

Fig. 8-7. Four independent cartridge tape mechanisms are combined in this modern single unit. (Courtesy of Sparta Electronics Corp.)

It has been traditional in the professional field to use the full width of the tape for monaural recording. The most favorable signal-to-noise ratio is obtained with the full-track approach, in contrast to the half-track system so common to home-type tape recorders. However, it probably will develop that certain individuals will prepare broadcast tapes on their own machines, as is often a common practice with ministers, county agricultural agents, and others supplying program material. When a half-track tape is played on a professional full-track machine, anything recorded on the alternate track is reproduced simultaneously and backwards, which can be

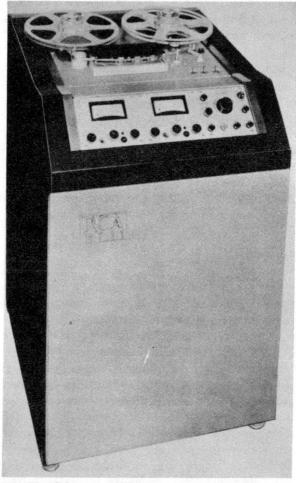

Fig. 8-8. This RCA reel-to-reel tape machine is designed to serve most studio needs.

most distressing to the attentive listener. For this reason many stations incorporate full-track recording heads for compatibility with other possible broadcast users with half-track playback heads to accommodate "home-made" tapes.

The tape picture has been complicated by the emergence of stereo. Professional applications divide the tape width into two tracks, while home-type machines have pretty well settled down to four. This means that there may be a situation where a station has to play a quarter-track tape (even if it's monaural, if it is made on a quarter-track stereo machine, it requires a quarter-track head for proper playback). There also is a matter of speeds: The NAB standards are written around a tape speed of 15 inches per second, but virtually all local stations have settled on 7 1/2. Most home-type machines offer 7 1/2 and 3 3/4 inches per second, and it isn't unusual for an outside tape to come into a station recorded at the slower speed, which the professional machine may not provide for its proper playback.

So, to circumvent the problems that can arise for stations using outside tapes, many invest in a good home-type machine offering speed and track facilities that—combined with the regular studio machines—can meet just about every contingency. Given time, it is entirely possible to dub such outside tapes onto the professional machines before airing, if by so doing the problems of production are reduced.

MICROPHONES

Every station needs an absolute minimum of one excellent microphone, which ordinarily serves the operator-announcer. Besides the control board, microphones may be needed for another control room position and one, two or three in the studio. If the station expects to do any remote broadcasts at all, it should have enough microphones to take along without pirating the studio complement. A portable tape recorder is best equipped with a microphone especially suited to packing up with it. Meeting all these needs, even a small station may accumulate seven or eight broadcast quality microphones, all of them moderately expensive. While this may seem a strain on the equipment budget, a good microphone—given the care a delicate instrument deserves—is virtually a lifetime investment, so that in terms of yearly upkeep and depreciation, it is among the least costly of a station's equipment needs. See Chapters 15 and 16.

SPEAKERS

Considering that a radio station's single product is sound, it is dismaying to find that many stations lack the means to evaluate that product accurately. Many a control operator is forced to balance and blend outgoing signals with his judgment impaired by highly inferior monitoring facilities. The fact that 90% of the receivers tuned in suffer from even greater aural shortcomings is no justification; they <u>need</u> all the fidelity of the incoming signal attainable.

No TV station would consider picture monitors that are nearly obscured by discolored and distorted glass; yet, $10 speakers in next-to-worthless public-address type wall baffles abound in radio control rooms! Stations limited to such inferior monitor speakers <u>don't</u> <u>know</u> <u>what</u> they're transmitting. The broadcaster wanting to measure his product expertly will equip his control room with a speaker system capable of reproducing the entire audio spectrum, in proper balance and true color. It will cost perhaps ten times as much as the poor substitutes so prevalent today, but less than two hundred dollars should suffice. The speaker, like the microphones, should be a long-term investment.

At least one manufacturer (Electro-Voice) has developed models specifically for control room monitoring applications (Fig. 8-9). According to the response curves published by the maker (which probably are as reliable as any) these

Fig. 8-9. Monitor speakers designed expressly for control room application. (Courtesy of Electro-Voice, Inc.)

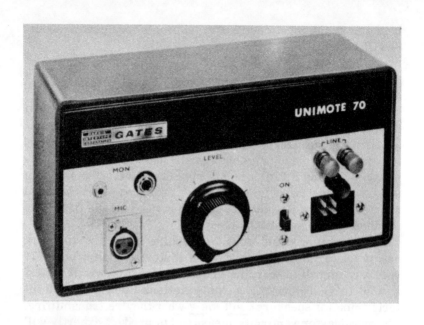

Fig. 8 -11. This novel remote amplifier mixes three microphone inputs, or as many as two turntables along with one microphone. (Courtesy of Collins Radio Co.)

speakers are remarkably uniform, or "smooth," and they should provide a highly accurate reference by which to judge outgoing sound quality. Moreover, despite their limited potential market, these speakers are less expensive than many consumer units of comparable sound quality. Gates Radio recently marketed a speaker line that includes units with their own matched and self-contained transistorized amplifiers. These, too, are aimed specifically at broadcasters, and there are many possible station applications for speaker-amplifier combinations.

The cost of one good speaker system (two, of course, for stereo) for the control room may be offset to a degree by employing very inexpensive speakers in those areas where fidelity is not of paramount importance. Cue and talk-back speakers in the control room need only to identify the content and starting points of various sound sources; in fact, a "penetrating" quality may enhance the utility of these speakers. The transmitter room probably does not need a good speaker, except perhaps for those stations where the transmitter plant is separate, but again, audibility is the prime requisite.

In some operations, quality speakers are used in the studios; yet, the principal need for studio speakers is to cue air personnel. This can be done admirably with a 6-inch, $5 speaker! Installing such a speaker in a recessed aluminum ceiling baffle, making of the ceiling a so-called "infinite" baffle, will produce sound quality far surpassing that normally expected of small, inexpensive speakers. While not high fidelity, the sound of even a small speaker, when mounted in a wall or ceiling so that the back is open to the attic or adjacent room area, is fullbodied and pleasing. Personnel won't find prolonged listening to be irritating. Of course, a studio that is to be used frequently for recording live musical groups should have high quality monitor speakers for the performers' critical evaluation of playback results, and a clients' room or visitors' lobby preferably should be equipped to present the station's product at its best. Those stations of limited means, though, should concentrate their speaker expenditures first and foremost in the control room.

REMOTE BROADCAST EQUIPMENT

The amplifiers and associated equipment available for remote (out-of-studio) broadcasting include a great variety of makes, functions, and costs. Figs. 8-10 and 8-11 illustrate a range of amplifiers, from single-microphone units for such as weather bureau pickups, on-the-spot action where lines are available, and other simple situations, through elaborate multi-channel equipment suitable for complex remotes.

Perhaps the smallest "remote amplifier" is one made by Altec Lansing that will fit in a pocket! It is a transistorized microphone unit that will slip into almost any standard telephone in place of its normal carbon "transmitter," providing greatly improved quality for spot news reports via the beeper phone. Many radio newsmen carry such units with them, ready for use whenever the occasion arises. At the other end of the spectrum, many stations equip trucks, vans, or trailers as complete studios on wheels. Such a unit is rolled onto or near the premises of those firms sponsoring remote broadcasts, and the advertising value of the prominently displayed portable studios is considerable—for the station! Whether they are equally as valuable to the sponsoring advertisers is a matter of some controversy.

Many broadcasters feel that a station can do a better job for

Fig. 8-12. Practically a portable control room, this remote production center typifies an increasingly popular approach to musical remotes. When not on location, it can serve the studios as a second console. (Courtesy of Sparta Electronics Corp.)

the sponsor when it sets up shop within the place of business. For this approach, complete broadcasting centers like the unit shown in Fig. 8-12 are popular. Offering turntable and microphone facilities, with cueing and a public address feed, the most important control room functions are transported to the remote location with this equipment.

If a station is active in doing frequent remote broadcasts from a variety of locations, the conventional use of leased telephone lines to carry programs to the control room can result in cumulative line costs of several hundred dollars a month. Like other forms of rent, line expenses are money down the drain once the services are used. Some stations prefer to put some of their remote costs into capital investments that eliminate the need for many lines. Typical of these is the remote pickup transmitter and receiver facility pictured in Fig. 8-13. This equipment is designed to send remote programs from their originating points to the station via radio.

For years, broadcasters have modified two-way radio equipment basically designed for nonbroadcast communications to serve their purposes. The results have generally been mediocre, because two-way gear intended for police, taxi, and industrial use is not easily convertible to broadcast quality. For "newsmobile" applications, modified equipment has sufficed, but the Marti unit shown in Fig. 8-13 is one of two makes specifically designed for high fidelity broadcast quality. Within its service range, which depends upon terrain, frequency, and antenna elevations, it will surpass in audio quality all but the most expensive of equalized lines. With a volume meter and accommodations for professional microphones, the broadcast-type remote pickup unit offers many advantages in return for its substantial cost (which may be offset by saving a few months' line charges). Of course, since it is a transmitter, it must be suitably licensed, logged, and maintained, but the requirements are minimal relative to those every broadcaster must meet.

Somewhat akin to the remote pickup transmitter is the studio-transmitter link (STL) which serves as the program path between studios and transmitter in split operations. Widely used in TV stations because of the complexity of TV signals, the STL has not yet gained wide application in radio broadcasting. In those installations where transmitters are highly

A

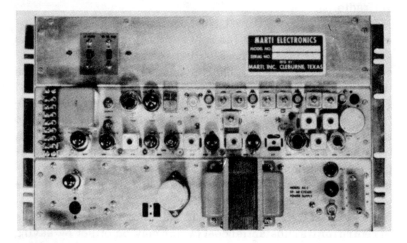

Fig. 8-14. A single dual-row jack strip.

inaccessible, the advantages are obvious; they are less so for those with more convenient locations. Yet, a telephone line equalized for full-range audio is costly over even short distances; stereo requires two very closely matched lines; and remote control facilities impose even more line requirements. A single STL can accommodate all these functions simultaneously. In view of the increasing use of stereo, it is likely that the number of STLs in use will rise sharply in the future. The STL, like the remote pickup transmitter, must be licensed and operated according to applicable regulations.

OTHER TECHNICAL EQUIPMENT

Some test equipment needs were mentioned earlier. Other maintenance needs include a variety of tools, an all-purpose test multimeter, and a limited stock of commonplace electronic parts. Odds and ends of hardware, wire, soldering equipment, all will be needed from time to time.

The supply of spare tubes necessary to assure prompt replacement of normal burnouts and failures can represent sereral hundred dollars, but this figure is declining as transistors supplant tubes in broadcast equipment. The station utilizing new solid-state apparatus should not have to stock spare transistors for some time; in general, their failure is rare. (Radio repairmen report that replacement of transistors is commonplace in automobile radios, which are subjected to extremes of temperatures, vibration, and supply voltages. Experience to date with broadcast equipment, with its professional design, uniform environment, and stable power sources indicates that transistor failure is no more frequent than that for other "permanent" components, such as capacitors.)

Many small stations completely overlook the flexibility afforded by "patching" facilities. Borrowed from telephone central office practices, the concept of the patch panel provides accessibility to every audio circuit by plugging into a jack field. If all microphone, turntable, remote line, amplifier, and speaker circuits are routed through the jack field, a fairly large panel space is required for the control room patching center, but isolated racks (at the transmitter site, for instance) may manage with a single dual strip like that shown in Fig. 8-14.

With every circuit available at jacks, rapid selection of alternate signal paths can be made in the event of equipment failure. Thus, if a single amplifier fails, an alternate can be "patched" in with a minimum of lost air time. Flexibility also is greatly increased for those unusual situations requiring equipment interconnections not provided by the normal switching arrangements. The typical small station practice of permanently wiring each amplifier and processing unit rigidly in their normal sequence means that the failure of one interrupts the entire chain until it is repaired, but a patch panel permits bypassing the faulty unit in the same way a telephone operator plugs into various lines. The wiring and installation of complete jack facilities is a tedious and lengthy job, comsuming much audio wiring in the process; yet, the resulting flexibility makes it well worth the extra effort.

Every station expecting to do remotes with normal telephone line facilities should invest in at least one line equalizer. This is a device designed to compensate for the losses inherent to all telephone lines, losses that are cumulative with increasing line length. Fixed and adjustable equalizers are available, with the choice being somewhat dependent upon the range of probable mileages to be encountered. As modern telephone plants have grown in the larger cities, smaller wire sizes have been installed in an effort to keep overall cable sizes down. Unfortunately, smaller wire size aggravates those normal line losses, so that a terminal equalizer at the station's control room is limited today in its effectiveness to a very few line miles. Greater lengths require equalization in segments by the telephone company, adding sharply to line costs and adding to the attractiveness of the remote pickup transmitter.

The old open-wire telephone lines strung on pole crossarms are surprisingly low in audio losses. One station on the outskirts of a small town still using such lines achieved flat audio response to 15,000 Hertz—FM quality—on all local remotes with a simple fixed equalizer, which also equalized a 30-mile remote studio line to 5,000 Hertz—comparable to network service Class A lines feeding radio and TV stations everywhere. In this instance, a variable equalizer was unnecessary; in others, the added flexibility provided by one may be necessary to accommodate varied line characteristics.

Among the miscellaneous equipment items considered by

many stations are auxiliary power generators. There is nothing quite so eerily silent as a radio station when the power fails. A little checking on the local utility's record of outages is in order for the new station builder; if peculiar circumstances indicate too high a risk of prolonged power failure, then emergency generation equipment to handle the transmitter and essential studio gear may be a necessary investment. Otherwise, except for participating EBS stations, emergency power sources seem unjustifiable.

Sometimes overlooked in the first outline of station equipment needs is the vital matter of clocks! Traditionally, radio is considered to be the source of the exact time, and there seems no reason to relax that tradition, so accurate clocks are a basic need. The Western Union clock used to be the standard in most radio studios. Leased from the telegraph company, the clocks are mechanically operated, being wound automatically from internal batteries. They incorporate a re-setting mechanism that is actuated by an hourly pulse from special Western Union lines. In some cases, stations extended lines from the nearest Western Union connection points at their own expense in order to have exact time available.

But in most areas today, such complexity is unnecessary. The ordinary electric clock is a perfectly accurate timekeeper when it is plugged into an exact 60-Hertz power line. With interconnection between individual power companies being almost nationwide, they find it necessary to maintain their frequency with great precision, so that the ordinary clock, once set, rarely deviates by more than two or three seconds from the correct time (except for power failure, of course). Many network affiliates manage their network "joins" with nothing more elaborate, and the local independent should have no difficulty in most areas with inexpensive electric clocks. The models selected should, of course, have circular faces clearly divided into 60 minutes, so that they can be read to the second.

For the broadcaster interested in something more precise, several firms make industrial clock systems that use slaves driven from highly reliable master clocks; it's even possible to synchronize some master units automatically with WWV, the Bureau of Standards station. If conventional electric clocks are to be used, it is helpful when wiring the station to provide a separate power circuit exclusively for them. The

master switch or circuit breaker for the circuit then simpli—
fies synchronizing them when power failure or Daylight Savings
changes make re-setting necessary.

NON -TECHNICAL EQUIPMENT

In addition to a full complement of technical equipment, the
new station must equip its offices with the usual assortment
of desks, files, office machines, and related items. Many
stations avoid the substantial investment in office equipment
by contracting with local dealers on a "trade-out" or exchange
basis. This is a valid and legal procedure, simply obligating
the station to provide advertising time for the dealer to the
extent of the retail value of the merchandise. The details of
the dealer's options as to times of use, frequency discounts,
etc., should be settled when the deal is made, and the accounts run through the books and billing procedure in a straightforward manner. Of course, no implication of station ownership as collateral should be made, lest the FCC raise a col-
lective eyebrow.

Many stations have found that lukewarm participants in
trade-out deals have been among the first to discover and exploit the advantages of radio advertising, often increasing
their patronage when the trade-out is satisfied. Others have
adopted a rigid policy of no trade-outs, preferring to acquire
their accoutrements on the open market.

Chapter 9
The Staff

Radio station ownership takes every conceivable form, from a lone individual to the vast, impersonal corporation. But whatever its structure, the responsibility for a station's operation rests squarely on that ownership, morally and legally.

For the individual undertaking his first flight at radio ownership, this requirement usually is met automatically. In a partnership, there usually is (and there certainly should be) at least one member who is a veteran of the business, and he, too, usually takes an active hand in the operation. His partners may be co-investors who are neither experienced or interested in the actual operation; or they may be inexperienced but highly interested, in which case they may choose to learn "from the top," presumably with due deference to the experienced member.

MANAGEMENT

Fig. 9-1 illustrates the interlocking organizational structure of most smaller operations. From this chart it is evident that management must exercise expertise in many areas. When the echelon is filled by a single individual, usually labeled the General Manager, he has his hands full with more detail work than he possibly can handle effectively. Despite this, it is almost axiomatic that the general manager in the average radio station also is sales manager, and he is expected to spend most of his day on the streets rustling up clients. In fact, almost the only way for an aspirant to attain general managership from staff ranks is via the sales route, unless he can accumulate the financial means to invest in a station and "buy" the position!

In most cases, underlying the selection of salesmen to the exclusion of other qualified radiomen is the profit motive. Recognizing that adequate sales efforts are vital to a station's financial success, ledger-minded ownership believes that only a successful salesman can, as a manager, assure those sales. However, vital as sales are, other requisites of management are of equal importance. Business acumen does not automatically accompany sales ability; orderly administration and executive tact are not necessarily learned from selling; a sense of production values and programming creativity do not inherently arise from pounding the streets; and as for engineering...well, most salesmen are highly inept at dealing with things, as contrasted to people.

The fact that many salesmen-graduated-to-general managers do head profitable and well-run operations is largely explainable by two factors: Many radio time salesmen have gravitated to that area following a stint in programming or engineering, giving them an overall grasp of broadcasting's needs. They are radiomen who happen to be in sales, not salesmen who happen to be in radio. Secondly, the station that operates smoothly in the day-long absence of its selling general manager, day after day, is staffed with competent people who know how to "keep the store" on their own. In

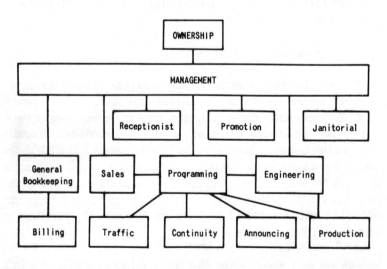

Fig. 9-1. **Radio's Typical Organizational Structure**

essence, that station is operated by a sales manager heading an autonomous staff.

Granted that it is heretical in some quarters to suggest that management sometimes may be drawn from other than the sales department, the thought nevertheless may give some station owners an idea that never before occurred to them. If the general manager must provide the bulk of the sales effort, the logical approach is that used by some stations—counter him with an operations manager to administer the balance of the operation. Under this arrangement, the management box in Fig. 9-1 would be occupied by two persons, the general manager, or more appropriately, the commercial manager, and the operations manager.

That this method is not used more widely attests to the prevalence of the erroneous concept that the prime purpose of radio is the making of money. It is not, to again revert to the heretical. A station must show a healthy profit to entice the necessary investment, of course, and it must be prosperous enough to afford the professional level of service to the community that distinguishes the best operations across the country.

The correct objective of ever-increasing sales efforts is that of improving the product and the rewards to all concerned. Despite the widespread opinion to the contrary, this view is practical, as many of the nation's biggest and finest stations exemplify. Not that excess profits are a problem to most beginning operations, to be sure. For most of them sales efforts are directed toward the basic problem of keeping the operation alive, and to this extent ownership's concern with ledger figures is not to be belittled. Especially in the new operation is executive attention to many non-sales areas required, particularly in the days when policy is being formulated and the staff acclimated. A general manager gone selling is of little help during this crucial period, and if a member of the ownership cannot be present during these formative months, there should be an executive on hand to develop his interests.

SALES

A strong sales department is an indispensable element of any staff, whether it is composed of a single salesman or a half

dozen. In this regard, it is my contention that a good salesman never costs his station a penny. His function is to sell
advertising, and (in radio, at least) his "cost" is a percentage (usually 10, 15 or 20 percent) of his gross billing. Thus,
for every dollar paid in commission, the operation receives
several in gross income. Only during the first few weeks is
a salesman on a "draw" basis, when he will not bring in as
much as he costs; if he is competent in his specialty—and if
the station's product is saleable—he should be earning his
draw and better well before it is demanded of him.

Since it always is difficult to discharge an employee, the
obvious way to avoid it is to hire only competent salesmen in
the first place. Unfortunately, there is no formula for so doing. Many salesmen, inept though they may be, manage to
sell themselves convincingly, and even the most seasoned
broadcast management is susceptible to mistakes in hiring.
If a radio salesman of known success can be lured away from
another market (there is an oft-violated ethic against pro-
selytizing employees of competitors within the same market
that seems not to apply in the case of separated, non-compet-
itive markets), one may reasonably expect him to pay his
way. But he must start all over in a new market, with a not
yet established operation; obviously, for a good man to make
such a change he must have strong personal reasons.

A very small market may be covered adequately by a single
full-time salesman, but most stations cover enough retail
businesses to justify two. Often one is responsible for the
principal town and another is assigned to the scattering of
smaller towns lying within the primary signal coverage, thereby leaving no local business prospect untouched. While it
may be true that a good salesman never cost a station a penny,
it does not follow that the commercial staff can be expanded
indefinitely. There must be enough undeveloped business potential to justify the addition of each salesman, since the
world's best cannot meet his draw if the market's prospects
are virtually all reserved.

Often an announcer or other staff member will show an interest in trying his hand at sales in his spare time. If it
doesn't run counter to station policy, there may be some justification to turning him loose on the "shirt-tail" remnants of
a market, since he is after experience and presumably earns
his livelihood by other duties. The experience he gains will

be excellent, and he may actually bring in a few dollars. If he lasts in the face of such discouraging prospects, he may develop the skill necessary to graduate to full-time sales and better account lists.

There are two sides to the practice of permitting or requiring announcers to double in sales. On the credit side is the indisputable fact that air names known in the community find that doors open more easily; the ice already is broken almost to the point of a first-name basis. Also, the announcer may be more at home in phrasing and timing than is the non-performing salesman, in the event that he is responsible for copy preparation. The biggest drawback to doubling in sales and announcing is the rigid, relentless advance of the clock. The announcer has an air schedule to meet, and it often necessitates an abrupt termination of a sales pitch at a moment when the client was on the brink of signing a contract. Some announcer-salesmen have avoided the problem by serving on the air during the early morning hours and then hitting the streets after their day's air commitments are over. Whether this can be maintained indefinitely depends entirely upon the particular makeup of the individual.

Whatever its size and alternate duties, the sales staff of the local station should be smoothly coordinated and directed by the commercial manager, or general manager, as the case may be. Since personalities enter into sales success, trading of unduly difficult prospects among the various salesmen sometimes brings different personalities to bear on the problems. Often a prospect that one man finds adamant turns out to be an easy sale for another. There is no point in protecting an individual's unproductive prospects unduly; if he doesn't sell within several calls, he has little to lose by relinquishing them to another.

One kind of sales force that the new station (or any, for that matter) would be well advised to avoid is the fly-by-night crew that invades a town with a high-pressured pitch to tie radio advertising in with some giveaway item. It has been done with clocks, thermometers, and countless other premiums, usually imprinted with the station's call letters and slogans. Local businessmen are offered attractive-sounding advertising packages in return for placing the premium items in prominent places, and the station is induced to share a commission with the foreign crew in return for all the "valuable advertising" the operation will receive from the displays throughout its area. While the premium items may be genuinely novel and effective inducements, somebody has to lose. Either the radio advertising package must be comparatively overpriced, which it rarely is, or—because the station is sharing a substantial percentage, like 50%, of the gross with the invading crew—the operation either cheapens its air product or loses money overall. In essence, the premium items are not worth the money the station pays in commission to the outsiders. The idea has merit, but the station might better buy from the firms specializing in promotional premiums and undertake their own campaign.

NATIONAL REPRESENTATIVES

Some stations are legitimately represented to remote prospects by other than staff members. The national representative firm is one which undertakes to sell a local station's services to national and regional advertisers in major cities. For a fee or commission, the national rep uses his location and experience on behalf of his client stations, endeavoring to obtain national and regional business for them. With the stations' help, he will do market research, prepare presentations, and in general serve as salesman to the big advertisers.

In an earlier era, it was my experience that the national representative was essentially worthless to the small-market station. In an attempt to update my information, a recent letter to a national representative ostensibly specializing in small stations said as much, inquiring if the situation is better today. Since I have received absolutely no reply, I can only assume that the representative was unable to offer any encouragement. The new small-market station will have to make its own inquiries and form its own conclusions about national reps.

ENGINEERS

In the usual operation technical duties seldom require 40 hours a week, once construction is completed and operation becomes routine, so that a full-time engineer usually is expected to double in other duties. He may perform any of a number of tasks for which he may be fitted. Many do announcing, some are part-time salesmen, others help out in promotion and bookkeeping, etc. As a rule, a man with the ability to cope with technical concepts is capable of doing many other duties as well, provided that he has no reluctance to do so. For instance, some engineers don't mind an announcing shift, while others hate it to the point of refusal. The same may be true for practically any nontechnical chores. Many engineers are interested solely in technical duties, and smaller operations that cannot keep them so occupied should avoid hiring those of that turn of mind. There are others, radio men interested in the total scope of broadcasting, whose interest may be primarily technical, but not to the exclusion of a keen interest in other phases of the operation. It is from the ranks of these that the smaller stations should search out their staff engineers.

Whatever his background, the station engineer is in the difficult position of serving two masters, for he must earn his paycheck from his employer and safeguard his license by compliance with FCC regulations. In a sense, he is an unsung representative of the FCC, for he may be the only staff member who understands many of the technical regulations, It then is his responsibility to persuade management to comply, justifying his position by interpreting the rules in a manner that the nontechnical can understand.

Chief Engineers, which is what those in stations having but one are called, should command a starting pay of at least $100 weekly in even the smallest market, although there are some working for less. According to the Statistical Abstract of the United States, 1966, compiled by the U. S. Department of Commerce, average hourly earnings of all radio-TV employees rose from $3.13 in 1960 to $3.70 five years later, reflecting an average annual increase of 3 1/2%. In late 1964, according to the Occupational Outlook Handbook (U. S. Department of Labor), the national average income for radio chief engineers was $126 weekly, which projects to a current figure of about $145 if the annual rate of increase remains constant.

Most FM and non-directional AM stations can operate well with but one engineer, but as regulations now stand, directional AMs need enough First Class men to staff their operating schedule for all but the times of nondirectional operation, and FMs using transmitters over 25 kilowatts also must have First Class operators on duty for all operating hours.

Staff engineers earn from $15 to $20 less per week than the "chief."

It is my belief that every radio owner-manager should hold a First Class license. Not that he necessarily should spend part of his time on a shift, but the license affords him a certain degree of assurance that he can maintain the operation in nearly any emergency. An unexpected resignation, strike, or prolonged illness can leave a station legally crippled (in the eyes of the FCC), and it seems unthinkable that a station owner should be powerless to operate his own property if conditions or precarious economics deplete his staff. There is a considerable convenience, too, in having another licensed man to supplement the chief engineer. It simplifies vacations, emergency technical repairs, and, usually, communications between engineering and management.

ANNOUNCERS AND COMBINATION MEN

Once upon a time, the distinction between the announcer and the engineer was clear. The announcer spoke into the microphone, and the engineer turned it on and off. Then, as stations occupied the smaller markets, where economics dictated combined studio-transmitter plants and smaller staffs, a new breed—the combination man—evolved. In the main, combination men were announcers who recognized the value of being "legal" engineers by possession of the then universally required First Class license, and who managed by dint of assiduous memorization to pass the exam (proving that nontechnical persons can do it, even though it is more difficult today than it was before FM and TV entered in). The combination engineer-announcer, or "combo man" for short, valued his "ticket" at about $10 in additional weekly salary. That he ordinarily really understood little of electronics and cared less seemed beside the point; he was legal, he filled two requirements virtually for the price of one, and everyone seemed happy.

Since then, as has been mentioned, licensing requirements for most small operations have been reduced to a mere formality and the need for combo men to one for announcers, although I know of no "combo" men who suffered a pay cut in consequence. The term "combo man" virtually dropped out of the radio vernacular. More recently, the pendulum of licensing requirements has swung back to midpoint, requiring an examination for those who would shepherd a broadcast transmitter as a part of their air duties. However, the actual technical knowledge required for Third Class license still is minimal, and it is inaccurate to refer to those announcers so licensed as "combo men," if by that is meant announcer-engineer.

As radio is today, the announcing staff includes disc jockeys, members of a specialized category that seems to offer the greatest fascination to the aspiring younger generation. While many oldtimers deplore the term and feel that, as modern performance goes, a disc jockey is a man who does a boy's job (someone needs to offer occasional commentary between records).

The true function of a disc jockey, as of any air man, is to lend interest and continuity to the program at hand. This properly is done by his selection of music—after all, DJ shows are, by definition, musical programs—and, if he has the talent, by interesting or amusing or entertaining patter. While some are truly creative and highly entertaining, for every one so endowed there are 50 whose stock in trade is limited to repetitious time and weather announcements and hypo jingles. Automation can replace this breed with ease.

The new station should obtain a nucleus of professional announcers whose experienced style and temperament are in tune with the station's desired image in its market. In keeping with the emphasis here on professionalism, even the smallest station should sound like radio, rather than a group of amateurs playing radio.

This nucleus of professional voices will cost a little more than the $75 to $85 weekly that the average small market announcer commands, but it can be justified in part by selecting men whose abilities can be used in other areas. The era of the chief announcer is pretty well past, but most stations do maintain the title of "program director." It is he who should have a hand in program creation, scheduling, developing saleable innovations, and—importantly—training of announcers. Usually the program director is an experienced professional announcer, well qualified to be the station's "main" voice and to coach his subordinate air men. Add to him at least another polished announcer, and the new station has the core of its beginning air staff. It might even be possible to locate a chief engineer who can double in professional-level announcing.

The emphasis on professionalism must be tempered with reality within the smaller operations for two reasons. First, beginning announcers must start somewhere, and relatively few break into the field in metropolitan stations. Secondly, as the new station develops the desired local identification with its market, it can be advantageous to add interested hometown boys to the staff as openings permit. Particularly in the very small towns, where everyone knows everyone else, the value of making opportunities for the town's aspiring youth may far offset the resulting lack of professionalism.

Announcers come in all personality types. Probably the "prima donna," is less a problem than was once the case, but the "drifter" remains. Experienced announcers whose average tenure at a given station does not exceed a few months are not good staff material; neither are those who will chafe at the limited entertainment afforded by most small towns. Unlike the practices of some professions, though, a history of an announcer's occasional discharge from a position is not necessarily stigmatic. Many announcers are fired because of circumstances not of their making, and honest ones will not hesitate to discuss the incidents.

Announcers are to be found in several ways. Personal acquaintanceship may offer one source; announcer training schools are another; and the classified pages of various trade publications are filled with ads placed by individuals representing a great variety of backgrounds. If all else fails, the station can place its own ads in those publications, inviting resumes and audition tapes. (If this is done, it is to be hoped that the station will have the common courtesy—all too sadly lacking among some broadcasters, it seems—to at least acknowledge those replies it receives, and to return those tapes for which return postage is included.)

The overall average salary for radio announcers appreciably exceeds $100 weekly, and the professional nucleus in any station most likely will command at least the national average. Statistics limited to smaller markets indicate that run-of-the-mill staff announcers may expect to start today at $80 or better, and even the eager local beginner, who might willingly work free for a time, must be paid at least the applicable Federal minimum wage.

A daytime station may get by in the short days of winter with a 3-man announcing staff, although it makes it pretty rough on the two remaining when one has a day off. In many areas, local college students with some ability and the necessary licenses are resorted to on the weekends, and this practice, if carefully planned, can be of great benefit to all concerned. The same source often serves to fill the extra hours most daytimers operate in the long summer days. Fulltimers, of course, must maintain correspondingly larger air staffs. Particularly in an independent operation, a straight 7- or 8-hour air shift is overly demanding, difficult as it is to make the layman believe it. In consequence, announcers usually are scheduled for only a few consecutive hours. If they are to put in a full day on the air, then they must work split shifts to break up their hours, and split shifts are highly undesirable in the eyes of most. This is where the man who doubles in brass has an advantage: He can devote periods of his working day to non-air duties rather than tolerating intervals on his own time that are too short to be productive in his personal pursuits. The possible exception in the matter of split shifts may be the college student who can dovetail class schedules into a broken-up day, probably working on a part-time basis.

CONTINUITY AND TRAFFIC REQUIREMENTS

Continuity is the formal term for the script used by announcer. The literal meaning of the word suggests a means of tying varied program elements together into a related whole, as was done consistently in the days of entertainment programming. Musical transcription library services provided scripted continuity with which the local announcer could relate assorted selections to a given program's central motif. Today, the intention seems to be reversed; presumably it is necessary to jolt the listener to gain his attention. Thus, the disc jockey schedules consecutive selections so contrasting as to be clashingly unrelated, and the commercial announcement yells, screams, or jangles abruptly without regard for the aural tone of the preceding and following material. Continuity, in the classic sense of the word, is virtually nil in most radio programming today, and when it is used at all, it usually refers to "copy."

Borrowed from newspaper jargon, "copy" in the radio sense

is not limited to written news material, but is applied also to written commercial announcements to be read by announcers. The continuity departments in most local radio stations are primarily concerned with the preparation of those announcements. Most local accounts lack their own advertising writers, and those that don't are apt to produce inferior radio copy. In the interest of economy, some stations have employed one or two girls who were recent high school graduates. Before the advent of the Federal minimum wage laws, they were available in smaller markets at minimal salaries, and with a little selection one or two could be found who were at least capable of passable grammar, but few who instinctively produced arresting copy.

Some stations charge their salesmen with developing copy for their own accounts, so that their sales days end with tedious hours over typewriters. This approach is predicated on the supposition that the salesman is the staff's most direct contact with the advertiser and that he should best know what is to be said. While there is some justification for this belief, the undue difficulty that many salesmen experience in putting that knowledge into polished, typewritten air prose suggests a different approach. After all, if the man is a good salesman, the best use of his time for all concerned is selling.

It is well known that an exceptional announcer can make mediocre copy sound good. It also is true that good, easy-flowing copy enhances the run-of-the-mill announcer's performance. But the combination of an average local announcer and mediocre copy adds up to sub-professional radio. Since powerhouse announcers cost more than competent copywriters, the station with limited means will do well to provide itself with at least one staffer who is at home in the copy (or continuity) department.

The duty of the traffic department is the scheduling of programs and announcements. Here the program schedules (which subsequently may become the program logs) are typed, hopefully at least a day in advance. Here, importantly, the sales contracts are translated into scheduled announcements and programs according to the stipulated terms, with all the necessary precautions to avoid time conflicts between competing advertisers, etc. Because a key selling point for radio is the flexibility it affords, insofar as an announcement can be on the air within minutes following a phone call, radio scheduling is becoming more and more a matter of last-minute changes. For this reason, traffic personnel must be on their toes to avoid missed and confused scheduling. The mechanics of typing the schedule, and producing copies, if necessary, then inserting changes as they occur right up to air time, perhaps also posting the previous day's business in the books—all place demands on the traffic department that cannot properly be met in odd moments. On the other hand, the small operation's traffic will not consume an employee's full time, and it usually is consigned to either the copy or secretarial personnel. Perhaps it most natually complements the duties of the copywriters.

BOOKKEEPING

Radio bookkeeping can be sub-divided into two aspects: daily business, and detail accounting. In radio, daily business is concerned with posting the commercial business actually aired to the respective advertising accounts, billing them, posting receipts, and petty cash transactions. The payroll accounting also may be included in this facet of bookkeeping, as may a daily report to management. At this level, bookkeeping requires no extensive accounting knowledge or experience; arithmetical accuracy is the prime requisite, and any competent staff member with the time to do it can be delegated to do so.

Detail accounting, concerned with the intricacies of taxes, depreciation, expenditure classifications, FCC annual reports, and profit and loss statements, is best left to an individual or firm experienced in such matters. Often a member of management is qualified to do the accounting, or the bookkeeping department of another business with which the station is affiliated can absorb the added burden. Lacking these possibilities, many stations retain local CPAs to keep their books in order. Alternatively, the NAB extends to member stations a jealously guarded outline of its uniform radio bookkeeping procedures.

RECEPTIONISTS AND SECRETARIES

Large radio (and TV) operations experience enough incoming

phone calls and visitors to keep a formal receptionist reasonably occupied, and associated executives may have enough correspondence to require full-time secretarial assistance. In smaller stations, though, the distinction between receptionist and secretary becomes indistinct. A girl hired solely to answer the phone and receive visitors finds idle time hanging heavily on her hands, and a given executive's secretarial requirements ordinarily are sporadic. In consequence, staff girls in small stations usually find themselves charged with a variety of chores. The girl at the receptionist's desk may be tending to traffic, copy, billing, or transcription of dictation during the substantial intervals between phone calls and visitors. Local girls hired for a radio staff, therefore, should be able to wear several hats with competence, and the right one may be worth a little more money than would be commanded by one solely suited for a single office duty.

JANITORIAL SERVICES

The sources of janitorial services available to small stations range from a full-time employee to simply calling in a neighborhood cleaning lady only when the dirt becomes absolutely intolerable. Whether many small stations can justify a full-time janitor at today's minimum wages is questionable. My experience with full-time janitors in small operations predates the minimum wage and inflation in general; very likely adequate cleanliness in the typical small station can be achieved in less than 40 hours weekly.

Many towns and small cities today have professional cleaning organizations, and some stations have made arrangements with such companies to provide periodic cleaning forays, once or twice weekly at least, on a trade-out basis.

Another entirely workable scheme that permits daily cleaning at a minimum cost can be practiced by any station. It is only necessary to hire a local student, either late high school or college, to devote a couple of after-school hours to the dusting, mopping, waxing, and glass cleaning. A possible bonus in this method, and it has happened, is the opportunity it offers to young persons interested in breaking into radio.

PROFESSIONAL VS LOCAL PEOPLE

It is an observable fact that townspeople in a small market

enjoy a vicarious "ownership" of their "own" station, and the broadcaster should nurture that proclivity by starting with the highest level of professionalism that he can muster. Thus, the new station should take to the air with its nucleus staff composed of able professionals. Since there are virtually no professional radio people among the citizenry of most small towns, management is justified in opening with imported personnel.

As the station becomes established, however, and its image becomes ensconced, community-minded citizens will come to view the operation in terms of other local businesses—a potential employer of local persons. If a station is to become a revered voice of its community, its public service must include providing local employment opportunities. Apart from janitorial and office-girl elements, which may be recruited locally at the outset, perhaps the first area suggesting itself to local personnel is that of sales. Certainly a native citizen who is known and respected by the businessmen in the community can be a tremendous ice-breaker for the commercial department, if one can be found whose sales qualifications appear promising. It is wise, though, to avoid an aspiring local salesman whose potential appears highly questionable; the discharge of a popular townsperson, no matter how valid the cause in the broadcaster's eyes, can be twisted by the local gossip-mongers into a reprehensible act.

EMPLOYEES AS PEOPLE

A radio station, more than an ordinary retail business, perhaps, is personified by its staff. The employees give a station its air personality, its community voice, and its advertising success. The ingredients leading to the overall image of the station are selected and directed by management and ownership, but in general they are implemented by employees.

Management rightly expects staff employees to act in the best interests of their station, giving their loyalty, duty and devotion to the goal of making it a financial success. Yet many executives seem to feel that a bread-and-butter paycheck (which, face it, is the lot of most radio employees) is—by itself—the only compensation necessary. In fact, an employee's conscientious devotion and loyalty are never bought! They must be earned through actions that satisfy the complex needs for individual human dignity, pleasure in his work, pride in his organization, and a sense of accomplishment and growth.

When, as sometimes happens, ownership asks employees to place the company's interests above their own, it errs. The company's interests are ownership's own, but the employee's personal interests must take precedence in his scale of values; otherwise he is not quite a whole individual. The secret is this: the more the company's interests enhance his personal ones, the higher he will rank them—and for most, personally interesting as money is, it alone is not enough.

This certainly is not to suggest that employees have to be coddled; that their unimportant whims must be indulged at the cost of the operation's efficiency. Not at all. It is to say that in return for expected adult responsibility, they are entitled to common courtesies. As an example, when admonition is necessary, as it is for everyone at some time or another, a straightforward, unemotional and private correction insults no one. The angry, name-calling and belittling harangue in the presence of others belittles an employee's human dignity. And, while the emergency schedule change arising from sickness, technical failure, or other unforeseen factors is understood and accepted by all staffers, the last-minute advisement by management of working schedule changes that could have been anticipated with reasonable notice is rightly resented.

While making a strong stand for management's consideration of employees, it must be emphasized that the need is not unilateral. Certainly employees are obligated to deliver commensurate value for payment received, even under less-than-ideal conditions. It is my belief that most radio men are dedicated to good radio, and that they will deliver to the limits of their ability for the sake of their own professional pride even when management attitudes may be stultifying. Many of them once would have worked for nothing for the chance to break into the business, and money—while it must be adequate—is not so important to their job satisfaction as are some of the other values mentioned here. Nevertheless, human nature being what it is, even these professionals will react favorably to management's respect for individual dignity by "going the extra mile" in return.

Chapter 10

Programming

Programming is radio's merchandise, and like any other product it is intended to attract the public's interest. Unlike most wares, though, it costs the customer nothing more than his attention, but even that is as scarce as cash in the face of modern life's demands.

Programming is at once the most difficult and most vital aspect of radio broadcasting. There is no really magic formula that automatically will assure vast listenership in any market, as some group operators have found through experience. The types of programming already available, the listeners' provincial tastes, and the broadcaster's own convictions all shape the fare that a new station will dispense.

In the multi-station market, the new outlet may narrow its choice of programming by avoiding those concepts already entrenched, concentrating instead on those areas in which other stations are deficient. This has been done with some success in large cities by new operations that specialize in continuous news, or by others that have brought country and western music to cosmopolitan markets. The station entering a large market with this philosophy presumably has ascertained to its satisfaction that the potential audience for such specialized fare is large enough to support its operation; yet many—particularly those specializing in classical music—have found the going very difficult in some parts of the country.

An alternative approach made by some newcomers to multi-station markets is that of programming similar to one or more of the established operations, apparently expecting to do it so much better that the listeners will be enticed permanently. Probably more new stations have submerged through this philosophy than any other (although it must be noted that not merely a few succeed in their aims).

THE SMALL MARKET

The problems of programming to smaller markets are quite different from those of the big cities. When there are but one or two stations offering local service, specialization may not be desirable—or even permissible in the eyes of the Commission. Again, it must be said that the broadcaster limited to a small market needs every listener he can snare, every minute of every operating day. If he is to justify his outlet as a mass medium in the eyes of his advertisers, he has to reach enough listeners with enough frequency to do the commercial job that radio can do. Basically, his goal is impossible: to please all the people all of the time. He will manage only to please some of the people some of the time, And the problem is to make both somes as large as possible. His programming—in content and in presentation—will determine his success.

Variety probably is the most widely used programming recipe in the small market, and the particular proportion of ingredients, the kinds and amounts of enhancing spices, and the manner of mixing comprise more combinations than it is possible to consider here.

As both listener and broadcaster during the growth years of TV, I long have contended that much of the blame of radio's abrupt demise should be laid squarely at the doorsteps of the radio broadcasters themselves! When an established business is threatened by competition, that's a signal for it to meet that threat aggressively and imaginatively with merchandising innovations and bold countermeasures. The business that tucks its tail under and cowers in dread defeats itself; yet that's just what radio did! (Some will object on the basis that all the merchandising in the world would not have prevented the demise of the horse-drawn buggy, which is true; it became irrevocably obsolete. The fact that radio today is very much alive is proof to me that early predictions of its obsolescence were highly premature.) Of course listeners were wooed by the novelty of the long-anticipated new medium. Of course a substantial—but temporary—audience desertion was inevitable. But was it good business for radio broadcasters (and, significantly, the networks) to accelerate that desertion by making their programming less enticing? Was it good business for radio's top people to flock to TV like rats deserting a sinking ship? Understandably, many had entered radio only for a related livelihood until television became a practical reality, but countless others found their fling in TV to be less rewarding in its satisfactions than radio had been. Some of them gravitated, with their invaluable experience, back to the older medium in due time, but had radio been more aggressive in the face of TV, they might have had the confidence to remain aboard and pilot a shorter course to renewed vigor.

The retrenchment that radio inflicted upon itself with the advent of TV indicated to many aspiring broadcasters that aural broadcasting was a dirt-cheap enterprise, and stations with limited resources began to mushroom across the dial. Thus entered a substantial element fundamentally oriented to inexpensive broadcasting, a complicating factor in any general effort to upgrade the variety and quality of programming. The cult of the turntable was infused with their increasing numbers, and radio leaned ever more to the jukebox-with-an-antenna concept so prevalent today.

To those who would accuse me of merely trying to turn broadcasting's clock back 20 years, I make this refutation: the programming of that era would not suffice today. In fact, I concede that a temporary retreat to the turntables probably was the better part of business discretion in the face of TV's compelling novelty. However, the emergency is over! Radio is very much alive today, and millions of listeners spend more daily hours with it than they do with TV. It is time, now, to venture into new areas of programming, with creativity backed by monetary investment, because radio is capable of so much more than playing the same records that are aired on 99 other channels. If it is to continue its hard-won survival, the medium must climb out of its circular groove. A few progressive stations today are successfully experimenting with programming suited to radio—controversial issues, interesting educational features, news in depth, editorializing—leading, by its thought-provoking nature, a modicum of variety to the radio fare in some areas.

MUSIC

Music, of the recorded variety, is the programming mainstay of by far the majority of American radio stations. This is true simply because a record (or tape) is a source of two or three re-usable minutes of rehearsed, professional entertainment at an absolute minimum cost. Enough of them manage to fill the hours of broadcasting time that cannot conveniently be filled by live entertainment, and the local station managing to produce unusual programming variety still will make extensive use of recorded music.

Certainly, music is a natural for an aural medium, since it is meant to be heard. There is little that is compelling in watching a band perform for hours on end; its sound is its raison d' etre. Happily, the American public seems to dote on musical fare of many sorts, but a swing across the dial sometimes is enough to create a suspicion that the entire radio industry is concentrating on music to the virtual exclusion of other commendable fare. Whatever the proportion of total programming it will occupy, music likely will be a staple item for most stations. Most of it will be recorded, and the nucleus of a record library must be acquired before a new station reaches its first broadcast day. A strictly "Top-Forty" operation may manage with only 40 beginning selections. An occasional station has been fortunate enough to obtain the stock of a defunct retail record store for a nominal per-record cost; others have been able to rely on personal collections of one or more of their founders; and many have leased transcription libraries.

Once commonplace in almost every station, the transcription library included perhaps 4,000 musical selections, ten or so to each 16-inch 33 1/3 RPM disc, all catalogued and cross-referenced by title, artist, tempo, category, and disc number. Auxiliary services included scripts for complete, integrated programs to be produced locally from the discs, sound effects.

The station building a new music library may rely heavily on the LP catalogs of the major labels. Rather than pay the thousands of dollars they represent at retail value, however, most stations contact the record manufacturers directly. Some have a package available to broadcasters, often with a completely open choice of titles, at nominal costs somewhere around a dollar or so per album. This brings the cost of a basic library down near the $500 mark, but since individual policies among manufacturers change with some frequency , it is necessary for the prospective broadcaster to inquire into them at the appropriate time.

Once it is on the air with its basic music library, the new

station is confronted with the problem of updating its files. The management whose previous experience is limited to big city outlets may be surprised to learn that the major record labels do not ordinarily supply <u>free</u> new releases to broadcasters in the smaller markets. This is understandable from the record companies' viewpoint: with over 4,000 radio stations, free distribution to all may entail more expense than is warranted by all but the biggest hits, and no one knows which they'll be until some time after initial distribution.

Yet, this in not entirely accurate; most of the major labels do accommodate the small-town broadcasters in some manner. Regular issue of all new single releases of a given label may be arranged at a flat monthly cost. It may be that a company's popular releases, for example, can be had for $10 or less monthly, with additional categories included, if desired, for a few dollars more. Some labels service their radio customers directly; others do so through their distributors. LP albums often are available on a station-selected basis for substantially less than retail costs, and the new broadcaster may receive an attractive opportunity to purchase them in quantity as a library starter. Ostensibly, the rates set for these release services is sufficient to cover only the record companies' costs of handling, bookkeeping, etc., which seems reasonable enough when a market won't justify free copies. However, to obtain comprehensive undating from, say, five major labels obviously will run around $50 a month, and in this era with its multitude of successful minor labels, it may not be comprehensive after all. Further, the full singles output of any label will include much material that is useless to a particular operation, possibly raising the cost of the usable releases close to the retail level. The broadcaster will have to decide, on the basis of his own needs and experience, whether the cost of blanket services can better be spent in selective buying, even at the retail level if necessary. $50 a month will buy a considerable number of 45's at the corner record store.

Oddly enough, small market broadcasters fare better on free releases from some minor record labels. Letters sent to as many of the smaller recording companies as the broadcaster may be interested in will get his station's call on at least a few free record mailing lists.

Several firms have developed music libraries on tape, principally for use with associated automation equipment. Some

firms are adjuncted to equipment manufacturers, while others
specialize in the programming aspect and supply equipment
adapted from other makers' lines. For conventional disc
jockey programming techniques, music on long reels of tape
is awkward to program from, but modern automation gear
can select a specific selection from within a reel of tape with
surprising facility. It is theoretically possible to arrange an
installation capable of delivering any selection from an entire
library on short notice and, while it would be expensive with
present techniques, such a system could combine the technical
advantages of tape with the selection convenience of a disc file.

As is rather evident from the foregoing, a discussion of
broadcast music must center principally around recordings,
because modern radio airs virtually no live music. Even those
metropolitan powerhouses that once maintained staff orches-
tras have, by and large, given them up for the economy and
variety of recorded music.

There is one area, though, where "live" music may still
work for some stations. It has been 20 years since one station, serving variety to a million-plus market via records
and transcription, first had an experience with the drawing
power of live musicians. Included in the variety offerings was
a segment of country and western styling, with the prominent
recording artists of the time. Mail requests were invited,
with only desultory response. Then one day a local man-and-
wife team applied to broadcast daily, free, for the exposure.
A sympathetic management agreed to give them 15 minutes
daily for a short trial run, somewhat to the dismay of station personnel, who felt that the pair's talents were limited.
To everyone's surprise, the mail response was enthusiastic,
even discounting the obvious "hypoing" by the pair's friends,
and their trial period stretched to 30 minutes daily for week
after week! Taking this lesson to heart, the management
opened the air to other local groups, and within a year no less
than five country-flavored bands were broadcasting daily, to
the accompaniment of sustained mail response.

There are many ramifications to the practice of airing local
"live" artists, of course. The station in this example could
not have paid the musicians union scale; it was fortunate that
the groups were willing to continue their appearances free,
and that it then was permissible under the local union procedures. Morally, of course, the station should have paid

for what proved to be strong programming services. And, apart from the ethics, there is a practical reason for a station to pay outsiders who appear on the air regularly in any capacity: they then are morally obligated to be available, prepared for their broadcasts. Where union restrictions do not intrude, modest fees within reach of the station's budget often suffice. It is wise for a new station to keep an eye open for opportunities to air "live" local artists, if only to enlarge the area of local expression.

When it comes to consideration of various types of music, there is little that can be said here. The decision to program classical, middle-of-the-road, contemporary popular, country and western, or outright rhythm and blues is best made by management familiar with the specific market under consideration. He will be influenced by other programming services available in the community, regional preferences, the audience age bracket he's aiming for, and even his own personal musical values (if he's as dedicated to what is, in his opinion, quality broadcasting as he is to pursuit of the dollar).

PERFORMANCE LICENSING

Whether live or recorded, most music is copyrighted and performance for profit—which its broadcasting is contsrued (and hoped) to be—entails royalty payments to publishers and composers. Since nearly all published music is controlled by three major music licensing organizations, most stations having blanket contracts with all three feel free to play any music that comes to hand without making a detailed investigation of its copyright terms. While this assumption in not 100% safe, it seems to be workable. Instances of prosecution at the local station level for inadvertent failure to observe copyright restrictions are few, although the laws do have teeth, should it be necessary to use them.

The traditional music licensing firm is The American Society of Composers, Authors and Publishers (ASCAP for short). Since 1914, it has represented the interests of many of this country's leading composers and lyricists, being instrumental in instigating court cases that established certain guidelines defining performance for profit. When radio became a substantial user of music, ASCAP permitted its broadcasting on a free or very nominal basis. Later, as radio advertising became profitable, music fees were imposed on all commercial radio broadcasters. (A similar procedure was followed during the establishment of television.) Today, blanket ASCAP coverage for a local radio station costs 2% of the gross income, adjusted for several exceptions like commissions, political broadcasts, etc. An additional "sustaining" fee is dependent upon station size. This blanket license covers the station for all ASCAP music played, be it much or little However, it does not automatically clear all ASCAP titles for broadcast; the Society maintains a list of specific numbers that, for various reasons, are restricted from air play.

An alternate ASCAP licensing arrangement is available on a per program basis, but it is of little interest to smaller stations since it entails a fee of 8% of the adjusted gross received for musical and variety programs and 2% for those using only theme, incidental and background music, along with a sustaining fee. While this arrangement might prove economical for the occasional station specializing in nonmusical programming, it does involve a considerable amount of logging and bookkeeping, placing considerable demands on the time of staff personnel. The ASCAP blanket agreement contains a clause giving the Society the right to require logging of actual music played, but I never have known a local station that was called upon to do so.

Listeners who are old enough can recall the period nearly 30 years ago, when their favorite radio programs suddenly blossomed forth with unfamiliar theme songs, and the public domain compositions of Stephen Foster were played incessantly. It was the year that broadcasters balked at continued support of what they then felt was ASCAP's strangling monopoly. To fill the void, some of them formed Broadcast Music, Incorporated, in 1940. The infant grew slowly over the years, until today BMI claims a stature fully competitive with the much older ASCAP, and it sometimes incurs criticism from its own founding industry. Blanket arrangements for BMI music are similar to those of ASCAP, except that the commercial fees are graduated from 0.84% to 1.35%, based on the station's gross. Per program licenses also are offered by BMI, with commercial fees ranging from 2.81% to 4.50%, in addition to graduated sustaining fees.

BMI determines its payments to its member composers and publishers in part by statistical analysis of titles actually broadcast. It derives its samples from logging reports obtained from a cross-section of the country's radio stations, with perhaps a hundred or so of them keeping per-performance logs in detail at any given time. As it works out, each station is faced with the sometimes onerous chore of logging specifically all music aired for a 2-week period about once every three years or so. In the small operation, where one man may be responsible for the simultaneous duties of announcing, cueing records, choosing copy, keeping the program log and the operating log, along with answering the telephone, the added obligation to log each song by title, label, and publisher or composer can be the proverbial last straw, and even 3-year intervals seem too short! Some stations manage to free or hire a girl specifically to handle much of the required BMI logging when those infrequent occasions arise.

The third music licensing organization to which most broadcasters subscribe began as the Society of European Stage Authors and Composers, now simply—and officially—SESAC. Founded in 1931 in the interest of, in the words of founder Paul Heinecke, "...improved international understanding," SESAC long represented only a small proportion of the music commonly played on radio. Consequently, some stations historically have attempted to avoid the necessity of fee payments by carefully screening all SESAC selections from their files. Apart from the chance of inadvertent violation, the time consumed in checking copyright sources probably is more demanding than the nominal fee required of small stations. The SESAC rates for blanket coverage range from as little as $90 annually for the smallest daytime operation to a possible extreme of $6,000 for the major market 50-kilowatt outlet.

Unlike ASCAP and BMI, SESAC actively produces and promotes recorded music services, including an LP program service designed expressly for broadcast, and specialized material developed as sales and production aids. There also is offered a series of short complete selections and other broadcast aids not readily available on ordinary records. Because of this aggressive promotion of SESAC music aids, the old idea that there is little to be gained from a SESAC license is no longer valid, if it ever was.

MUSIC INDEXING

The station that would receive the greatest utility and economy of staff effort from its record library will institute an indexed filing system to expedite music selection. Most libraries are indexed at least by song title, although some operations strangely prefer to index primarily by artist. Preferably, the file system should be cross-indexed under both headings, and packaged libraries intended for broadcast use usually come accompanied by an extensive index. The problem in most stations arises when pressing duties delay the filing of new releases as they are received as approved, until a considerable backlog of unindexed material is at hand. The task of catching up then is a formidable one.

The physical requirements of a perpetually growing music library also should be anticipated. Whether discs or tapes, or both, are used, they must be stored. As years pass, most stations find themselves adding shelves to every available wall area in a mad race with accumulating records and tapes, and the practical expedient of an annual weeding out of dead material is instituted. Systematic storage, well labeled and kept clean and temperate, is imperative to convenient recorded musical program preparation. A safety note: Records in quantity are heavy. Shelves and cabinets that may hold thousands of discs or tapes must be exceptionally sturdy and tip-proof. A falling transcription cabinet or wall cupboard can seriously injure the hapless employee caught in the way.

Chapter 11

Other Program Types and Program Logs

This Chapter must be prefaced with a statement of my personal bias favoring national networks. Perhaps because my first infatuation with radio dates to its "golden" era, when the networks served an endless variety of program content and locale far beyond the reach of the then few independents, a radio station without a network affiliation still is to me something less than complete.

With radio in general growing more conscious of the need for greater programming diversity across the dial, networks are making a belated battle for survival. The American Broadcasting Company, which owes its very existence as a distinct network to an earlier governmental edict forcing its divorcement from the parent NBC network, recently obtained FCC dispensation to provide four disparate program services tailored to as many programming concepts. If ABC succeeds in what many consider to be a do-or-die attempt, it may become commonplace for a single market to have as many as seven radio outlets offering the programming advantages of national network affiliation.

In an earlier era, a network was a source of appreciable revenue only to affiliates in larger markets, while those in smaller towns hoped to break even. In terms of network revenue balanced against assorted costs such as sustaining fees and line costs, the small market outlet rarely had much to show on the books. However, the intangibles sometimes were overlooked: the network provided many hours of programming, freeing station personnel for greater concentration on local programming periods. There was a certain prestige among certain network offerings that made adjacencies (spot announcements immediately preceding or following a particular program) easier to sell, and perhaps worth a premium rate.

Inexpensive technicians could operate a station during those times when programming was simply a series of network feeds interspersed with recorded announcements. Smaller news and production staffs were needed for a given level of programming. In general, when a network provides a substantial portion of an affiliate's programming it eases the problems of operation much more than is reflected by the cold revenue figures.

Network affiliation once was restricted almost entirely to full-time stations (when night-time radio was considered choice time), but many arrangements with daytimers have been made in recent years. The diminished importance of night listenership and the scarcity of willing affiliates in some markets have led the networks to offer many concessions. Included are eased requirements on option time (certain hours guaranteed to the networks), and the provision of some chain programs available for local sale. This last concession, incidentally, is potentially remunerative. Network compensation for nationally sold programs traditionally has been low; perhaps 25% of the affiliate's rate card. Obviously, network calibre programs available for local sale offer the lure of full card rates at minimal program cost, and some stations have justified affiliation handsomely on this basis alone. Others, it must be admitted, have not found network fare easily saleable.

Apart from national chains, regional radio networks have abounded. For some reason, many of them proved to be so marginal that they were abandoned, with but a handful sustaining prolonged profitable operation. The cost of wire lines was a large handicap to earlier "live" networks, and some have managed since World War II to remain active by utilizing their affiliates' FM adjuncts for live intercity relay. In fact, certain FM regional networks have prospered, once the technical complexities were mastered. Ideally, the FM network is technically superior to the conventional land-line feeds of the national chains. The regional network concept parallels that of the national chains, offering a ready-made lineup of outlets for regional advertisers. Unfortunately, the required combination of network-calibre production and sales forces, coupled with a plentitude of prospective regional advertisers, is rare. For all its apparent merit, the regional network concept has proved generally unworkable.

Some regional "networking" is done via tape, with modest success, although this approach more nearly approximates "syndication." There is one area, however, that seems to be exploited but little: tape programs that are interchanged among the properties of group owners. With some prominent exceptions, stations under common ownership rarely exchange program features. Yet, each should have an outstanding personality or an exceptional program concept within its staff, and it seems logical that each station's long suit could be beneficial to its sister stations through a suitable tape interchange. In this manner, all of the group's outlets' programming would be strengthened with a sprinkling of the best from each. That it is not done more commonly may indicate that there are too many problems involved in such fraternal syndication.

SYNDICATION

Just as newspaper features are syndicated to subscribing independent papers, radio and TV programs are syndicated to broadcasting outlets. However, while TV program syndication enjoys considerable popularity, its radio counterpart never has been of much consequence. Some of the daily serials of the '30s were syndicated, and Ziv (a firm offering such material) attained some circulation of several radio features in the late '40s, but they joined in the demise of variety programming in general. It is unfortunate that radio syndication is at such a low ebb. Theoretically, it is capable of supplying all the variety and exceptional (and therefore costly) talent once monopolized by network radio, except for timely news and special events coverage.

The underlying cause of inadequate radio syndication is the usual one: financial. The syndicator ordinarily sells program content to subscribing stations, which then must develop their own sponsors. The syndicator would like to sign a number of stations to moderately long-term contracts in order to justify the development and production costs of a particular program series, but individual broadcasters are reluctant to obligate themselves when they are uncertain of continuous sponsorship. Small stations are notoriously loathe to pay for sustaining material.

In contrast, network programming has been embraced by

affiliated stations because, in general, it comes pre-sold. A net not only packages the program (or procures it from outside packagers), but it customarily sells the advertiser as well, leaving the local station little to do but air the feed and accept the fee. It seems safe to say that if independent program packagers could offer stations their products already sponsored, radio syndication would skyrocket. Until that situation comes to be, syndicated program production must be paid for by its users.

Radio syndication may yet have a future. It must have one, if radio is to meet the challenge of increased program variety with quality fare, since few stations can afford the necessary calibre at the individual local level. Before this can happen, though, local radio managements must realistically face the necessity of paying reasonable fees for the material they are paid to broadcast. The virtually painless combination of free records, a pair of turntables, and a $6,500-a-year disc jockey has lured most of them into miserly attitudes.

Syndicators must bend some, too. With current radio committed to short features, a la NBC's "Monitor," and repetition —like hit records—to accommodate audience turnover, a single per-program sustaining fee should prevail. Without restrictions on the frequency of usage, a pattern of repeats would pare station costs to mere pennies for each unsponsored airing. Added to the sustaining fee would be some percentage of the station's revenue from a program's sale to an advertiser. Sponsored repeats would produce a tapering return for the syndicator, much as the "residuals" function in similar areas. Admittedly, the bookkeeping and policing would be complicated, but some similar approach seems necessary to minimize the local station's obligation for contracted programs that go unsponsored.

Lest my pro-network and pro-syndication comments here should appear inimical to an overall emphasis on local expression, it must be noted that most small markets simply don't have enough activity of local interest to fill all of a station's operating hours with pertinent local expression. Consequently, most broadcasters have resorted to records to fill the great bulk of their air time. Certainly there is a place for musical programming directed to all listeners' tastes; I merely contend that too many stations are duplicating the musical programming of competitive signals, to the point of excluding other valid concepts.

TALK PROGRAMS

Most metropolitan centers now have radio outlets specializing principally or entirely in talk programming, contrasting sharply against a preponderance of musical fare. Appalling as the idea is to some listeners, others find it a refreshing change. Some veteran broadcasters view talk programming as a step toward re-establishing radio as a <u>foreground</u> medium, since it requires the listeners' attention; music often is dialed for background listening, so that loud gimmicks are required to command attention to commercial announcements.

Not that just any talk will command attention, of course. The "interest quotient" for talk material must be consistently higher than that of general music, since it must maintain devoted attention. Therefore, the station of limited means instituting some talk programming will do so judiciously, attempting only that which it is equipped to do well.

INTERVIEW

The very word "interview" immediately conjures images of the stilted, dry, and utterly boring question-and-answer programs all too common to radio in bygone years. This is unfortunate; almost any interview can be done interestingly. The first rule of good interviewing is to throw away the script. The written interview, planned to the last comma, invariably sounds as mechanical as a printing press, completely devoid of personal enthusiasm. If the <u>participants</u> project no enthusiasm, certainly none can be expected from the listeners.

Ordinarily an individual is interviewed because he possesses some particular ability, knowledge, interest or position, and the interviewer who approaches a discussion with only guide-line notes and a genuine interest in his guest's specialty soon will draw him into an earnest, spontaneous response that will evoke attentive curiosity among many listeners. The local station, then, need not shy from airing interviews, if it will develop the technique and schedule them only when there is a good subject available, which may be only occasionally.

PANEL DISCUSSIONS

Closely related to the interview is the forum, or more informally, the panel discussion program. The key to interesting panel programs is controversy, requiring participants who represent opposing views, and who do so articulately. Each of several clear-channel powerhouses capture late night listeners in 30 or 40 states on the strength of their discussion programs. The local station ordinarily will not have access to panelists of the prominence of those appearing in major cities (many of whom are authors of recent books, with their radio appearances arranged for publicity value), but there are local controversies in almost every town, and there are partisans who can be induced to appear on the air in support of their positions. Again, it perhaps is better to program such discussions only when there is some local ferment over an issue. Panel discussions artificially inspired simply to fill a regular program schedule soon fall flat.

A serious fault of many panel shows, including some of those on the major outlets, lies in the moderators' inability to allow but one panelist to speak at a time. When eagerness to press a point leads to two or more talking simultaneously, the listener becomes lost. An individual participating in such a group can "tune out" interferring cross-comments to a marked degree, but when radio transmission intervenes, that ability to discriminate is lost (at least for monaural reproduction). A panel show moderator should keep that limitation in mind and firmly exercise his authority in the interest of intelligible discussion.

"TELEPHONE" SHOW

Another form of talk programming that is enjoying considerable popularity is the telephone show. Its prime appeal, perhaps, is that of inviting the listener to participate. Just as some persons find playing in a sandlot game to be more satisfying that merely observing major league baseball, some listeners find that telephone participation makes a local program more interesting than one of greater professional polish.

I was doing beeper phone shows in 1954 without the insurance against profanity of the now commonplace tape-delay technique. Fortunately, the small-town public then still observed the traditional air taboos, and the particular program did not invite controversial arguments, either. Today, the tape-delay mechanism for telephone shows is virtually mandatory, so that any violation of good taste can be excised during the several seconds available before it reaches the transmitter. In this way, the broadcaster maintains the control to which he is obligated.

The telephone facility may be used in conjunction with panel and interview shows, inviting questions directly from the audience; it may seek information from listeners, as in the problems-and-solutions format; or it may be used for polling public opinion on the question of the day. Some stations have incorporated "conference" telephone facilities, whereby the principal guest on a panel or interview program may be aired via phone from his home or other location, often with the facility to hear queries from local listeners and studio guests and return with answers, with all sides of the conversation being broadcast. This technically complex arrangement might be useful to the local station whose market rarely is visited by prominent people. If you can't bring a guest to the program, it is in this manner possible to take the program to him via phone, all at no more cost than that of a lengthy phone call.

A pitfall common to telephone shows in small towns is the tendency for a certain few of the listeners to monopolize the discussions day after day. There always are a few of the most avid who eagerly await the chance to call daily, and if care is not taken, the program series will lose interest for most of the other listeners. Some control of repetition should be exercised.

Other talk program material is provided by both of the major wire services in the form of features written for delivery by local announcers. Most stations use this material sparsely; yet periodic surveys indicate to the wire services that enough stations find enough of it useful to justify their continued transmission. The station looking for talk program material may find selected wire features entirely suitable, but they may be enhanced by a little dressing up. Two voices, a little production, mood music sometimes, perhaps a dramatized line or two—a little time and creativity invested by the staff can minimize the monotony of a single voice droning on at some length. If there are competent staffers not ordinarily heard in the course of the day's programming, their voices can add to the variety value of wire service material.

EDITORIALIZING

An important avenue now open to the broadcaster is that of editorializing. Ideally, it will not add substantially to the quantity of talk programming to editorialize, since short, succinct and arresting statements are most effective. It should, however, add materially to the significance of the stations' programming, provided that editorializing is practiced only when there is an issue at stake. The power of the editorial should not be diluted with trivia.

OTHER SOURCES

One facet of talk radio is virtually dead today: drama. Those concerned with the production of drama, being theatrically oriented, naturally envision it to be complete only with visual reproduction to complement the aural, thus their general exodus to television. Admittedly, much of the old radio drama was of the much-maligned "soap opera" or "private eye" calibre. Yet, popular criticism of TV drama by those who would impose their own values on the public at large has not measurably induced audiences to seek more than light entertainment on the television screen. Radio drama, if it were to revive, probably would be similarly oriented.

There are many areas that lend themselves to creative talk programming, dependent upon audience tastes, station policies, and staff capabilities. There is, for instance, a great variety of subject matter in the daily newspaper columns, and established features retain their continued circulation only because of sufficient reader interest. Conceivably, any of these time-tested subjects could be developed for radio talk programming. How about book reviews? Hobby features? Medical problems? Market analyses? Travel features? Scientific and technological frontiers? Fashion notes? Newcomers to the community? The daily papers find all these topics to be of interest; surely they and many more are adaptable to the needs and interests of particular radio markets.

NEWS

In various formats, news is second only to music among the

major ingredients of modern radio programming. A 5-minute news summary at least once hourly seems mandatory, apparently in response to an American desire to keep superficially abreast of headline events.

One of the most effective measures a station can take to achieve a local image is to become a voice of its community through local news programming. Like any other air offering, it is best done well or not at all, of course, and the metropolitan stations exploiting local news to the hilt keep a horde of radio newsmen circulating at all times. The operation in the small community can't afford such a top-heavy news staff, and generally newsworthy happenings don't occur that frequently in a small town anyway.

The veteran broadcaster accustomed to metropolitan news concepts may be surprised by the comparatively inconsequential nature of the events that can interest the small-town listener. Where neighborliness borders on nosiness, innocuous events comprise the bulk of the "news," and the local broadcaster must re-orient his news values accordingly. The line between local news coverage and gossip-mongering is a delicate one, and of course the broadcaster's good taste, respect for privacy, and unflagging veracity must prevail.

The small-market station should cultivate the favor of the local police department, whose venerable chief may incline toward resentment of queries by something as new-fangled as a radio station. The blotter should be routinely available to station personnel, and a station monitor on the local police radio channels is highly desirable, if a staff member can be freed to track down any newsworthy leads so acquired. In this connection, it is vital for the broadcaster to appreciate that FCC regulations specifically forbid the divulgence of information gleaned from point-to-point radio—which includes police channels—to any but the intended recipients. Thus, the police radio monitor is only a source of leads for station personnel to check out, either personally or by official release by the law officials; it is not by itself a source of news stories.

Another source of news with strong local interest is the hospital. A daily check of those within the station's coverage area spices the local news with admissions, births, and deaths. This one source has provided a substantial part of many stations' local news, and—maudlin as the idea strikes some—a few have managed reasonably good taste, along with ready sponsorship, with an "Obituary Column of the Air." Of such is the stuff of local news. For regional and worldwide news, nearly all stations rely on one of the two major wire services: Associated Press, and United Press International. (Some network-affiliated stations concentrate solely on local news, leaving the national and worldwide coverage to their network programming.)

The wire services are networks in their own right. Most national and worldwide news is fed from a central point to subscribers across the nation, with periodic "splits" during which the circuits are taken over regionally by "local" bureaus central to their respective territories. Thus, the wires strive to cover all but strictly local events. Standard radio wire fare includes not only broad and timely news coverage, but also a multitude of special and regular features for women, sports enthusiasts, investors, farmers, and others with special interests, along with material on weather, religion, automotive developments, and news material.

In addition to standard news and features, the wire services also provide special circuits for financial reports, business news, sports and race results, play-by-play ball games, and a variety of other specialties to radio stations choosing to pay for them. For several years, UPI has augmented its teletype coverage with an audio service that provides "actuality" reports of the news happenings in the voices of the principals, or voice coverage by on-the-scene reporters. Involving some expense, this optional audio service offers many network news advantages to non-network stations. The station subscribing to UPI Audio ordinarily delegates a tape recorder to automatic operation from the incoming audio line, with periodic editing and airing of the received material. With UPI claiming over 300 audio service users, competitor AP recently inaugurated an audio service of its own.

The cost of a basic radio wire service from either of the two news organizations is determined by market size. Also, rates historically have been negotiable, so the new broadcaster should encourage competition by inviting quotations from both. He also should evaluate the applicability of each service's offerings in the light of his particular operation's needs. In the end, he should obtain his choice of the basic radio teletype wire for less than the cost of an inexpensive announcer.

WEATHER

The weather is a vital aspect of radio news. In most areas, the U.S. Weather Bureau maintains a teletype weather wire for interested parties, with airports, highway departments, and radio and TV stations among its subscribers. There is no charge for this weather wire service where it is available, except for a proportional share of the wire and teletype costs. If there are several existing subscribers in a station's proximate area, the expense of joining the service may be quite small.

There are private weather forcasting services vying with the U.S. Weather Bureau for prognostic accuracy, and certain radio services are available from them, too. Costs may be higher, and there well may be commercial connotations in using the name of a private concern, but some broadcasters feel that some private forecasters have a better track record than does the government bureau, and they have utilized their services. Live weather broadcasts, aired remotely from the nearest U.S. Weather Bureau center by Bureau personnel, long have been a staple of radio. Since the Government cannot practice favoritism, if the nearest Bureau is providing live reports for any station, it is obligated to do as much for another. The expenses incurred in line charges and equipment are the responsibility of the broadcaster, and he may have to settle for sharing simultaneous feeds with his competitors.

Most small towns have official weather observers who record the local precipitation and temperature extremes for the U.S. Bureau. Often it is a weather-minded individual who assumes these unpaid duties, but the Bureau prefers to assign them to a local radio station. While keeping weather records is an added burden to the small staff of the typical station, there is something to be said for having official conditions to report at all times.

SPECIAL EVENTS

A special event is, by definition, an unusual occurrence.

Thus, special events do not lend themselves to regular scheduling (unless yearly scheduling of an annual affair can be called regular). Every area has its special events, many of which can be aired as live remotes, while others can be taped, edited, and broadcast at a station's later convenience. The daytimer, in particular, can lend substance to its regular programming by assigning a staff member to tape many of the community events, occurring mostly at night, when the station is silent, and airing edited highlights the following day.

The special event may include a visit by a prominent personality or performer; a forum on local issues; a traditional local celebration, fair, rodeo, or trade show; a church or school cantata; a race or parade; or any digression from the small-town humdrum. The local special event may not seem exciting to the cosmopolitan radioman, but in a small town even the most bland diversion from routine is exciting. If it draws a crowd, the event is potential broadcast material.

RELIGIOUS PROGRAMS

Conventional religious programming seems to be on the wane. With the emphasis ever more on music and news, station after station has reduced or eliminated its religious programs in the belief that they repel far more listeners than they attract—which probably is true. In consequence, a few stations have swung to the opposite extreme, catering to the small but fervently loyal religion-oriented audience. Excepting a few stations stubbornly dedicated to programming traditions, the specialty outlets are virtually the only ones available to ministers and their spokesmen. However, religion still is important among the FCC's programming expectations, although the pressures of certain militant atheists threaten to wrap the whole issue in controversy.

Many small stations make their facilities available to the local Ministerial Association, often donating a daily quarter-hour devotional period for rotating use by the member churches. Others have restricted their free religious time to a weekly church service, broadcast remotely and consecutively from the Association's member churches. However, once free time has been made available to Ministerial Association members, some stations have found that churches outside the organization feel entitled to equal free time. In some cases, it has been given; in others, the broadcaster has discontinued all free religious time.

Paid religious time is another matter; one that the religious specialty stations rely upon for profit. The small-town station may prefer to shun all paid religion, especially those programs not directly related to local churches. Or it may clear "painless" time availabilities (those hours considered not commercially productive) for a limited amount of religious fare. Some stations have encouraged religious expression by offering a flat rate discount to all, although there may be some question of the business propriety in so doing. (The practice of giving discounts or rebates to special-interest advertisers might be construed as similar to the now illegal practice of setting premium rates for political broadcasts. However, there can be no objection if certain hours are offered at cut rates, if they're available to all advertisers.)

PUBLIC SERVICE

In its broad sense, public service is the reason for a radio station's existence, and insofar as listeners derive some benefit from its offerings, it is serving its purpose. In the programming sense, though, public service has come to mean a more limited category, comprised mainly of announcements and inducements on behalf of government and other non-profit enterprises. Every station applicant promises a certain number of public service announcements (PSAs) when he files with the FCC, and he is expected to show actual airing of at least that many when license renewal time comes.

Since the Commission now is interested in the number of public service announcements, rather than the former criterion of percentage of program time so allocated, the broadcaster has no particular inducement to "sponsor" whole blocks of time for worthy purposes. Strictly speaking, the quarter-hour transcription supplied by, say, the U.S. Air Force to further its recruiting campaign credits the broadcaster with but two or three actual announcements devoted to specific recruiting messages. The rest of the time is simply sustaining programming. This, perhaps as much as general program trends, has hastened the adoption of the 5-minute "public service" program.

Because the number of public service announcements is the

important factor, the dull wordiness so common to many of them can be reduced to a succinct 10 seconds of essential information. This practice generally improves the pace and flow of the surrounding programming. Since most listeners make no distinction between public service announcements and commercial spots, shorter PSAs allow more paid announcements per hour before the audience becomes sated with messages.

PSAs may meet the letter of the law, but the dedicated broadcaster will offer programs that provide genuine public service to his listeners. The characteristics of each market will suggest several sources of local interest public service. In rural areas, most agricultural "county agents" are equipped and eager to provide specialized program material of interest to farmers, stockmen, and homeowners, for instance. In many states, land-grant colleges produce several series for syndication to area stations. Most of them are done in a low-keyed but smoothly professional manner.

Local schools are an important source of public service programs. The metropolitan radioman may be aghast at the idea of turning a group of small-town high school students loose on the air, but with a little professional guidance the results are good enough to attract many parental listeners. School news, discussions of student-faculty differences, debates, sports interviews, dramas, and the inevitable disc jockeys all permeate school broadcasts, and school administrations, along with the community in general, are most appreciative of the opportunities offered to their youths by the local station.

In non-academic fields, radio coverage of town council meetings, promotion of worthy projects undertaken by fraternal and civic clubs, and exposure of countless other happenings that are far from earth-shaking but are of local importance can contribute to a station's public service image.

SURVEYS

One of the more difficult problems confronting the broadcaster in his program evaluation is that of determining how many listen to which ones. Lacking a better criterion, metropolitan stations subscribe to the professional surveys conducted by the several private polling concerns. These surveys purport to determine listenership by statistical extrapolation of a small sampling, giving audience size by number.

Recently, the need for more knowledge of audience characteristics has been recognized, and the rating services are attempting to classify audiences in terms of age, economic level, and other aspects important to potential advertisers. Apart from the oft-raised question of the survey's partiality to the stations paying for them, the cost of a reputable one taken in a single-station market is prohibitive for most such stations. Besides, the sales value of a favorable rating, so vital in the cities, may be limited by the local businessman's unfamiliarity with audience numbers, leaving the principal function of the survey limited to merely pointing up programming strengths and weaknesses. Vital as this function is, it cannot justify the cost of a professional single-station survey.

On the other hand, it may be most difficult for a station to conduct its own, from both the standpoint of mechanics and the matter of validity. How many listeners, knowing they were being queried by the station itself, would give an unbiased answer? An independent polling agency is far preferable.

One small station obtained a useful survey by approaching the appropriate faculty members of the local junior college with the concept of a survey as a class project. As it finally was arranged, the station provided an office and a telephone for shifts of students who undertook to call most of the town's residents regarding their listening habits. The caller was identified with the survey as a project of the college, encouraging unbiased responses, while the participating students were paid by the station for their time. The result was a comprehensive poll of most of the principal town's adults, dignified by the name and academic impartiality of the college, all for a few hours' cost at the prevailing minimum wage. The report meant as much to most local businessmen as would have one by any of the recognized broadcast rating services, and its revelation of programming effectiveness was of considerable value to the station.

PROGRAM LOGS

Whatever may be a station's programming structure, accurate and complete logging is essential. The FCC requires that logs be kept in such a manner that interested parties can reconstruct the nature and general content of programming at any instant of the broadcast day.

Since an advance program schedule is necessary to most operations, it is customary to prepare it so that it becomes the log as the broadcast day progresses. The program log is, in essence, a detailed record of the general nature and commercial content of a station's broadcast day. The Commission's detailed regulations for AM program logging begin with Paragraph 73.112 (Vol. III), and are repeated virtually word-for-word in the FM rules. They stipulate standardized abbreviational nomenclature for several program and announcement categories, and the broadcaster unfamiliar with them should refer to the official definitions. For that matter, so should those experienced broadcasters who have not done so in recent years; some of them still are following logging procedures that are at variance with current requirements.

In essence, each program is to be identified by title and sponsor, if any, along with entries showing actual beginning and ending times. If timeliness of a recorded program may be misconstrued, the necessary Mechanical Reproduction Announcements (MRA) are to be noted as given. When an entire program is sponsored, the individual performance times of the actual commercial messages are not logged, but the total minutes and seconds within the program devoted to commercial continuity (CC) are entered. Actual CC in such a program might be three or four minutes, and the Commission now is interested in commercial minutes per hour, be they sponsorship messages or commercial announcements.

The ubiquitous spot announcement is logged either as a Commercial Announcement (CA), or as Commercial Continuity (CC), with the entry giving the duration and either the specific time of airing or a clear indication of the quarter-hour segment in which it was included. (Perhaps most stations will prefer spot performance times logged to the minute for their own convenience in determining compliance with guaranteed time contracts, sufficient separation of competing products, and general internal control.) Duration times need not be logged precisely; a 62-second and a 57-second spot both qualify as nominal 60-second announcements. However, logging of "nominal" durations is not to be used as a mechanism for consistently airing more CC per hour than the log reflects.

There is no longer a logging distinction between live and

recorded announcements, although a station almost certainly will need to make some distinction for the operators' procedures. It is important to note that a recorded commercial announcement is not to be logged MRA, as some operators persist in doing. An announcement made free on behalf of a nonprofit organization, civic or government activity, or similar local or national cause, is a Public Service Announcement (PSA).

The logging practices of some broadcasters notwithstanding, time signals, routine weather reports, and station promotional announcements are not PSAs. In fact, there is no specific logging category for these repetitious announcements (so long as they're not commercial), and therefore no requirement to log them at all, though they may be included on the daily log form for scheduling purposes. A weather report may legitimately be listed as a "news" program if it is long enough to serve as more than a passing interruption to the program in progress.

The Commission has set forth eight basic categories within which it is expected that all program content will fall. By their official designations, these program types are:

A: Agricultural, addressed primarily to a station's agricultural listenership.

E: Entertainment, including music, drama, variety, quizzes, etc.; the bulk of most stations' programming.

I: Instructional, intended to further "cultural" appreciation; occupational and vocational instruction; and other programs not included in the A, N, PA, R, S and O types.

N: News, including weather, stock markets, commentary, and sports news.

O: Other, a catch-all category for those programs not included in the other seven basic types.

PA: Public Affairs, such as talks, commentaries, speeches, political programs, editorials, forums, panels, and similar programs.

R: Religious programs, including sermons, religious news, religious music and drama, church services, and related religious fare.

S: Sports, including play-by-play, pre- and postgame action, separate programs of sports news, instruction, etc.

To further clarify the nature of some programming, further "sub-types" are added to the basic ones above. They are defined thus:

ED: Educational institution. Those A, N, PA, R or I programs that are prepared by or for, or in cooperation with educational institutions, organizations, libraries, museums, PTAs, etc. Sports are specifically exempted from this sub-type.

EDIT: Editorial, stating positions of the licensee. The basic type for most EDIT programs is PA.

POL: Political. Presentations of candidates for public office, or programs which express views (other than EDIT) on candidates or public issues subject to public ballot. Usually a sub-type under PA.

Official logging designations for program sources, once numerous, have been reduced to just three: Local (L), Network (N), and Recorded (REC). Those programs originated or produced by the station that use live talent for more than 50% of the air time are logged as L. They include remotes and those locally produced on tape for subsequent airing. Newscasts read live from wire copy are, contrary to older practices, also L programs. And, while most disc jockey shows are less than 50% live and therefore do not fall under the L source designation, there may be sub-programs (such as news programs) within the body of a disc program that are logged as local.

The NET classification includes all network programs carried, whether they are originated by national, regional, or special networks. Those delayed on tape for subsequent broadcast still are logged as NET. The third source category covers everything not included in the L and NET columns. All recorded programs are logged as REC, including those using tapes, transcriptions and recordings not produced by the station or a network. Most syndicated material joins record shows in this comprehensive designation. Specific logging procedures for station identifications, political announcements, filing applications, and other requisite entries are detailed by the regulations.

As is true of the other official logs, program logs are to be kept by those employees with actual knowledge of the necessary

KWZZ
PROGRAM LOG

DAY __Wed.__ DATE __9/11/66__ PAGE __2__
ALL TIMES E S T

ID: Call Letters & Location

ANNOUNCEMENTS:
CA: Commercial, Identified
PSA: Public Service
POL: Political
MRA: Mechanical Reproduction

COMMERCIAL MATTER:
CC: Commercial Content
CREDIT: Sponsorship Identified

PROGRAM SOURCE:
L: Local
M: Mutual Network
N: Other Network
REC: Recorded

PROGRAM TYPE:
A: Agricultural
E: Entertainment
I: Instructional
N: News
O: Other
PA: Public Affairs
R: Religious
S: Sports

SUB-TYPE:
ED: Educational
EDIT: Editorial
POL. Political

OPERATOR   ON   OFF
                _E30A_   _1130A_

                _1130AM_

ANNOUNCEMENTS & COMMERCIAL MATTER

ID	SCHEDULED ON	SCHEDULED OFF	PERFORMED ON	PERFORMED OFF	CA	PSA	POL	MRA	PROGRAM	CREDIT	SPONSOR	DUR Min	DUR Sec	SOURCE	TYPE & Sub-Type
830	830 A	855	830	855	X		X		MORNING MELODIES	✓	Crayton Mills			REC	E
844	845		843				X		SENATOR IVES TP 5		County Demo. Committee		60	L	N
	855	900	855	859					WEATHER SUMMARY		no				
900	900		859						ET - 2		Smokey Bear			L	
900	900	915	900	915		X		✓	CHURCH OF THE AIR	✓	Lakeside Baptist	0	0	REC	R
915	915	945	915	944				✓	KWZZ FORUM		no			L	PA
931	930		931		X				TP 3		Ford Dealers		60		
945	945		944		X				M - 32A		Clark Associates		30		

Fig. 11-1. A Program Log form devised to simplify scheduling and log It is customary to type commercial entries in red.

187

information. Erasures are not permitted among the required entries, although they are permitted for other information that may be included but not required by the FCC, such as billing information, operator's instructions, etc. Abbreviations are to be clarified by a suitable legend on each log sheet, and entries are to be legible. Each person maintaining a program log is to sign it at the time he goes on duty and again when he goes off, although the common practice of initialing each consecutive entry is not required by the Commission.

Because the man on the board is so occupied with a multitude of duties, his program logging should be made as simple and fast as possible. Assuming manual logging, he must record actual air times for programs, whatever their scheduled times may have been, and those few additional notations that can be made only at the time of actual performance, such as sponsorship identification, mechanical reproduction announcements, and station identifications. Other pertinent information can be pre-entered when the schedule is typed, subject to subsequent correction by the operator if actual performance deviates from that which was planned.

Similarly, typing of the daily log can be a tedious process if too much detail must be repeated time after time. The easiest log form, while it may run to an awkward size, is one that permits simple Xs or check marks in appropriate columns, thereby speeding both the pre-typing and actual performance logging. The log form in Fig. 11-1 provides such columns for several categories, making it more demanding in design but faster in execution than are some other popular log forms. However, it seems unnecessary to assign individual columns for the eleven types, since most of them can be designated by a single letter, although the most frequently used category—REC—is an exception. It might be desirable to provide a column for it alone.

The TIMES SCHEDULED columns of the form in Fig. 11-1 are wide enough to facilitate the indentation of scheduled "programs within programs," as is suggested by the FCC. Filling in of the AIRED times by the operator signifies that performance was accomplished, although it may be permissible, in the interest of logging convenience, merely to enter check marks in the AIRED columns when performance time coincides with scheduled time.

Chapter 12

Sales and Promotion: Getting Off the Ground

In common with other businesses, radio must rely for permanence on repeat sales. This basic fact rules out the opportunistic approach of the carnival barker who hawks inferior merchandise to his temporary audience. Radio's audience is more permanent, and its merchandise is programming. Unlike a retail business, though, it gives the product away to the public, so that in turn it can sell its audience to advertisers. But even free merchandise must be attractive if it is to survive the competition from myriad offerings by other outlets.

Strong programming, alone, is not enough. In the early days of my captivation by radio, I naively supposed that advertisers clamored at the doors of every radio station with eager hopes of finding a commercial availability or two in the glamorous medium. Many subsequent years as an insider have strongly impressed on me the importance of the radio salesman.

Bearing in mind the need for a sales staff of ample quantity and quality, the prospective broadcaster will have organized his commercial force well before—from 45 to 60 days, say —his projected air date. He will have briefed them on programming and general station policy, and turned them loose on his market. If his advance and concurrent promotion is effective, his operation should be comfortably commercial on its opening day. Even in smaller markets many stations have begun operation with as many as 75 signed accounts on the books, bringing prosperity from the outset. A combination of effective sales efforts and attractive programming prospects will do as well for any promising market.

COMPETITION

Again in common with other businesses, radio is faced with

abundant competition. In fact, that competition is felt on two fronts in broadcasting: rivalry for the listeners' attention, and competition for the advertisers' dollars. Unfortunately, the practical effect in recent years has been a cheapening of that product to meet a price, but there are persistent signs that the trend may be reversing itself. How otherwise can one explain the increasing instances of steady prosperity for operations selling spot announcements for a minimum of, perhaps, $3.50 against competitors that give them away for 50 cents? Which station is the better equipped to deliver a superior product in terms of programming and audience? Which one must be, to survive its premium prices? In point of fact, radio's worst competitive enemy has been radio!

The new operation in a market with an already established radio station may find the going difficult for a time. The established station either will be in a financial position to mount a hard competitive fight, thanks to respectable rates, or it will be floundering near the financial surface with a giveaway price structure that will have "spoiled" the market for the rates a responsible operation warrants. Of the two extremes, the former is to be preferred. A clean and forthright battle for listeners, coupled with inflexible rate floors, is a credit to all concerned.

TV's competitive nature often differs from that of other local radio stations. Because TV's overhead is many times greater than radio's, the metropolitan station cannot afford to compete in price with the local radio broadcaster. Further, most local businesses cannot "use" the total market area covered by the TV station, so that paying its full rates would be highly uneconomical advertising. Thus it is dollars-and-common-sense for local advertisers to favor the medium with coverage and rates tailored to their needs, leaving TV to metropolitan and regional businesses.

It doesn't always work this way, of course. The most popular method of small market exploitation used by metropolitan TV (and radio) stations is the cooperative package, which gives local dealers throughout the major area rotation mentions tagged onto general spots for nationally or regionally advertised name brands. Alternatively, small businesses sometimes are signed up for quickie "billboard" mentions at nominal rates that seem, at first glance, very favorable. Local advertisers who have participated in these TV promotions often have found, to their dismay, that little selling can be done in a fleeting glimpse on the screen.

The situation is considerably different when the radio broadcaster has a <u>local</u> TV outlet in his market. The market then is basic to the television operation, just as it is for the radio station, and the local businesses are fair game for both. Under these conditions the radio operator must convince his prospective clients that TV's admittedly stronger viewer impact falls short of justifying its necessarily much higher cost. Based on advertising results <u>per dollar</u>, a good radio operation can compete with television.

By far the most formidable competition in those lesser markets where local radio and TV have not penetrated is the newspaper. There are about as many small town weekly or semi-weekly papers as there are radio stations, and newsprint has the advantage of having been the traditional advertising outlet for about 200 years. Local businesses, often operated by stay-at-home descendants of their founders, are geared solely to that advertising tradition. The new broadcaster in such a market will have to mount a relentless campaign to perforate that tradition and inspire fresh thinking among his potential customers. He must show them how radio affords greater penetration among <u>all</u> levels of the public; how repetition is effective in offsetting radio's transitory nature; how the human voice—the most persuasive sales tool extant—surpasses cold print; and how radio's continuous operation provides a timeliness excelling that of even a daily paper.

Ordinarily, newspapers, radio and TV are the major sources of competition to the new broadcaster, but there are several other media clamoring for the advertising dollars, too. In many markets, those mentioned here are more likely to be nuisance factors than serious budget diversions. It still comes as a surprise to some big-city-bred individuals to learn that small town citizens were seeing color commercials thirty years ago—on their local theater screens. Interspersed between the newsreel, short features, and previews of coming attractions, these movie ads long have been mainstays of the small movie house. Most of these commercial films are "custom" made, and the local advertiser opting for them is signed to a binding long-term contract. Like any other form of advertising, movie spots have pleased some clients and soured others. Much the same can be said for other advertising methods, such as billboards, park bench backs, and cab cards, most of which sell on long-term contracts.

The "shopping guide" throw-away enjoys an intermittent life in many smaller towns, soliciting advertising during its active periods. It may actually receive larger circulation than the newspapers it competes against, but somehow it rarely becomes a substantial financial success. On the other hand, some radio stations have supplemented their own merchandising efforts by publishing throw-aways that combine the usual shopping guide contents (with ads for air sponsors) and summarized news reports. Sometimes these are updated daily and distributed to local restaurants, hotels, and motels.

Direct mail advertising still is used to some extent. Rising postal and clerical costs, however, must serve to make this form of advertising ever less attractive to most small businesses, with the probable exception of those whose appeal is of a very specialized nature and is best aimed at selected prospects. In general, no radio station should have any difficulty in showing a favorable cost-per-impression relative to direct mail.

SALES METHODS

It certainly goes without saying that a salesman must be personable, in order to sell himself readily. Even the most affable, however, occasionally will meet a person with whom he simply doesn't click. When this happens, a system of limited account protection among a station's various salesman will afford an opportunity (after several fruitless calls) for another sales representative to take over the prospect. It often happens that the second salesman can establish the requisite personality rapport and eventually make the sale, and jealousies within the station's commercial staff should not be permitted to prevent account switching when negative results persist.

In addition to being personable, a salesman should be organized. This is a characteristic that seems to be at odds with the nature of many salesmen, with the result that their sales and service calls become a pretty haphazard affair. Yet, one of the secret ingredients of sales success that works for even the untalented salesman is regular calls. The representative who is not actually offensive and who has a reasonable product eventually will sell a surprising proportion of his prospects through a technique of sheer repetition. The necessary regularity of calls requires organization on his part.

That regular effort should not end with the sale, either. Regular <u>service</u> calls on every active account, scheduled at intervals suitable to the nature of the business, may mean the difference between renewal and dropping when the contract expires. A salesman is prone to consider the newly signed account a finished conquest and resent the time that service calls take from cultivating additional accounts, but the fact is that it's usually much easier to re-sell an active account than it is to sell a new one. If his commissions are to snowball to the level of his dreams, a salesman must cultivate his already productive soil to maintain its fertility, while he also plows new ground. Only in this manner can his total active acreage continue to expand. Sometimes, an operation will engage a young employee specifically to service active accounts, in the belief that copy changes and other service needs can better be effected this way. There is some merit to this, particularly for grocery stores and other accounts requiring frequent copy changes, <u>provided</u> that the account salesman does not abdicate his courtesy calls completely. He still is the liaison between client management and station management, psychologically, and he cannot be replaced in that capacity by the station's "office boy."

A salesman's first call on a new prospect usually is just an icebreaker, by which he makes himself and the station known, sizes up his prospect's personality, and endeavors to learn something of the firm's advertising needs. Then, on subsequent calls he should be armed with a well-planned campaign that is slanted toward the prospect's specific needs. Radio advertising, being an intangible of sorts, is more readily sold when it is couched in a specific, organized plan. It should at least include typical copy that has been expressly prepared for the client. Even better is a procedure that too often is neglected by many stations: presentation of a complete recorded audition, which does much to add tangibility to a proposal.

Whether reel or cartridge, the salesman's audition equipment should be capable of excellent sound quality for the sake of maximum impression, and auditions should be produced with all the care that the program and engineering departments can muster. For pre-air-date selling (before studio facilities are usable) staff connections may enable audition preparation at some other station. While not every prospect will be deeply impressed, the effect on most small businessmen of hearing a polished, professional radio presentation incorporating their names and their product lines is most salutary, and it goes a long way in helping the salesman's closure.

When a sales prospect finally capitulates, the businesslike practice is to get his signature on a formal contract. Most stations have printed sales agreements, usually patterned after the standard AAAA contract. (American Association of Advertising Agencies, 200 Park Ave., New York, N. Y. 10017). The signed agreement should clearly set forth the nature of the programs or announcements contracted for, the earned rate, and any pertinent data that will clarify the nature of the order for the client, as well as for the bookkeeping and production departments.

In many small towns, radio is sold on the more informal basis of a verbal agreement, and there is something to be said for the mutual trust that the practice implies. However, the signed contract, properly executed, is preferable. It often settles disagreements arising from misunderstanding or faulty memory, and it is substantial proof of commitment if legal action to collect ever should be deemed necessary.

The usual rate card reflects a diminishing unit cost with increasing frequency of usage, and the standard sales agreement provides a short-rate option. This obligates the advertiser who cancels his schedule before it has run its course to be billed at the frequency rate actually earned. Thus, if he signed for 260 announcements at an earned rate of $2.25 each, and then he canceled after using only 52, he could be billed at the 52-time rate of $3.00 each. When the cancellation is for good cause, many stations in the smaller markets prefer not to invoke their short-rate privilege, feeling that to do so would create antagonism and thereby jeopardize future business with that advertiser. Still others forsake the conventional frequency discount structure and charge a uniform figure for all local advertisers, regardless of the number they contract for.

Conversely, it is not uncommon for a client to sign initially for a short schedule at the card rate and then extend it before expiration. It probably is good business then to apply the new rate retroactively to the original contract, refunding or crediting the difference. After all, provided that the new order actually is a continuation of the old, the station has nothing to lose and much to gain by so honoring the increased business. At least, this should encourage the repeat business that long-range success requires.

INTERNAL COMMUNICATIONS

Teamwork among various departments is essential to a well-run station. Each one exists only to serve the others, after all, and a systematic interchange of requirements, changes, and availabilities is essential. In many operations, "Program Director" is nothing more than a title. It should be just what its name implies, and the staffer so designated should be responsible to management for the entire program day. He should be competent to develop new programs and logically organize the programming sequences. He is the one properly charged with approval of program changes, even to the extent of rejecting those unsuitable to the station's program policy or to certain time periods, their salability notwithstanding. This would force the salesmen to consult with the program department before bringing in a contract for some non-existent program he has conceived on the spot to make a sale. (Most program schedules tend to grow willy-nilly, evolving from signed contracts turned in by the sales department. Thus, programming is determined by what can be sold, rather than by what will garner the greatest audience.)

Similarly, the engineering department exists to convert Programming's efforts to a broadcast signal. Given the time and money, almost any program demand can be accommodated technically, but the engineering department needs to be consulted while a novel idea still is in the concept stage. This not only gives the technical staff time to design and make any installation modifications necessary, but it gives the production department the benefit of engineering suggestions that may simplify and improve operating procedures.

This list of examples could be expanded indefinitely, but these typical ones serve to illustrate the vital need for unrestricted and continuous interchange among the departments of even the smallest radio operation.

INITIAL PROMOTION

As has been noted before, a radio station—like an individual—assumes an image, or "personality," intentionally or not. The principal medium for pre-air publicity ordinarily will be the local paper(s), distasteful as it may be to some broadcasters to buy newsprint advertising. The papers will carry the FCC release on the local grant as a matter of pertinent news, and a prepared press release made available in advance to tie in probably will be used liberally by the papers to make a rounded story. If the broadcaster-to-be has already signed a contingent order for regular pre-air-date advertising, he can rest assured that his press releases will be given every consideration.

The purpose of early promotion is to lay the foundation for the stature the station hopes to reach in its performance. In the smaller markets a very informal tack seems to work well. A regular display ad series in the form of near-personal newsletters will keep the public informed as to construction progress, personnel profiles, and proposed operating philosophy. One station, during its construction in an agricultural community of 5,000, used such a series. They were chatty and light, sometimes to the point of self-deprecation. Bouquets were handed to local construction people by name; the accumulating staff members were introduced as they arrived in town; and programming plans were discussed. When the local electrical contractor inadvertently mis-wired the tower lights, so that night greeted the amazed staffers with a steadily burning top beacon and flashing side lights, the episode made a humorous report that excused him for his unfamiliarity with radio tower lighting conventions. And when the engineering department impatiently awaited delivery of the overdue transmitter, the delay was explained to the public with a truthful report of the problems encountered in finally tracing it to the Kansas City trucking dock, where it had sat forgotten for ten days.

In brief, the petty annoyances and the successive accomplishments that are normal to any new installation were shared week by week with those who soon were going to share their days with the station. By the time it took to the air, the station's local public already had a vicarious stake in the success of an operation they had been priviledged to "watch" through its birth pangs.

Other promotional efforts that may prove beneficial may be undertaken during the construction period. If at all possible, at least one staff member should be available to participate in community meetings of all kinds. Since the sales department presumably is occupied with potential advertisers, the engineering force is struggling feverishly with the installation, and the General Manager is trying to whip the entire confused mess into a smooth, interlocking organization, perhaps it is from the production staff that the "club envoy" can be drawn. His job is that of wangling invitations to address the local civic, fraternal, business, social, and school groups. In the course of two or three months during construction, most of the influential and leading citizens in the home community, as well as many in outlying ones, will have had the opportunity to hear the station's story in person.

Obviously, the station members designated to conduct talks at meetings must be very thoroughly grounded in every aspect of the proposed operation. They will have to field questions concerning power and signal radius, advertising rates, program philosophies, personnel, music selection, and a few thousand others pertinent and impertinent to radio. As the station's image personified, a representative must reflect professionalism, expertise, and personable informality in a single package.

If personnel time permits, principal staff members should discuss their own specialties. Certainly the General Manager and the Commercial Manager should address the Chamber of Commerce, Junior Chamber, and Retail Merchants Association. Any meetings of local radio-TV servicemen, radio amateurs, and similar groups rate talks by the Chief Engineer. If there is to be a Women's Director, she would be at home at various ladies' club functions. The Program Director might meet with school assemblies, drama and music clubs, etc. A staff member who is a natural humorist can be big at fraternal club meetings. There are so many opportunities to meet prospective listeners and advertisers personally in even the smallest of towns.

Some broadcasters like to whet interest in an upcoming station with a contest of some sort. While there is nothing wrong with a well planned contest, the careful preparation required can interfere with the details vital to construction, and it may be prudent to postpone the idea until a semblance of routine is achieved. Post-opening contests may be conducted to choose a slogan fitting the call letters, or the best program suggestion, or the name of a mystery personality—the possibilities are limited only by management's ingenuity. And, whether early or late in its history, a station contest should offer worthwhile prizes. They need not be highly valuable, but they should have quality and utility. Small appliances and household conveniences in the $15 to $25 retail bracket often can be acquired at cost or less from local participating sponsors (some will voluntarily provide them gratis), and they are very well received by secondary winners. The grand prize should be an item or gift of substantial value, and its winner should be gracefully exploited for all possible promotional value.

The broadcaster who postpones contests until after the operation is rolling will concentrate all possible effort during construction on that first day on the air. If he thinks in terms of a ceremonious sendoff, he probably will want recorded or live congratulatory tributes from prominent citizens such as the Mayor or City Manager, Congressional Representatives, Senators, educators, and perhaps even other radio stations. He might consider leavening the fare with similar tributes from the Main Street shoeshine boy or the refuse collector; the image of the local station never should border on the pompous!

Whatever ceremony the first day's operation may include, the programming and production must be flawless. With considerable money and effort invested in leading the public up to the day of debut, it would be foolhardy to present a blemished first impression. Some new operations spend the last few days before "D Day" rehearsing the entire schedule in complete detail, right down to playing records and timing out the program segments. Since the first day presumably reflects the regular program schedule, this practice serves as rehearsal for succeeding days as well. The problems of production and interpersonal cooperation get ironed out privately, so that the public first experiences the polished, professional product that the pre-air promotion promised.

Speaking of promotions, the first post-debut effort could be a "Sponsor Speaks" day. A few weeks after the station has begun, long enough that the internal operation is running smoothly, a day is designated for all the active advertisers to make air appearances. Most advertisers in smaller markets are one-man proprietorships, and it is from their ranks that the day's air staff is drawn.

Well before the day arrives, the clients are advised of the procedure. Some scheduling according to their preferences is required, since only three or four will be on duty at the studios during any given hour of the day. (The confusion and inconvenience incurred by having them all available all day long would be intolerable to all concerned.) A few will still hold the radio microphone in enough awe to refuse flatly, and of course they should not be insistently urged. Most will condescend to go along with the idea, with some misgivings, and a few will be delighted at the prospect. When the day arrives, the first contingent of sponsors puts the station on the air at its regular time (with the station staff handling technical operation, of course, as well as directing, coordinating, and perhaps providing shuttle transportation as the sponsor-announcer shifts change). Each sponsor prefaces his announcements with his name and business affiliation, and, whenever possible, he is required to deliver his competitor's commercials—never his own. This procedure is followed until, by sign-off time, advertisers and listeners alike have experienced a day that they long will remember.

Dubious as the merit of "Sponsor Speaks" day may seem to the uninitiated, it actually provides a programming highlight than can be highly amusing, arresting, and memorable for all concerned. It is a listener hook, certainly, but more to the point, it establishes a certain rapport between station and advertisers that can be gained no other way. They leave their air shifts with a new appreciation of the business of broadcasting and a better understanding of its demands.

Chapter 13

The Engineer: Part of the Management Team

While a radio operation is by nature quite compartmentalized, the engineering department often seems the most disparate. The once-common separation of studio and transmitter contributed to this, but there sometimes seems to be a more fundamental gulf between engineers and other staff members. It often seems to the engineer that announcers, salesmen, and management all consider him to be a sort of nuisance whose contribution to the operation is secondary to their own. The impression has led on occasion to interdepartmental friction, with its inevitable detrimental effect on the whole operation. With the gradual elimination of separate transmitter crews and the assimilation of engineers into the ranks of combination men, the sharp distinction between the technical and other departments has become blurred; yet, in general, there is a basic difference between the technician and other staff members.

I believe this arises from a fundamental difference in thinking patterns: The typical technician is prone to be object-oriented, while other staffers—salesmen in particular—are more likely to be people-oriented. This means that the engineer likes to apply his mind to the orderly world of the physical sciences, where a given mixture of causes consistently produces a predictable effect, while the salesman, say, prefers to engage in the more tenuous arena of social action and reaction. The engineer may be a perfectionist at heart, showing impatience with equipment shortcomings, while the salesman finds human foibles to be a source of fascination, with the idea of perfection bordering on the abhorrent.

THE ENGINEER AS AN IDEALIST

References have been made here to the engineer as being a

perfectionist, or idealist. Again, individuals differ widely, and some technicians are as pragmatic as the most crassly commercial salesman. However, insofar as broadcast operations go, the engineer's prime responsibility is the anticipation, location, and correction of equipment faults; in other words, he is dedicated to the quest for perfection, in the sense that perfection represents the absence of defects.

From management's viewpoint, this professional idealism can be both beneficial and detrimental. On the one hand, the engineer dedicated to technical perfection will maintain his station's equipment at peak performance on his own initiative, but he may, on the other hand, clamor for new apparatus because its imperceptibly superior specifications leave him discontented with that at hand, even though the older equipment still may offer many years of potentially first-rate service. It's easy to study literature on a fascinating new piece of equipment and long to incorporate it into an operation, since the substantial matter of its purchase price is usually a personal intangible to the engineer. Management, though, is prone to look first at the numbers following the dollar sign and wince, wondering why the present equipment suddenly is no longer airworthy. Driven by their idealism, many engineers manage to convince a technically ignorant management of the need for rapid equipment turnover when none exists. It also is true that many engineers are forced to nurse worn-out and obsolete equipment along for years after it has served its useful life simply because management is not cognizant of genuine new equipment needs.

If he is the station's sole engineer, the Chief is responsible only to management (and his own professional integrity), and as such he really is a right-hand member of the management "team." Viewing his job from this position will lead him to those day-to-day decisions that are most beneficial to the operation and therefore, presumably, to him as well. If there is a staff of engineering subordinates, the Chief Engineer then is charged with a double responsibility: To ascertain that management receives conscientious and responsible staff effort at all times, and that subordinate employees are not unjustly exploited by management.

As a member of the management team, the Chief Engineer usually is looked upon as the FCC expert, at least insofar as technical regulations go. It is he who must explain to nontechnical executives the steps necessary to comply with them, and it is upon his assurance that management assumes complete compliance. It also is he who must shoulder the blame if an official inspection turns up infractions. Because his license and his professional pride are at stake, the Chief Engineer will at all times endeavor to keep his operation completely legal, even to the point of forcefully resisting possible executive pressures to engage in expedient irregularities.

THE ENGINEER AS A SALESMAN

With some notable exceptions, engineers do not engage in station time sales. Yet they are "salesmen," in the sense that they routinely do come into contact with businessmen and other community leaders on behalf of their employers. Ordinarily, it is the Chief Engineer who is responsible for negotiations with telephone and power utilities, and those discussions may on occasion extend to the local utility managers. Also, the engineer often is the second personal contact an advertiser has with a station. When a salesman sells a remote broadcast the usual procedure is for the engineer to install the equipment on the client's premises in advance of broadcast time. In the process he almost certainly will meet and consult with the client's management.

In these situations, it is important that the engineer play his role as ambassador with the same friendliness and courtesy as the salesmen do. A surly preoccupation with the technical duties at hand can prove detrimental to his station's image.

EQUIPMENT RELIABILITY IS GOOD MANAGEMENT

The engineer's first responsibility is the maintenance of a solid and reliable broadcast signal, the means by which his station delivers its product. The industry record for reliability is excellent; the American public is accustomed to finding the usual signals available as a matter of course. The design and durability of modern broadcast equipment makes this consistent performance relatively easy. In fact, many stations maintain remarkable signal reliability in the face of rather haphazard maintenance procedures, but the conscientious engineer will develop and practice regular routines that will wring the greatest possible reliability from his equipment. If, as many engineers do, he doubles in some other station capacity, he may find that time limitations prevent top-flight maintenance, in which case he will have to reach an understanding with management as to acceptable maintenance procedures.

Whatever the cause, signal failure may result directly in lost revenue. Some commercial content, scheduled for the interval of failure, cannot be made up later, while some can. But even during sustaining times, signal failure is costly in terms of audience loss. Anything more than a momentary interruption inexorably results in a multitude of dials being switched to active channels, there to remain for indefinite periods. Thus, once the fault is cleared and programming resumes, it is reaching a diminished audience. An occasional signal failure is inevitable, but the station that experiences one after another with undue consistency is bound to find its audience growing permanently smaller.

FAR-SIGHTED TECHNICAL PLANNING IS ALSO GOOD MANAGEMENT

Time was when an installing engineering staff looked forward to the moment of completion, when their chores would settle down to routine operation and maintenance for several years. 'Tis no longer so; our snowballing technology produces a steady stream of equipment that is not only materially better for established broadcast procedures, but which also opens the door to new ones.

Excessively rapid equipment obsolescence is unduly expensive, and good management requires the exercise of considerable far-sightedness in planning. It's difficult to anticipate which of all possible trends will be embraced by the broadcast industry, but the engineer who is widely read in his field and who maintains a program of continuing self-education is better equipped to do so than is one who is tied to technical tradition. He can keep abreast of his industry because it has been a little slow to adapt those advanced electronic techniques developed for other fields in electronics. In recent years, though, technical innovations have been undergoing shorter gestation periods before bursting upon the broadcast world.

Occasionally, too, the radio industry develops its own innovations. A case in point is the development of the cartridge tape, and an early contender for recorded spot applications —

the wide-belt machine marketed by Gates Radio. It was capable of containing 101 separate announcements of up to 90 seconds, any of which was pre-selectable by the simple motion of a lever and the press of a start button at air time. The industry made it clear, however, that the cartridge was to become the standard. The cartridges themselves have been improved to the point of consistently good performance, and the use of multiple machines has reduced the chore of loading them to one of relative infrequence.

Difficult as it may be to predict specific innovations, the general future is signaled by the present. It seems highly probable that automation will grow to encompass more and more of the typical radio installation, with increasingly complex and miniaturized logic circuitry replacing manual operations almost entirely. Insofar as possible, new equipment should be selected for compatibility with sophisticated electronic control techniques in order to better incorporate it into future programming systems. Test gear and hand tools will have to be applicable to integrated-circuit equipment. Wiring ducts and conduit must be available for an increasing quantity of DC control wiring, some of it leading to areas not presently used for electronic apparatus. RF repeater terminals for the telephone company may, in time, replace a multitude of wire lines and consume floor space presently allocated to other uses. Automatic equipment may tie the transmitter and program circuits to an EBS override system activated through press service teletype lines or direct wires from a Regional Defense Headquarters, as networks now override local programming for hot bulletins in some operations. These and many more future possibilities must be weighed by the Chief Engineer in his capacity as a member of the management team, all in an effort to strike a reasonable balance between premature equipment obsolescence and the investment of excess current capital in a future of uncertain trends.

The evolution (or revolution) of electronic technology demands a constant up-grading of the engineer's knowledge, attained through several channels. Jobbers' catalogs in themselves do much to educate, through a sort of painless osmosis, since even bare specifications for new products give substantial clues to their capabilities and applications. The various trade periodicals usually get around to article series that give at least a cursory exposition of technical innovations. A more positive approach is to seek out books on particular developments. They usually are available in treatments ranging from elementary explanations keyed to the level of the practical technician to the sophisticated mathematical language of the engineering graduate. Most electronic parts houses list a comprehensive assortment of books on numerous facets of electronics, and public libraries can locate some of the more obscure ones.

Broadcast engineers seriously concerned with up-dating their grasp of the more exotic theory might take a page from their brothers in industry, many of whom have resumed their formal educations through enrollment in selected courses at nearby colleges or universities. Most of them are able to schedule their classes around their working hours, and frequently their employers offer plans to defray some of the tuition costs.

If management is agreeable and the operation is satisfactorily solvent, the engineer may convince his company to underwrite the cost of an expanding technical library. Since technical books are costly to produce and are restricted a very limited sales potential, they are prone to be expensive in terms of an individual's purchasing power; a station-sponsored library would insure that necessary references were available. This approach is particularly commendable in the smaller towns, where public libraries simply don't stock technical references in depth. However, he manages to continue his education, the radio engineer thus far has one advantage: The broadcast industry's lag in adopting innovations gives him an opportunity to at least hear of new developments before he is called upon to service equipment incorporating them. A few subscriptions to publications serving the space and missile industries will keep him well ahead of most of his fellow broadcast engineers, and the time lag also gives authors and publishers the opportunity to get suitable books on the market before he really needs them.

Chapter 14

Fidelity: The Product's Showcase

Because radio's only product is sound, it is important that it be merchandised as attractively as possible. This was forcefully brought home to me in connection with the debut of a new AM station over a dozen years ago. With the combined plant, so that no intervening program lines with their sometimes restricted audio range were necessary, the overall turntable-to-antenna frequency response was flat within a decibel or so from 30 to 15,000 Hertz. With a new library of modern LPs and a conventional transcription service to program from, I knew that the signal was good. However, I was surprised to receive numerous unsolicited complimentary comments. The man in the street didn't praise the frequency response, or the low noise and distortion; he simply said something like, "Your records are so clear." These were people who had been accustomed to a wide selection of radio (and TV) signals for many years, but they somehow were subliminally aware of superior fidelity when it came along. For each who commented, it is safe to assume that there were many others who never bothered to analyze just why that station was more pleasing to hear.

FASHIONS IN FIDELITY

The development of the electro-dynamic speaker and house-current-powered receivers provided a vital breakthrough in audio quality. The earlier horn speaker, essentially a headphone unit with its diaphragm motions amplified in megaphone fashion by the horn, had a very thin sound (it lacked the extreme high frequencies, too, which were not even transmitted then, but the drastic deficiency of the low end was most objectionable). Magnetic speakers, with their large cones, did far better, but it took the voice coil motor and the electrically powered magnet to bring real bass into the home. Suddenly radio's ethereal, telephonic voice became a booming, stentorian colossus that commanded the rapt attention of entire families grouped around massive and ornate consoles.

The reign of the radio console ended with World War II. After civilian shortages were eased and consumer electronic items again appeared in the stores, the table radio emerged victorious. A population grown mobile and anticipating TV's impending arrival chose the economy and portability of the smaller sets, evidently no longer addicted to sound they could feel. Lacking the cabinet volume and speaker size necessary (at the time) for real bass reproduction, many table radios nevertheless possessed a pleasant aural balance. Their tone controls, if any, were mild in their action, and the whole trend was actually a step forward in the fidelity of voice reproduction.

By this time, the high fidelity cult had matured enough to exert some influence on the technology, with an emphasis on improved reproduction of the higher frequencies. This may have been, in part, a united reaction to the years when the intentionally mellow sound held sway, and in part a clamoring for equipment capable of handling the extreme audio "highs" that had been beyond the general state of the art previously. The lower extremes had not been beyond capability. The carbon microphones of early broadcasting possessed low-frequency performance that puts some modern ones to shame, and by the mid-'30s, audio transformers and speakers were available that would deliver respectable bass. It was in the upper reaches, from 10,000 to 15,000 Hz, that technology had lagged.

With the arrival on the radio scene of the format programmers, who believe that enthusiasm is denoted by yelling (which always reproduces "thinner" than does conversational level), the traditional pear-shaped tones were displaced by countless downy-cheeked voices across the AM dial, all surrounded by the metallic overtones of tortured steel guitar strings amplified to the point of ear injury. And finally, the whole business was compounded by the advent of the pocket transistor radio, with its half-dollar sized speaker, finally driving reproduction of the lower frequencies completely out of fashion.

AM TRANSMISSION IS HIGH FIDELITY

It seems to be a well-kept secret outside the industry that modern AM radio is capable of high fidelity transmission. Even articles in specialized electronics publications, whose editors certainly should know better, often quote the "5,000 Hertz limitation" on AM broadcast transmission. I believed this, along with most budding audio-philes, until 1942. That was the year that the Chief Engineer of a 5,000-watt station with a composite transmitter told me that his station's audio response was flat, from microphone to antenna, to better than 11,000 Hz! I was dumbfounded by this revelation.

It seems reasonable, with assigned channels only 10,000-Hz wide and with double sideband modulation, that the traditional 5,000-Hz presumption should apply, but it doesn't. So far as I know, the AM broadcast band is the only radio service where substantial radiation outside the assigned channel limits is condoned by the FCC. There is no regulation restricting AM broadcast stations to 5,000 Hz of audio. There is one requiring greatly subdued radiation beyond 15 kHz (See Paragraph 73.40 (a) (13), FCC Rules & Regulations), and another prohibiting objectionable interference outside the assigned channel, but it's rare for an AM station to encounter complaints leading to enforced audio frequency limits.

This is due, in part, to the relatively low amplitudes of the upper audio frequencies in most program material, and the fact that AM does not exaggerate them during transmission with pre-emphasis. Thus, the out-of-band energy normally radiated is usually a pretty small proportion of the total signal, although the absolute value still must be substantial in the case of 50-kilowatt stations. Earlier AM transmitters had their limitations built in. The transformer necessary for conventional high-level modulation posed design difficulties at the upper audio frequencies, and the problem sometimes was circumvented by complex circuitry. As far back as the early '40s, Western Electric's modified Doherty system gave a response down not more than a db or so at 15,000 Hz, with distortion throughout the audio range of the order of 1% and noise levels in the -50 db bracket. This performance is comparable with today's FM requirements, and improvements in modulation transformers and feedback circuitry have enabled modern AM transmitters to equal it with simple circuits.

A glance through manufacturers' AM transmitter specifications today show most of them rated to at least 12,000 Hz, with satisfactorily low noise and distortion levels. Since these ratings are generally conservative, most actual transmitters exceed them, and many are capable of a full 15,000-Hz when transmitting normal program material. Thus, provided the antenna system is sufficiently broad in its response, the AM station can transmit audio quality that is, for all but the professionally hypercritical ear, indistinguishable from that expected of FM.

It must be conceded that AM radio almost never is <u>received</u> in high fidelity. The limiting factor is the typical AM receiver, in which the audio response is rarely flat as high as 5,000 Hz, and which often introduces appreciable distortion. AM reception is highly prone to noise, both man-made and natural. Since the relationship of noise to the desired signal is a function of the channel bandwidth employed, and because audio pre-emphasis is not used in AM, the most effective method of reducing noise and interference is that of limiting the received bandwidth.

If, then, most listeners are unable to <u>receive</u> everything an AM station transmits, why the insistence on high fidelity? Because of one characteristic of receiver selectivity curves: they are gradual. With the exception of some communications receivers, a response that is, say, only three db down at 5,000 Hz may still be only 10 or 12 db down at 7,500. This means that some of the 7,500-Hz signal transmitted is going to be heard, albeit at a reduced level. As a rule of thumb, the less expensive the receiver, the broader its selectivity.

A similar argument can be made for other deficiencies that are responsible for gradual roll-off characteristics, such as small speakers at the lower frequencies, amplifier droop at either audio extreme, etc. The practical effect is this: the ordinary receiver will reproduce a wider range when the source is a high fidelity signal than it will for one of limited range. A difference between a transmitted range limited to 5,000 Hz and one flat to 10,000 <u>will</u> <u>be</u> <u>discernible</u> with most receivers, even though they may be nominally flat to only 4,000 Hz or so. (Whether the extreme top, from 10,000 to 15,000 Hz, really is of any consequence to AM broadcasting is debatable. From the audio purist's viewpoint, the professional way is to transmit the best attainable, absolving the broadcaster from contributing any weak links to the chain of transmission and reproductions.)

The only way for the broadcaster to reduce distortion in his listeners' receivers is to reduce his modulation percentage. For other reasons this is not desirable, leaving him little recourse but to be sure he is transmitting at the lowest possible distortion, giving the receivers a clean signal to start with. Beyond that, he cannot be held accountable. So AM transmission, at least, can and should be high fidelity. Were this fact to be stressed more frequently in technical publications, American ingenuity eventually would devise better receivers to take advantage of it.

IN THE FIDELITY FOREFRONT

The enhancement of reproduction is a separate consideration entirely. Technical gimmickry to make a reproduced sound "better" than the original enters into the area of artistry and is not entirely in the engineer's domain. This long has been my principal objection to tone controls on consumer equipment; they permit the listener to flavor an artist's performance with his own conception of how it should sound, something he cannot do in the concert hall. On the other hand, it's probably a basic human right to exercise some freedom of choice not only in what he hears in the privacy of his home, but also how he hears it! But again, the broadcaster perhaps should leave that choice to the listeners through the practice of transmitting the true nature of a performance, or is he to foist his conception of how it should sound on the unwitting public?

The field of sound enhancement has been highly cultivated in recent years by the recording companies, particularly in the arena of popular music. Many of the sounds heard on records today cannot be duplicated by their performers in person; they are an amalgam of the original performance and a liberal salting of technical artistry. Walt Disney unwittingly started it back in the '30s when he used 32 microphones and a multitude of optical sound tracks to record Fantasia. The modern recording studio (which once resembled a conventional broadcast studio in its facilities and operation procedures) is littered with equipment that is practically unknown to the radio industry, as are its manufacturers. Elaborate consoles incorporate numerous insertable reverberation and equalization circuits, and feed as many as eight separate tape tracks simultaneously (24-channel tape recorders now are being offered to the recording industry). In addition to squeezing the original sounds through all manner of electronic shaping, it is even possible (I'm told) to correct a singer's single off-key note!

Through repeated mix-downs and stringing together of the best parts of several takes, a final recorded product emerges that bears no more relationship to the original sounds than does an artist's copy resemble the photograph from which it was painted. The painting may be, in the opinion of some, more pleasing to behold than is the photo, or its original subject, but it is <u>not</u> high fidelity. Just as the artist gets credit for the painting, the control room staff should receive artist billing for some of today's recordings.

While sound enhancement techniques form a challenging field of endeavor, they should not be confused with the broadcast engineer's responsibility to high fidelity of radio transmission. For a radio station to technically enhance those performances under its control is a form of misrepresentation. If too many presentations need aural improvement, the professional solution is to acquire performers who don't. <u>Doctoring in the control room is not a satisfactory remedy for inferior performance</u>. (This is not to be confused with doctoring those audio sources wherein <u>technical</u> shortcomings may be minimized, so that the listening is easier. In some cases this requires intentionally restricted frequency response, equalization for transmission losses, etc.)

In summary, then, the broadcast engineer must strive at all times to attain the highest fidelity of transmission within his means, without indulging in colorations bordering on artistic judgment. In a transmission system, the objective is the delivery of a commodity without alteration of its content.

Chapter 15

Microphone Basics

The radio broadcast engineer's knowledge mainly embraces the techniques of manipulating voltages and currents. He can amplify them, transpose their frequency domains, demodulate them, delay and distort them, and in general control them with great precision. But in doing so, he is dealing only indirectly in his product—sound. The microphone is a transducer; its job is to translate sound vibrations into their electrical analog, and the precision with which it does so determines how true a facsimile it generates.

ESTABLISHING STUDIO MICROPHONE STANDARDS

The perfect microphone is yet to be invented. Even though many demonstrably excel the human ear in sensitivity and frequency response in the laboratory, there is none that can routinely and perfectly substitute for ears in every sound pickup situation. In the meantime, practical selection is based on many factors, including application, cost, engineers' subjective preferences, and insufficient information.

There is a profusion of professional models available, among which is at least one eminently suitable for each specialized use, at a price within reach of the small station. The temptation, when establishing a new operation on a slender budget, to cut corners on the investment in the basic complement of studio microphones makes little sense. Given reasonable care, a studio microphone is a 10- to 20-year investment, so that a few hundred extra dollars spent on good ones reduces to a very small annual price for superior sound. Within today's cost structure, careful selection should equip studios with excellent microphones for a maximum ranging around $150 each.

It would be convenient if microphone characteristic curves could be drawn with a ruler from 20 to 20,000 Hertz, like those of professional amplifiers. Since electro-mechanical devices inherently are irregular, the problem is that of setting acceptable limits of deviation from that ideal. The frequency range of a microphone needs only to include that of the sound it actually will be called upon to reproduce. For general studio applications, it should be capable of accommodating live music without perceptible degradation. That this requirement can be a demanding one is demonstrated by the fact that the largest pipe organs generate frequencies from 16 to 16,384 Hz!

That 16-Hz lower limit is a little extreme; however, there is some controversy as to whether the auditor hears that lowest pedal note or feels it. In any event, it's a little academic here, since such a pipe organ is unlikely to be found in small radio stations. A more practical broadcast consideration is the piano, commonplace among studio furnishings. Its lowest note is about 27 Hz; lower, surprisingly, than the bottom extremes of the bass drum, tympani, bass viol, and bass tuba. A transmission system flat down to 35 Hz will do reasonable justice to most piano bass. At the other end of the audio spectrum, the oboe runs the big pipe organ a close race, with prominent harmonics up to 16,000 Hz, while numerous other instruments trail not far behind. It is the harmonics (overtones, in musical parlance) that characterize the various instruments, so that good high-frequency response is vital to accurate musical reproduction.

From the purist's view, then, it appears that a microphone-to-antenna response quite flat from 35 to 16,000 Hz is required for true high fidelity transmission. However, the conventional limits assumed by the broadcast industry are based on the old textbook statement that the range of human hearing is from 30 to 15,000 Hz. As a practical matter, the top 1,000 Hz or so lost by bandwidth requirements is the least important segment of the audio spectrum, for the average listener, at least. A further limitation is implied by the FM standards, which require the low-frequency capability to extend only to 50 Hz. This was adopted because certain difficulties with FM carrier stability were experienced with some circuits at very low modulation frequencies. The newest FM transmitters will handle 30-Hz audio, though.

Considering the limitations of AM receivers, the AM-only station may settle for microphones good from 30 to 10,000 Hz, if economic considerations demand, while the FM or AM-FM operation rightly should be equipped to broadcast the full 15,000-Hz spectrum, as will be seen. (It seemed a bit ironic when a few years ago a popular equipment manufacturer was "packaging" entire FM stations that included a unidirectional public-address type microphone, often used by small stations, which wasn't even rated above 10,000 Hz.)

Having decided upon a range of 35 or perhaps 40 Hz (relatively few microphones are rated below 40) to 15,000 Hz, the engineer will find a great many professional models for which the catalog specifications blithely indicate such coverage. Unfortunately, few of them list the output tolerances above and below the 1,000-Hz reference, and with good reason: compared to electronic equipment, the variations are large. While a deviation of plus or minus 1 decibel over the audio range is an easy amplifier requirement, it is an unusual microphone that digresses as little as plus or minus 2 1/2 db throughout the important frequencies. Relatively good as this is, different models of similar stated specifications may sound quite dissimilar. Fig. 15-1 shows how two hypothetical frequency response curves, both within 2 1/2 db from 50 to 15,000 Hz, can differ by nearly 5 db, which is a very audible difference.

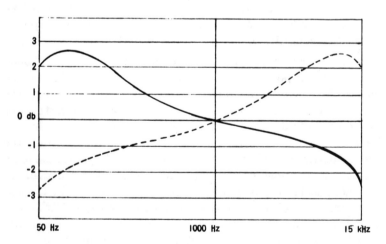

Fig. 15-1. Two microphones, similarly rated within ± 2½ db over the range from 50 to 15,000 Hz, can deliver quite dissimilar sounds.

As an actual case in point, consider a popular non-directional dynamic microphone widely used on TV network panel and news shows. Made by one of the most respected names in the field, its frequency response is listed as 50 to 15,000 Hz. However, reference to the typical response curve in the manufacturer's catalog shows it to have a rising response through the fundamental voice range, with its 120-Hz output a full 10 db less than that at 4,500 Hz. This particular microphone is not broadcast quality at all, although it would serve admirably for communications, where intelligibility, not naturalness, is the criterion. Another microphone, a ribbon-velocity type, is stated in the same reference to possess a range of 20 to 20,000 Hz. In this case, the manufacturer's curve shows that, referred to its 1,000-Hz level, the output at other frequencies is:

    20 Hz—0 db (rare performance at this frequency)
    80 Hz—+3 db
   100 Hz—+2 1/2 db
    15 kHz— -3 db
    20 kHz— -5 db

This is pretty good microphone performance; even so, the variation over the stated range is +3, -5 db. It is within ±2 1/2 db only from about 100 to 10,000 Hz. More to the point, both microphones look quite acceptable from just the simplified catalog listings, and they may be (and are) intermixed in the same studios. A balanced and consistent sound product cannot be obtained from transducers so disparate in their properties.

It is clear, then, that ordinary catalog listings are useless for selecting microphones. The manufacturers' response graphs are necessary to arrive at an informed conclusion, and even they have limitations. In the first place, the curves are "smoothed" averages of countless minor irregularities in actual output. Secondly, there is no assured uniformity of measurement methods among the various manufacturers, and the difficulties of precise measurement in the field make it nearly impossible for the user to check performance quantitatively. Last, the published curves are only "typical," so that actual units may deviate somewhat (the reason that stereo microphones should be used in matched pairs, selected by the manufacturer), and different curves may accompany the same model from year to year in the manufacturer's own catalogs. This is why microphone selection often is a matter of personal choice among engineers.

There is a further, and often overlooked, consideration: FCC requirements. While the element of uncertainity in microphone characteristics prevents the Commission from enforcing it, Paragraph 73.317 (g) (ii) (2) of the FM regulations states:

"No specific requirements are made with regard to the microphones to be employed. However, microphone performance (including compensating networks, if employed) shall be compatible with the required performance of the transmitting system."

Thus, for an FM station, a range of 50 to 15,000 Hz is a basic microphone requirement. The permissible digression from flatness over this requisite range can be inferred from the FCC tolerances specifically set forth for the overall system. They are given in Fig. 15-2, the FM pre-emphasis curves. To remove the confusion factor of pre-emphasis, these curves can be straightened out. Assuming a perfect demodulator incorporating precisely complementary de-emphasis, the permissible overall system limits become those of the shaded area in Fig. 15-3. If the entire electronic system is utterly flat, Fig. 15-3 then indicates allowable microphone tolerances. It is evident that a latitude of 3 db applies over most of the range, increasing respectively to 4 db at 50 Hz and 5 db at 15,000. At first glance, this doesn't seem too restrictive, until it is noticed that there is no positive tolerance. Since most microphone response curves show output levels both above and below the 1,000-Hz reference value, this means that they must be transposed to a new reference taken at the frequency of greatest output. When superimposing such a curve on Fig. 15-3, this new reference must coincide with the flat upper FM limit, and it then becomes apparent that the microphone cannot be over 4 db down at 50 Hz, relative to its point of greatest output; likewise, the 15,000-Hz end may not droop more than 5 db from the same reference. In other words, no point on the microphone's response curve can extend beyond the shaded area of Fig. 15-3 over its 50- to 15,000-Hz range.

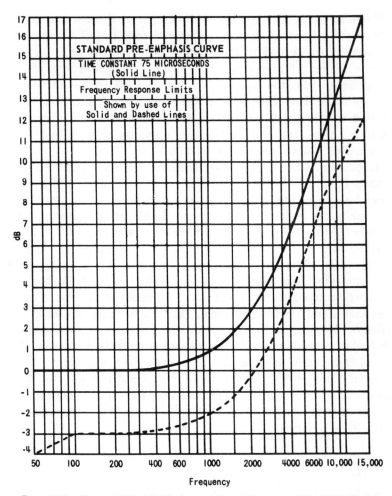

Fig. 15-2. The standard FCC pre emphasis curves set the permissible
audio response tolerance for the entire system, including microphones.
(From FCC Para. 73.333, Fig. 2)

This is a difficult criterion for actual microphones to meet.
Specifically, for the dynamic microphone above, referring
zero db to its maximum output at 4,500 Hz puts its 120-Hz
level a full 7 db shy of the FCC minimum! By the same measure its 15,000-Hz output approaches 5 db below the legal
minimum for that frequency. Yet this unit is blithely rated
in the catalog listing to cover 50 to 15,000 Hz. To a lesser
extent, this problem arises with many units. Most diaphragm-
operated microphones display a rise approaching 3 db some-

where in the 3,000- to 10,000-Hz range, and most are prone to slope off enough at both audio extremes to fall outside the tolerance suggested by Fig. 15-3.

For direct AM transmission, where no pre-emphasis is introduced into the system, a minor rise in the mid-high range is entirely acceptable. However, the limitations imposed by pre-emphasis in an FM system, and different but similar pre-emphasis techniques common to tape and disc recording, aften are overlooked.

Of course, a peak at lower frequencies also can lead to overload, but it will show on the control board operator's meter and he can correct for the excessive level. The insidious factor in the high-frequency range is that pre-emphasis normally <u>follows</u> the studio level meters, as it should for proper mixing and balancing, and system overload can occur without the operator's knowledge. In recent years, excessive overmodulation of high frequencies has forced many FM broadcasters to adopt limiters that can anticipate the effects of pre-emphasis and limit accordingly. The FM station has its modulation monitor to indicate overmodulation at any frequency. but what detects overload due to pre-emphasis following the level indicators in tape and disc recording systems? Evidently it sometimes is only the ear, when it is subjected to a distorted playback. With the modern, wide-range equipment common today, a 3 db peak in a microphone's upper response should be avoided.

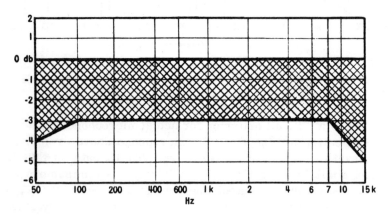

Fig. 15-3. The tolerance limits of Fig. 15-2 prior to pre-emphasis. In the case of ideally flat electronic components throughout the system, this figure defines requisite microphone performance.

No doubt microphones will be improved in time, perhaps one day approaching the flatness already common to electronic equipment. A recent effort in this direction borrows a technique from speaker designers by using two distinct generators to cover different portions of the spectrum. Their outputs are combined through a crossover network, providing what appears to be a remarkably smooth, wide-range response. According to the most recent manufacturer's curve, one such unit—a unidirectional dynamic type—conforms to the FCC tolerances for FM use. (A.K.G.'s Model D-202E, presently $130 net.)

An alternate approach for the purist is to select models that can be easily equalized for flatter response (using the "corrective networks" of the FCC paragraph). Removal of a mid-range peak or valley is difficult, but a gradual droop at either end of the spectrum is readily corrected electronically. For instance, the ribbon unit mentioned above will be 3 db below tolerance at 15,000 Hz if zero reference is taken at its 80-Hz point of maximum output. Since the intervening characteristic is a gradual downward tilt with increasing frequency, a suitable rising amplifier characteristic is all that's required. Another microphone might require an opposite amplifier slope. In any event, smoothness of the response curve is an important requisite for simple compensation. A station using such methods would do well to equip all studios with the same microphone model, so that all preamplifier channels in the plant could be identically equalized, thereby facilitating microphone and amplifier interchangeability.

THE FALLACY OF THE "VOICE" MICROPHONE

In every radio station, there are certain microphone positions that are used for nothing but voice pickup, and it is commonplace to choose less expensive units for this application. The station dedicated to fidelity will do so with caution. It is true that voice frequencies do not extend from 30 to 15,000 Hz, Tests made many years ago showed that, with the equipment then at hand, male voices suffered no perceptible degradation when they were reproduced through a system flat from 100 to just over 8,000 Hz. The corresponding limits for female voices were 130 and 10,000 Hz. Obviously, by these criteria a general voice range requires flat response from 100 to 10,000 Hz.

It has been my observation that differences can be detected beyond these empirical limits. A male voice sounds more vital and "live" when the microphone responds to 15,000-Hz than only 7,500, as older tape recroders will show (only the upper audio limit is changed by the recorder's speed of operation, and direct comparison yields a perceptible difference). Further, a sharp 6 db, 70-Hz peak introduced within an amplifier has been noted to produce a notable difference in a baritone voice, suggesting low-frequency sub-harmonics, perhaps weak but nevertheless present. A flat response of at least from 100 to 10,000 Hz seems necessary, then, for quality voice reproduction. This appears to be less demanding than the requisites for general use, but there is an important further consideration. Speech, far more than music, is composed of complex transient sounds, and their proper reproduction places stringent demands on a microphone. A peak or valley in response corresponds to certain mechanical resonances or anti-resonances in the device and these, like any resonance, are shocked into "ringing" by excitation at appropriate frequencies. During musical intervals of relatively sustained tones, a "peaky" microphone may sound passable, but the coloration it lends to speech transients is highly undesirable. In fact, I rate smoothness of a microphone's response on a par with total frequency range as a criterion of good voice reproduction.

It is a general rule of thumb that quality of transient response in a transmission system is directly related to its bandwidth, so that in general the wider range microphone will display fewer objectionable peaks. This consideration brings the requirements for high fidelity voice reproduction very near to those for music, and the concept of the "voice" microphone as one requiring only desultory performance is seen to be fallacious. For that matter, the FCC paragraph on FM microphone requirements makes no exception for those that are to be used only for voice pickup.

Many smaller stations have considered fidelity of voice reproduction to be less important than the few dollars more that an initial complement of good microphones would cost. Yet is is the "local" voices that set a station apart from the record and network fare available anywhere, and it is they that will be selling local advertisers' wares. It seems only good business to give those voices the benefit of the best transmission. The small station announcer may be intrinsically handicapped by a voice and delivery less professional than those of his metropolitan counterparts, and an inferior microphone only adds to the contrast.

MICROPHONES OUTSIDE THE STUDIO

Studio microphones customarily are used under the most favorable circumstances. They are handled principally by professionals, who should know how to care for delicate precision instruments (although I actually have seen experienced radio men blow into them in checking for liveness!). Equipment for remote broadcasts, however, is far more vulnerable to adverse weather conditions, handling damage, poor acoustic surroundings, and even theft. For these reasons it may be justifiable to forego the elegance of studio quality in favor of greater durability and reduced risk. With the possible exception of indoor presentations of serious music (for which studio quality microphones should be very carefully transported and set up and telephone lines should be equalized to take advantage of them), ultrawide-range reproduction adds little to remotes but excess noise. So, for knockabout remote use the ruggedness of the modern dynamic microphone will serve well. To minimize uncontrollable acoustic conditions, a unidirectional pickup pattern (see Chapter 16) is effective in those situations where close talking is unnecessary and where wind conditions are not severe. Alternatively, for really severe conditions of noise and weather, the last resort is to speak very close to an omni-directional dynamic. For complete remote flexibility, both types should be available among a station's equipment complement. Eminently suitable microphones are available, with careful selection, in the $40 to $75 range.

It sometimes is possible to select suitable remote microphones from among a manufacturer's public address line at considerable savings. Some manufacturers offer different models in very similar pairs, possessing nearly identical appearance and specifications. The engineer is cautioned, however, that in some other makes there has been no performance comparison between professional and public-address versions of similar appearance and specifications, so that prepurchase trials are recommended.

A specialized microphone application that is much overlooked is that of the remote _radio_ pickup. The mobile equipment used in cars and airplanes for on-the-spot broadcasts often is, to be bluntly forthright, lousy! It is no great problem to equip these mobile transmitters with passable microphones and modulation controls so that they transmit a _clean_ signal, even though it may be limited in its response by the radio channel width. The muddy distortion so prevalent in these transmissions shouldn't even be permitted on the communications channels, let alone being relayed on the broadcast band. A suitable close-talking dynamic microphone and the necessary modification of the mobile transmitter audio circuitry to accommodate it would be of great benefit to these pickups.

Another source of poor microphone quality often heard on the air today is the telephone. While the carbon "transmitter" in a modern telephone is a marvel of reliability and durability, the widely varying currents and the physical abuse to which it is subject do take a toll. Under amplification, most telephone microphones display excessive distortion, and it is this, rather than the restricted audio range, that is most annoying on the air. There is little to be done for incoming calls from the general public (except for the equalization suggested in Chapter 17), but there is a partial remedy for those stations whose staff personnel make frequent beeper phone reports on the air. That is to equip them with units made by Altec Lansing (Model 697A) that are designed to replace the conventional telephone "transmitter." Employing a dynamic microphone and transistorized circuitry, one can be temporarily installed in any conventional phone in seconds, and removed after use. Each staffer expected to make phone reports can carry a unit in his pocket and be assured that, with its use, his voice will be aired with undistorted clarity. Even though the frequency response falls short of studio quality, the improvement is worthwhile. (A few years hence, an improved transmitter will be standard telephone equipment. The latest advances in the technology of the electret, a membrane possessing a permanent electric charge, have led to a laboratory prototype unit using a condenser microphone with integrated solid-state amplification, designed for ultimate telephone use.)

OTHER TRANSDUCERS

Another transducer vitally important to broadcast quality is the turntable pickup cartridge. Like the microphone, it is subject to all the problems of electro-mechanical conversion; however, the relatively rigid coupling of the stylus to the motivating force (the undulating record groove) provides much closer control of the pickup's characteristics than does the tenuous medium of air, the actuator for the microphone. Because of this, the problems of resonance and compliance are more readily surmounted, and any modern magnetic or dynamic pickup should display a very flat response over the entire audio range.

Apart from the obvious factors such as stylus condition, tracking force and arm bearing freedom, the most important consideration in good turntable quality is proper equalization. For reasons of physical geometry, discs are cut with a "constant velocity" of stylus motion over part of the audio spectrum, and "constant amplitude" throughout another part. Additionally, high frequencies are pre-emphasized in the interest of signal-to-noise ratio. This then requires playback equalization of exactly complementary characteristics to produce a net flat response. Fortunately, the great variety of distinct recording characteristics, requiring selectable playback equalization with its attendant perpetual missettings of controls, has been largely supplanted by the RIAA curve. As a result, broadcast tables today need but a single, fixed equalization characteristic.

Like the microphone, the frequency response from a turntable should conform very closely to the flat ideal if high-frequency problems with FM pre-emphasis are to be avoided. A reputable test record (CBS Labs produces a number of them) in good condition, played through the console, will provide a check of the frequency response.

Another transducer common to broadcasting might be termed an electromagnetic-mechanical device. This is the tape playback head, which converts magnetic variations into electrical currents, with the mechanical help of the transport mechanism. Apart from head azimuth adjustment, perhaps the biggest response problem with tape equipment is the lack of compatibility between different makes of machines. Modern professional machines are more or less standardized on the NAB equalization standards, but there still remain many instances where a broadcast engineer is confronted by the failure of tapes made on one machine to play well on others.

Chapter 16

Secondary Characteristics
of Microphones

When two persons converse in an ordinary room, it matters little whether they are separated by one foot or eight; neither ordinarily is distracted by random voice reflections or moderate extraneous noise. However, when a microphone replaces one of the individuals and it in turn is heard elsewhere via a speaker, the listener will perceive a marked intrusion of noise and reflected sound for all but very small separations.

A good microphone can be shown to be linearly responsive to its sound environment, so the sounds reproduced by the speaker actually exist in a similar relationship at the microphone's position, whether it be occupied by a mechanical device or a human ear. Then why doesn't the ear hear them? The explanation lies in the subjective combination of ear and brain. There is no doubt that, physically, the ear senses all the sounds, but the brain suppresses an awareness of those outside its immediate attention. It does this largely through an innate ability, in conjunction with human binaural hearing (two ears), to sense the directions from which sounds emanate and to disregard those that at the moment are immaterial. Because the reflected sounds come from numerous directions, no single one ordinarily is strong enough to prove distracting to the ear-brain complex.

When the microphone substitutes for the ear, however, reflected sounds arriving from random directions add to a total amplitude that makes their presence quite apparent when reproduced from the same point in space—i.e., the speaker —as the desired sound. In other words, when random indirect sounds are concentrated into a single source coinciding spatially with the origin of the direct sound, as is typical of electronic reproduction, the human ear-brain mechanism is deprived of the directional information that normally enables it to discriminate between them. If the reflected sounds could be electronically separated from the direct ones and reproduced in the proper amplitude and phase relationships from numerous directions in the listening room, the original acoustic environment might be re-created accurately enough for the ears to "focus" as they would in live presence.

Long before stereo was developed beyond the point of a laboratory curiosity, efforts to improve the directional discrimination of the microphone bore fruit, leading to the selective varieties available today. To better understand the advantages and limitations characteristic of the several approaches to directional discrimination, some discussion of microphone electro-mechanical principles may be in order.

PRESSURE-ACTIVATED MICROPHONES

The ear is basically a pressure-sensitive device, responding with some amplitude and frequency nonlinearities to the rapid pressure changes produced in air by sound. Since technology usually emulates nature, the earliest microphones electrically "measured" the effect of pressure changes on a metal diaphragm. From this beginning came the carbon microphone, in which the diaphragm vibrations vary the compression of a cylinder filled with carbon granules. The corresponding changes in the electrical resistance of the carbon "button" provided the electrical analog of the diaphragm's motion. (With appreciable refinement and specialization, this is the device that still serves as the "transmitter" in the modern telephone.) The carbon microphone used for early broadcasting was capable of good sound quality, as the state of the art then stood, with its major drawback being a high "hiss" level arising from the energizing current's flow from granule to carbon granule. It also was sensitive to motion when energized, being prone to "pack" and became inoperative in the midst of a broadcast.

A short-lived successor to the carbon unit was the early condenser microphone, which was designed to eliminate the problem of internally-generated noise. As its name implies, the condenser model is based on the electrical condenser (which we now call the capacitor) formed by a diaphragm and a stationary back plate spaced very close to it. Since the capacitance of a given capacitor is inversely proportional to the distance between its plates, displacement of the diaphragm by air vibrations produces a corresponding variation in the capacitance of the microphone. When supplied with a polarizing voltage, those capacitance variations induce corresponding changes in the charging (or discharging) current which, when dropped across a large resistor, produce usable voltage variations. The condenser microphone eliminated the faults of the carbon, while adding a few of its own. It delivered sound quality comparable to the carbon microphone, minus the hiss, but the capacitance of a practical diaphragm is so small that the dropping resistor must be quite large. In other words, the device is one of very high impedance and scarcely suitable for use directly with long cables. In consequence, a "head" amplifier was incorporated as an integral part (in most models) of the microphone, with a couple of stages of vacuum tube circuitry and a reasonable output impedance. With the technology of the time, the electronics necessarily made a bulky package for a microphone; further, the filament and plate voltages had to be supplied from an external source through a multi-conductor cable, so that studio microphone installations then were only a little less awkward than are today's TV camera requirements.

In some climatic conditions, the high polarizing voltages and high amplification necessary for condenser microphones led to noise problems when moisture invaded the dielectric area. It was the practice in some operations to remove the active microphone heads and store them in desiccant enclosures when they were not in actual use. Despite these ungainly drawbacks of condenser microphones, their performance justified their adoption by the more affluent broadcast operations. Although they soon were supplanted by other types for broadcast applications, certain condenser microphones remained laboratory standards for a number of years. And, as improvements were made in European models, they became widely adopted in post-war years by recording studios. Now, with the advent of the field-effect transistor, adaptable to very high-impedance circuitry, and the attendant elimination of external power supplies through self-contained battery operation, modern condenser microphones promise to again invade broadcast studios. With at least one available now in the $100 price range, even the smaller operations can afford what many consider to be the finest means of sound pickup.

The early broadcast tenure of the condenser microphone was shortened by the development of the dynamic version, wherein a small coil of wire attached to the diaphragm moves in a strong magnetic field in much the same physical configuration as the "voice coil" in a speaker. This resulted in a generator free of the noise and delicacy of the carbon type, and (since it can be wound for low impedance) one that could be separated from bulky amplifier equipment by a simple cable, giving an advantage over the condenser unit.

The emergence of the dynamic microphone as a broadcast contender might have come earlier, but for a basic complication. Since a simple diaphragm tends to undergo a displacement that is proportional to the pressure applied, the generator it drives should be <u>amplitude</u> sensitive if its voltage is to be a replica of the incident sound pressure. In the carbon microphone the resistance is more or less proportional to the compression of the diaphragm, and the condenser also produces a voltage proportional to its diaphragm displacement. For these two microphones rather simple and basic mechanical configurations produce relatively good performance. The dynamic type, however, generates a voltage that is proportional to the <u>velocity</u> of the coil's motion in the magnetic field. In a progressing sound wave the velocity (or pressure gradient) is a function of both pressure magnitude <u>and</u> frequency, and the dynamic microphone—being fundamentally velocity-sensitive—tends to increase its generated voltage as the frequency of the incident sound rises. Practical models had to await the development of techniques to compensate that characteristic. Specially corrugated diaphragms exhibit modified displacement linearity; tuned "labrynth" tubes extend low-frequency response, and tuned cavities augment innate deficiencies and damp out resonances. Out of all these efforts to doctor its basic nature came a usable dynamic microphone good enough to displace its more ungainly predecessors.

The finest dynamic models today are capable of very flat, wide-range performance coupled with the basic advantages of ruggedness, durability, and simplicity of connection; however, drooping low-frequency response and irregular mid-highs remain common faults of many. Perhaps the greatest improvement of recent years lies in the development of non-metallic diaphragms, with their greatly reduced tendency toward resonant peaks. Fig. 16-1 illustrates an inexpensive and proven non-directional dynamic that is quite flat throughout the important octaves of the audio spectrum.

The microphone development discussed this far has been limited to the basic pressure-operated generator. In all instances, the diaphragm has been exposed to sound pressures on but one side, and it cannot discriminate as to the direction of the sound source. Sound pressures arriving from behind, for example, simply flow around the housing and deflect the diaphragm at its front surface. The basic pressure microphone is variously termed non-directional and omnidirectional, although it actually does show some high-frequency directional discrimination that is dependent upon the size of the diaphragm and the size and shape of its housing.

Other pressure microphones include the Reisz, an obsolete carbon type once common in Europe, the also obsolete inductor type, and the crystal unit. (The crystal microphone is popular in public address and household applications because of its relatively good quality in low-priced models. The crystal being an amplitude-sensitive device, good bass response is readily attainable—if it is terminated by about five megohms—but high-frequency resonances are more difficult to control. Because early models were highly sensitive to temperature variations and excessive humidity, because

low-impedance devices are more adaptable to broadcast practices, and because at the professional level other microphones excel the crystal, it has been used but rarely in broadcasting.) It was the early microphones, highly sensitive to sound from all directions, that led to the total draping of studios. With reflections eliminated from all directions, the omnidirectional sensitivity of the microphones posed no problem.

VELOCITY-ACTIVATED MICROPHONES

While the dynamic microphone was moving into the radio studio, a radically different type emerged from its developmental stages. Instead of a conventional diaphragm, a long, narrow metallic strip suspended in a strong magnetic field serves as its active element. This metallic ribbon usually has transverse corrugations that provide flexibility and prevent appreciable selfresonances. Sound waves impinging directly on the ribbon impart a motion that generates a corresponding current. The ribbon is a very low impedance generator, so that—unlike some dynamic microphones— a stepup transformer always is necessary.

Like the dynamic, the ribbon microphone generates a voltage that is proportional to the velocity of its moving element. However, unlike the diaphragm in the conventional unit, the ribbon is open to air on both sides and responds to differences in pressures acting on it. It turns out that its resultant motion then is proportional to the velocity of impinging air particles, and the net result is an output voltage that is proportional to ambient sound pressure. Thus it is linear in its basic form, without the compensations necessary to the conventional dynamic generator. This permits a simplicity in the ribbon velocity microphone that is shared by few others. There are no enclosed cavities to modify the response, and diaphragm resonances are avoided by making the ribbon's natural frequency lie well below the audible range. No polarizing voltages or self-contained amplifiers are necessary, and humidity conditions pose no problem. In fact, the ribbon microphone is so straightforward that a simple homemade one will deliver surprisingly good sound. Low-frequency response is limited only by the quality of the necessary transformer, while the upper extremes are dependent upon the flexibility and mass of the ribbon and the shape of the pole pieces. Out-

Fig. 16-2. This RCA velocity model and its immediate descendants once were the predominant device of most network studios.

put variations through the important mid-ranges are small and gradual, giving a smooth, if not always flat, response. Fig. 16-2 shows an early ribbon velocity microphone that, with its immediate descendants, once populated a majority of the radio network studios. It has evolved into its present-day relative, shown in Fig. 16-3. The latter unit has excellent output as low as 20 Hz, and the manufacturer's curve indicates useful response (down 5 db from reference) at 20 kHz.

The velocity microphone differs from the earlier types in one major respect: it is directional. Fully responsive to sound waves striking it from either its front or back, the ribbon is not moved by those arriving at its edges, since the instantaneous pressure then is equal on both sides. Thus, the microphone has a bi-directional pickup pattern displaying equal sensitivity to the front and rear and none at the sides. This characteristic offers some advantages over the essentially nondirectional pressure microphone. For randomly diffused indirect sound, it can be "worked" at a distance of 1.7 times that of a pressure unit to achieve the same ratio of direct-to-reflected sound in the reproduction. In those acoustic situations where it is possible to turn a dead side of a velocity unit toward an offending noise source, the discrimination will be much greater. Conversely, when used for a stage performance, for instance, the live back of the velocity microphone will be highly sensitive to audience noise and public address system feedback, even more so than the ordinary pressure microphone which does display slight rearward discrimination.

Another convenience of the velocity microphone's two-faced nature is its ability to pick up voices from opposite sides of a table with equal facility, sometimes eliminating a need for two units. Of course, it also will pick up troublesome reflections when placed with its rear side too close to windows, equipment panels, or other hard surfaces.

The virtues of the ribbon microphone don't come without their price, of course. The fundamental characteristic that must be borne in mind when using a velocity unit is the proximity effect. This arises from a basic acoustic relationship"—the linear ratio between pressure and velocity of sound in

Fig. 16-3. The present-day descendant of the RCA 44A pictured in Fig. 16-2, the BK 11A delivers usable response from 20 to 20,000 Hz, and is priced at just over $100. (Courtesy of RCA)

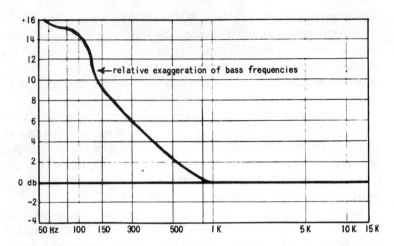

Fig. 16-4. From the manufacturer's curves for one specific velocity mic-rophone model, this proximity effect can be inferred for a sound source distance of six inches. Other models may display different degrees of proximity effect.

air applies only to a plane front. For spherical wave fronts, the velocity is exaggerated, giving rise to over-emphasis of low frequencies when a velocity microphone is positioned too close to a sound source. For music this rarely is a factor, since anything over three feet can be considered adequate. For voice, however, the otherwise "flat" velocity unit will tend to emphasize the lower frequencies at speaking distances under two feet.

While some stations have maintained two-foot speaking distances, most have neither the acoustic excellence or the low noise levels to do so. However, a studio working distance of one foot, or over 15 inches, is an entirely practical value and, to make velocity microphones sutiable under such conditions most professional models incorporate switches (or strapping terminals) that select one or more bass reduction circuits internally. Their designations range from the two position M - V (for Music or Voice) choice to those offering M, M_1, V_1, and V_2, representing progressive degrees of bass attenuation.

Fig. 16-4 indicates the exaggeration of bass frequencies for one ribbon velocity microphone model situated six inches from a sound source (other models may display different proximity effects). If the bass cut switch happens (in the V position) to

232

exactly complement this rise, the net result will be flat. However, this correction will be accurate only at that distance. If one announcer moves up to three inches, his voice will be reproduced with exaggerated timbre, while another who moves back to, say, 10 inches will be penalized by insufficient bass. Because of this, ribbon microphones should be investigated as to correct working distances for the bass-cut switch positions, and then those distances should be enforced.

Another misuse of the M - V switches on microphones so equipped arises simply from oversight. It frequently happens that a microphone switched for voice use subsequently will be employed for musical pickup without its settings having been checked. The result for all ordinary orchestral working distances will be unduly thin reproduction, unless it is used for solo brass or other instruments in the higher registers.

The ultra-free suspension of the ribbon in a velocity microphone makes it highly susceptible to air movements, whether they result from natural wind or puffs of breath. When one is opened and all wind screens removed, the ribbon undulates visibly just from convection air currents in the room. The enclosure protects it from damage under ordinary conditions, but the ribbon's proclivity for excessive wind noise makes such microphones unsuitable for outdoor use, and they're prone to "pop the p's" when spoken into too closely. The ribbon microphone also is more critical in relation to its electrical termination than most others, as is discussed later in this Chapter.

UNI-DIRECTIONAL MICROPHONES

The non-directional pressure microphone, historically the first, and the subsequently-developed bi-directional ribbon type, suggested a way to obtain yet another directional pattern. An instantaneous positive sound pressure arriving from the front of a pressure-operated microphone presses its diaphragm inward to generate a voltage of a certain polarity. That same sound pressure acting on an immediately adjacent velocity microphone presses its ribbon to the rear, and its electrical output may be paralleled with the same polarity as the pressure unit's, so that sounds from the front produce additive voltages in the combined connection. When a positive sound wave arrives from the rear, it must travel around to the front of the pressure diaphragm to deflect it, again producing a positive voltage. However, that wave deflects the ribbon forward, acting as it does on the rear surface, and the resultant voltage so generated is a negative one. In this manner, if the two generators are electrically balanced, their outputs cancel each other for sounds arriving from the rear, producing a uni-directional sensitivity pattern. When graphed, such patterns give a more or less heart-shaped curve similar to a geometric cardioid; hence uni-directional microphones often are said to have a "cardioid" pickup pattern.

The uni-directional microphone opened new possibilities of discriminating against unwanted sound, permitting working distances over twice those for non-directional microphones for the same reproduced ratio of wanted-to-unwanted sounds. The earliest uni-directional microphones employed two distinct generators within a common housing. Fig. 16-5 shows an early professional model using separate ribbon velocity and dynamic pressure units. Through electrical switching their outputs can be selected or combined to give a choice of non-, bi-, and three different uni-directional patterns. This model has survived a change of manufacturers and is available today. Another early (and surviving) approach to uni-directional operation uses but a single ribbon, with a mechanically adjustable shutter behind it. When half of the ribbon is covered behind, the segment responds to pressure, while the remaining half is velocity actuated, and the combined output produces a uni-directional pattern. A fully open shutter position provides a conventional bi-directional velocity pattern, while a fully closed condition results in an essentially nondirectional sensitivity. Intermediate positions give various cardioid shapes. This is the familiar microphone in Fig. 16-6 which has nearly doubled in price over the last decade.

It also is possible to obtain uni-directional operation from two dynamic generators if one is modified and open to the rear to provide a velocity characteristic. The earliest public address models took this approach. The one shown in Fig. 16-7 appeared nearly 30 years ago; it did not incorporate a simple switch that would have permitted a pattern choice. As a rule of thumb, the multi-pattern microphones deliver their flattest frequency response when set for their various uni-directional patterns, since they were designed principally

Fig. 16-5. An early professional multi-patterned microphone, this one uses a ribbon element and a diaphragm dynamic element, with switchable combinations. Originated by Western Electric, the 639B survives today as an Altec product.

Fig. 16-6. An early and familiar multi-directional microphone using a single ribbon element and mechanically adjusted apertures to provide its various patterns. It, too, survives the years and is available today. (Courtesy of RCA)

Fig. 16-7. An early unidirectional microphone incorporating two diaphragm dynamic generators, one of them modified for velocity response, stacked one above the other. A simple switch, not included, could have provided a choice of three patterns. With good directional properties, its inferior frequency and transient response made this public address unit unsuitable for broadcast purposes.

Fig. 16-8. A public address model with a frequency response entirely suitable for most remote applications, this Electro-Voice 676 obtains its unidirectional properties with a single diaphragm dynamic element and distributed rear ports acting through an acoustic network. Under $60.

for such use. The bi-directional setting will tend to be relatively dull, while the non-directional mode tends to be thin; when combined, the generators complement each other's deficiencies for more uniform performance.

Since these early developments, the art of microphone design has advanced so that the modern uni-directional microphone (with the exception of some condenser models) employs but a single diaphragm, driving a dynamic generator. Directional discrimination is obtained through internal acoustical phasing or delay networks. Sound ports behind the diaphragm sample the sound arriving from the rear and delay it so that it will cancel its own arrival at the front. For sound originating from the front, cancellation does not occur; hence a unidirectional pattern results. (When such units are used as hand microphones, care should be taken to avoid covering the rear ports.) Most recently, distributed openings have been designed to phase out rearward-originating sounds more uniformly. The louvered characteristic of this method of porting are visible on the microphone of Fig. 16-8, which is a public address dynamic suitable for many remote broadcast purposes. A similar phasing method is used in the professional model of Fig. 16-9, which costs nearly three times as much and is (according to the manufacturer's curve) very flat from 100 to 15,000 Hz. Typical of TV-era design, it is down about 5 db at 50 Hz.

Being either a mixture of two basically different generators or incorporating acoustic networks limited by physical size, it is not surprising that the unidirectional microphone may not be as flat in output as either a good pressure or good velocity unit. In general, it is much more difficult to make a uni-directional one ultra-flat over a very wide range. However, with front-to-back discrimination ranging from 15 to 20 db, the improvement possible under difficult acoustic conditions more than offsets minor irregularities in output.

Since a velocity characteristic is contributory to uni-directional performance, it is not surprising that cardioid microphones display some wind sensitivity and proximity effects, although they are less pronounced than the basic ribbon velocity. Their degree differs greatly among the various models, with the distributed-opening version being the least offensive.

THE CONTROL ROOM MICROPHONE

There is no set approach to meeting control room microphone requirements. Some stations use non-directional units positioned for close talking. Since proximity effects are no problem with a pressure unit, the operator can work in the neighborhood of two or three inches distant and simply override the background noise, even though his microphone is omnidirectionally sensitive to it. This method has the disadvantage of severely limiting the operator's range of movements while he is speaking. The bi-directional microphone

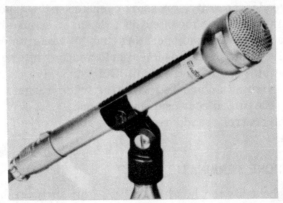

Fig. 16-9. A professional unit using the distributed rear port method of obtaining unidirectional performance. The manufacturer's curve shows the Electro-Voice RE 15 to be very smooth, but its TV-era design puts the output down about 8 db at 40 Hz. (Courtesy of Electro-Voice)

is well suited for minimizing noise pickup from its sides, where the turntables and tape equipment may be located. However, its live back almost certainly will cause trouble with the indirect sounds reflected from the studio window behind it. Further, the proximity effect requires either long working distances, meaning higher gain settings which bring up the noise, or the use of a bass cut switch, which again restricts the operator to an exact working distance.

The uni-directional microphone eliminates the window reflection problem and reduces the proximity effect, especially if it is of the distributed porting type. It will be somewhat more sensitive to noise from its sides than would a ribbon velocity, but overall noise reduction will permit, in many control rooms, sufficient working distance to give the operator relative freedom of motion while remaining on-mike, and minimal proximity effect.

It has been suggested that the board operator wear the lavalier microphone common to television. In my opinion, the control room microphone requirements are too important to condone inferior equipment or inferior techniques, and the lavalier is a compromise. To offset the effects of its indirect positioning, the lavalier unit must possess a doctored response that reduces chest rumble and compensates for lost high frequencies. The result is a restricted and inconsistent performance scarcely suitable for a radio station's principal microphone. An alternative might be a miniature unit of genunine broadcast quality, pressure operated so that it possesses no proximity effect, mounted on a headset boom similar to those used by telephone operators and TV cameramen. This would give good signal-to-noise performance while permitting total operator motional freedom. Unfortunately, there seems to be no such miniature unit with truly wide-range response, so that the uni-directional microphone, properly situated above the control board, remains the most workable present solution.

MICROPHONE TERMINATION

Throughout his technical education, the engineer has been taught that it is necessary to match impedances in transmission systems; that is, to terminate a given source with a load equal to its own internal impedance. It comes as a shock to some to learn that there are important exceptions, of which microphone termination is one. The principle of matching holds only when the objective is maximum power transfer. In audio work it often happens that considerations of distortion and/or frequency response take precedence over that of power transfer. Because the microphone is a voltage generator, rather than a power device, its frequency response and output level ratings usually are determined in terms of open-circuit voltage.

This means that a 250-ohm microphone should not be terminated by 250 ohms; to do so is to lose a theoretical 6 db at the outset. The load it is rated for is a transformer designed to work from a 250-ohm source and into an open circuit such as a vacuum tube grid. A check of professional tube-type consoles will reveal that the microphone input transformers operate with unloaded secondaries. For this configuration, the primary impedance "seen" by the 250-ohm microphone ranges to perhaps 10 times that figure. Thus, the generator "sees" what is, for practical purposes, an open circuit.

Microphone amplifiers employing inferior input transformers may incorporate loading (or "matching") resistors across the secondary windings to swamp out audio resonances and other transformer deficiencies. These, and some transistor circuits, present impedances of the same order of magnitude as a microphone's source impedance. So do low level mixers, wherein each input is terminated directly by an attenuator pot of a resistance equal to the source rating.

The quality degradation caused by such improperly designed equipment is related to the type of microphone involved. It may be permissible, and even necessary, to terminate a condenser type in its rated impedance, since the actual transducer is "buffered" by the internal preamplifier or impedance-converter stage. For the dynamic microphone, however, a low-impedance termination will reduce the available output and therefore reduce the system signal-to-noise ratio. Because the pressure-type dynamic generator is internally "resistance controlled" to damp out diaphragm resonances and other non-linearities, loading its output reflects little additional resistance into the mechanical system, and the frequency response will not be seriously affected. For the non-directional dynamic under normal conditions, then, termination by its rated impedance will not seriously degrade its performance.

The situation is quite different for the velocity generator, which is "mass controlled"; i.e., the impinging sound waves work mostly against the physical inertia of the ribbon (or diaphragm) itself, which must be very free of restraint within the limits of normal deflection. When this generator is loaded by a low impedance, the ribbon's freedom becomes limited by the dynamic braking effect of increased self-induced current flowing through it (just as a DC meter prepared for shipment will suffer far less violent pointer movements enroute if its terminals are shorted, or as the self-resonances in a speaker are damped out by a low internal impedance in its driving amplifier). The dynamic braking suffered by a terminated ribbon is greatest at the lower audio frequencies, which approach the sub-audio resonance of the moving element. For this reason, a ribbon velocity microphone that is loaded by an impedance less than several times its own suffers not only reduced overall output, but a considerable change in frequency response as well. If the full rated bass capability is to be realized, it must be terminated in a relatively open circuit.

Because uni-directional microphones must include velocity characteristics to some degree, it follows that their frequency response will be more susceptible to adverse effects from improper loading than is true of the basic non-directional unit. The degree of susceptibility varies widely from one model to another; the best way to avoid the problem is to use only unloaded input circuits. This raises a question pertaining to the modern practice of inserting a 10 to 15 db loss pad between modern high-output microphones and their amplifiers in those applications where very loud sounds may overload the input stages. Ordinarily a conventional "T" or "H" matching pad is recommended, whereas a simple "L" pad would better meet the open-circuit condition for which microphone specifications are given.

These unique aspects of microphone impedance loading are not widely publicized in the literature. The RCA audio equipment catalogs for years have included a good explanation in their microphone sections, standing almost alone as purveyors of information that is basic to all broadcast interests.

Chapter 17

Construction Notes

Nowhere does the installing engineer's professionalism show more strongly to another engineer (and less so to management) than in the meticulous procedures of construction. The key ingredients of good installation are knowhow, organization, and time. It is the latter one that is almost certain to conflict with management's desire to get a new station operational so that revenue can be harvested at the earliest date. Construction cannot begin until the CP is officially granted, by which time a considerable investment already has been made. As a staff accumulates and payroll obligations deplete cash reserves at an alarming rate, there is likely to be increasing pressure to meet an optimistically-set air date. The engineer who is rushed may resort to temporary installation measures, by which he can make the plant operational much sooner. To sate his professional pride he will plan to re-do the job permanently on a piecemeal basis once the pressure is off and routine sets in. But despite all good intentions, temporary installations tend to become permanent. So long as it's functioning, a sub-standard aspect of an installation is prone to occupy a low priority in relation to those other more pressing engineering demands that, in number, always exceed expectations. Further, once a station is operational, many of the circuits can be replaced only during off-air hours, and certain wiring complexes require more than a single evening to transfer.

There is a psychological factor, too. Most engineers would rather wire a new station from scratch than to re-wire one already in operation. This is true particularly when there are no reliable records to identify cable pairs, terminal numbers, and other essential bits of information that are likely to be lost during hasty construction. This factor certainly contributes its share in putting re-installation low on an engineer's must-do list.

The point that management seems to overlook is that a hasty, temporary installation is very poor long-term economy, for it actually amounts to paying twice for the same job. For every minute saved by a temporary initial installation, there will be two minutes added to the subsequent permanent one because it must be done without interruption of daily operation. And if the "temporary" job drags into permanence, there ultimately will be excessive lost air time because failing equipment cannot be expeditiously bypassed or another unit cannot be substituted by patching, or even its wiring connections readily identified. Adequate time, then, is requisite to a good initial installation. A few extra weeks make an investment in a technical plant that is well planned and executed, right down to the most obscure solder joint and the smallest conduit.

Management should appreciate the fact that there is a good bit of time-consuming detail work that doesn't meet the casual eye. When a transmitter is dollied in and set up, there is ample evidence of engineering accomplishment, but when 227 soldered connections are made deep in the bowels of an equipment rack, it appears to the uninitiated that the installing engineer has been dallying on the job! In the conventional full-facility plant, there is a great amount of such detail work which, once done rightly, will need no further attention until expansion or equipment changes are made.

PRELIMINARY PLANNING

Once the selection of specific equipment items is firm, the engineer is faced with determining their physical layout in terms of building floor plans. With an eye to functional convenience and maintenance accessibility, he will sketch several projected arrangements close enough to scale to permit selection of the best one. Having done this, he then should "wire" the entire complex on paper, being sure to include all audio, power, control, and RF paths. From this, he can anticipate the necessary conduit runs, wiring ducts, distribution panels, and junction points, preferably well before building walls are finished or floors are poured or constructed.

At this point, potential future needs should be considered.

It is impossible to anticipate in detail those that will arise several years in the future, but it is relatively inexpensive to include an extra conduit or two running to each equipment location before a concrete floor is poured or a wall is finished, and it can be a virtual lifesaver when unforeseen expansion needs do occur. This pre-planning of wiring runs, if routed to reasonable scale in a sketch, will enable the engineer to make a surprisingly close estimate of necessary wire and cable needs for the entire installation. If perhaps 3,000 feet of audio wire are estimated, the actual need may come to within 50 feet of that figure. This ability to estimate closely avoids unnecessary overstocking of wire that may not be readily returnable nor immediately usable, or, conversely, the annoying problem of lacking just a few feet to complete a job at three AM, when none is available.

The location for larger equipment items should be prepared in advance. The transmitter manufacturer will, upon request, provide detailed dimensions and wiring point locations prior to the unit's shipment, from which the installing engineer can prepare the foundation, place the conduits and pull and label the wires. When the transmitter does arrive, it then is simply set in its prepared place, the appropriate connections made, and it is ready for checkout procedures in minimal time.

It is a good practice in transmitter plants and other areas of strong RF fields to cover the floor areas under transmitters and equipment racks with solid sheet copper, tied into the station ground system. Power, audio, and control circuits are brought up through the floor and ground sheet through various conduits, also solidly grounded. The transmitter proper customarily is set upon a wooden frame fashioned from 4 X 4 lumber, and associated racks are set on similar bases, perhaps made of 2 X 2 material. This method of installation provides ample room between the rack bottoms and the building floor for the incoming wires to be fanned out and routed to their appropriate destinations, while the cabinet floor above and the ground sheet below afford reasonably good shielding. (When moving heavy equipment cabinets, a liberal spraying of a liquid silicone lubricant onto the wood surface will facilitate sliding them.)

Effective grounding procedures in combined studio-transmitter operations are very important to keep RF out of the audio equipment. Transistors, with their more abrupt overload characteristics, are especially prone to detect stray RF, and it is highly frustrating to have modulation or RF noise present in audio circuits. Heavy copper strap should tie every rack and equipment cabinet to the station ground as close to the actual earth as possible. FM frequencies, in particular, can be troublesome, because just a few inches of wire can possess a substantial impedance. It may be necessary to install filters on incoming power and control circuits for every rack, and microphone cables—despite their shielding—manage to deliver RF to input stages. Very careful attention to consistent and adequate grounding during station construction will avoid many later headaches.

PRE-WIRING

The audio circuits probably are the most demanding part of the initial wiring job. While there is a temptation, under the pressure of time limitations, to simply mount the various items of audio equipment and wire them directly from point to point, the end result is bound to be an impenetrable rat's-nest of intertwined wires that is not only unsightly but which also is impossible to trace through when the need arises.

The time-honored telephone practice of bringing all audio circuits to central terminal blocks in the rear of a rack still is used in wiring broadcast racks. The usual block possesses 80 terminals, accessible at both ends. All jacks are assigned terminal numbers on one side of the block, with equipment connections to appropriate jacks being made to the corresponding terminals on the opposite side. In this manner it is merely a matter of changing connections on the block's equipment side when future developments require jack re-assignment. Fig. 17-1 illustrates the jack side of such a terminal block that serves circuits to 24 jacks, several amplifiers, and inter-jack distribution circuits. As can be seen, many of the terminals on this one are unused. Circuits grouped near one end of the block carry nominal +10 dbm levels; those at the other are assigned to the higher levels to be found in various monitor speaker circuits. (It is good practice to separate audio wiring, both at terminal strips and in cabled groups, into similar levels. Differences of about 30 db or greater should not be permitted in the same cable group; a separation of at least two inches is desirable.)

The wiring of one of these terminal blocks is a tedious process, since a full one means stripping, preparing and soldering no less than 160 wire ends at the block, and another 160 at the corresponding jack and equipment terminals (a solderless technique could be devised for this operation). However, a little prewiring can minimize the hours an engineer plays the contortionist inside a rack. The jack-to-block wiring and that from the block to the equipment within the rack can be done at the workbench. The jack strip and the terminal block are temporarily mounted on a simple wooden jig in the relative positions they will occupy in the rack. Wire is reeled off the spool, soldered to the jack terminals, and laid between guide nails on the jig as it is routed to the terminal block. In this manner, the entire strip is wired to the block and the individual wires are laced into neat cables. Then another jig is arranged for pre-wiring the cable runs to the rack-mounted equipment, with suitable wires fanning from it like river tributaries (vis-

Fig. 17-1. The considerable effort required to do a professional rack wiring installation results in improved appearance, easier traceability, and simplified modification procedures. Here, the terminal block nestles low in the rack, serves many more circuits than haphazard wiring.

RACK #2 JACK PANEL
FRONT VIEW

	CONS. 1 OUT	UNI LEV. OUT	LIMITER OUT	CONS.1 BR OUT	MOD. MON.OUT	CONS. 2 OUT	L1 RACK 1	MULTIPLE	MULT.
TOP ROW — CKT. DESIGNAT.	CONS. 1 OUT	UNI LEV. OUT	LIMITER OUT	CONS.1 BR OUT	MOD. MON.OUT	CONS. 2 OUT	L1 RACK 1	MULTIPLE	MULT.
JACK PR. #	1	2	3	4	5	6	7	8	9
TB #	1 – 2	5 – 6	9 – 10	13 – 14	17 – 18	21 – 22	25 – 26	TIED AT JACK STRIP	
NORMAL THRU	↕	↕	↕	↕	↕	↕	↕	↕	↕
BOTTOM ROW — CKT. DESIGNAT.	UNI LEV. IN	LIMITER IN	XMTR IN	MON. AMP 2 IN	MON. AMP.1 IN	SCR– TERM.	L 2 RACK 1	MULT.	MULT.
JACK PR. #	13	14	15	16	17	18	19	20	21
TB #	3 – 4	7 – 8	11 – 12	15 – 16	19 – 20	23 – 24	27 – 28	TIED AT JACK STRIP	

TB#s refer to Term. Board 1, Rack 2.

Fig. 17-2. When wiring jack strips and terminal blocks, a simple chart relating terminal numbers to one another provides a convenient check-off as wiring is completed, and subsequently serves as a permanent interconnection reference for the diagram files.

ible in Fig. 17-1) to meet the equipment terminals. In this manner, the bulk of the rack wiring can be done at the bench. It is possible then to mount the entire assembly in the rack, tie in the wires to the equipment, and connect those circuits entering and leaving the rack in a short evening. This is about the only way to re-wire a rack already in daily service when temporary wiring is to be replaced.

When wiring a jack strip-terminal strip combination, a checkoff chart is most convenient. A simple form similar to that shown in Fig. 17-2 provides a way to check off each connection as it is made. It then may be retained as part of the permanent diagram file, giving an instant reference for terminal numbers associated with specific jacks and equipment. A simple additional chart that relates inter-rack connections to respective terminal board numbers permits immediate identification of cables and wire pairs between racks.

Most broadcast audio jack circuits are "normaled through." Supposing this to be common terminology to all broadcast engineers, I once was surprised to fine one of many years' experience at a loss to understand my routine request to wire certain jacks in that manner. Perhaps a brief explanation will clarify it for others, as well: it is customary to bring an amplifier's output, for example, to a designated jack pair, and to assign the pair directly beneath the output pair to the amplifier's normal load, which might be the transmitter's audio input. To avoid the necessity of connecting the two sets of jacks by a patch cord for normal operation, contacts within the jacks are used to connect the upper ones to the lower when they are empty. Inserting a plug into either will break the "normal through" contacts and bring either the amplifier's output or the transmitter's input, as the case may be, out through the patch cord to enable some alternate connection. Fig. 17-3 is a schematic of the conventional normal-through connection. It may be made directly at the jack terminals, or, if extensive future changes are anticipated, the normal-through contacts can be wired to the terminal block and jumpered there.

It is conventional practice to employ shielded twisted pair for all audio wiring, cabled and run in conduit (outside of equipment racks). Modern wire products simplify the problems of preparation by using a foil shield material and a ground wire, and physical size has been reduced over that of older

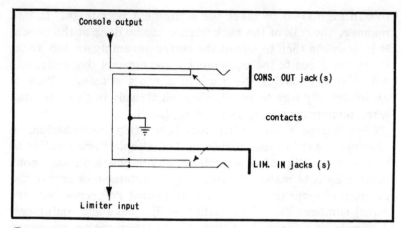

Fig. 17-3. When cascaded devices are connected in this manner, their normal interconnection is broken when a plug is inserted. Plugging into the upper jack brings the console output to the patch cord; similarly, the lower one makes the limiter input accessible. This is but half of the usual double-jack non-balanced circuit; the other half is symmetrically identical.

types, permitting more pairs to be pulled through a given conduit. (In this connection, it always is a good idea to include a few extra, unassigned audio pairs in the initial conduit runs, coiling and labeling their ends for future use.)

There are two schools of thought regarding shield grounds. One advises bare-shield wire, tightly bound and bonded to ground at every opportunity. This is the brute force method, which contrasts with the single-ground philosophy: all shields are insulated from each other, from conduits, from chassis, etc., and are physically grounded to a common grounding point at <u>one end only</u>. Each approach has its adherents; I prefer the latter. Using insulated shielded wire and grounding the shields at the point of lowest ground potential (usually at the terminal block in the base of a rack) eliminates troublesome ground loops, possible rectification of RF at corroded shield-to-conduit points, and other difficult problems. This method works very well in AM plants, although in strong FM or TV fields a long shield grounded at but one end may be far from ground potential at the other. If it can be done positively, the brute force grounding method theoretically affords better protection against short wavelengths.

Consideration of polarity in monaural audio wiring gets little attention, and perhaps is unnecessary, except for microphone circuits where phasing becomes important to multiple mike studio pickup. However, I contend that inter-equipment wiring should be made phase-consistent at the time of installation, particularly for the station that may later adopt stereo. A simple system will suffice. Most audio wire is color coded, having one red wire and one black, perhaps, and by settling on a procedure when wiring jack strips and terminal blocks, future confusion regarding audio polarity can be minimized by uniform patching procedures. Just putting "red on the right" for every pair of terminals pre-wired, and "red to red" when connecting to the equipment side of a block, will maintain consistency of polarity at the jack strip. Then, if it becomes important, the actual phase polarity delivered by various equipment items can be determined and their terminals connected accordingly. Since patch cords have polarity indicated on their plugs, patching at a consistently wired jack strip should turn out right the first time.

The matter of polarity is one of great importance where unbalanced circuits (those having one side grounded) are concerned, which brings up a problem of nomenclature. The term balanced, when dealing with audio distribution systems, causes no confusion; it always means that the various input and output transformers have their center taps grounded. However, an unbalanced circuit may be either of two configurations: one side grounded, or else nothing grounded. I consider the latter to be a nonbalanced form. Fig. 17-4 indicates a suggested confusion-free nomenclature.

Most inter-equipment broadcast audio circuits are nonbalanced, with important exceptions, including some microphone circuits, which may be balanced; mixing networks and busses, which frequently are unbalanced; voice-coil impedance amplifier outputs, which also may be unbalanced; and any high-impedance circuits, which are certain to be unbalanced. From a practical standpoint, a nonbalanced circuit may be patched successfully to either a balanced or unbalanced one, but a balanced circuit cannot be connected to an unbalanced one, since a short circuit across half of one transformer would result. Where this situation may arise, an isolation transformer should be available at the patch panel.

Other desirable patch facilities are either fixed loss pads or an attenuator, a VU meter with a range multiplier, and a "multiple" of three or four jacks simply paralleled with each other to facilitate interconnection of more than two circuits

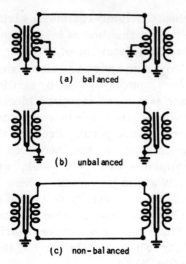

(a) balanced

(b) unbalanced

(c) non-balanced

Fig. 17-4. The terminology here avoids the confusion caused by indiscriminate reference to both (B) and (C) as "unbalanced" circuits.

simultaneously. Given these facilities and patch field representation of all control room audio circuits, practically any unusual circuit arrangement and temporary bypass configuration can be patched through.

Jack designations should be clear and coded in some manner to identify different audio levels and/or impedances. It may be effective to label normal program circuits in red, recording and remote jacks in black, monitor circuits in blue, and high-level speaker feeds in yellow, or some such method of distinction. Color coding minimizes inadvertent interruption of active program circuits and mismatching of extreme levels and impedances. The ingenuity required to label jacks clearly in the limited spaces provided is almost as great as that necessary to plan the actual wiring.

THE RF POWER DIVIDER

Recent changes in regulations requiring—or permitting, as the point of view may determine—operation by daytime AM stations at reduced power between 6:00 AM and local sunrise have raised a new problem for station engineers. While many transmitters include provisions for power reduction to half- or sometimes quarter-power, permissible pre-sunrise radiation may be a very small fraction of normal daytime values. 500 watts is the maximum where interference conditions allow, while some stations have been licensed for pre-sunrise outputs of less than 10 watts!

Such greatly reduced power is not readily available from a conventional AM transmitter. Changing loading coil taps is not a practical daily procedure, so until transmitter manufacturers incorporate infinite control of power output in their products, the broadcaster faced with greatly reduced pre-sunrise wattage has a choice of either a second transmitter of suitably low power output, or a power-divider circuit to reduce the power fed to the antenna.

Usually, the power divider is by far the simplest and cheapest solution. It merely diverts the proper proportion of the transmitter's normal output into a dissipating resistor, which may be the station's dummy load, while feeding the balance to the antenna. Figs. 17-5, 17-6, 17-7 show different views of one mounted outboard on an air duct atop a 5 kilowatt transmitter. I am indebted to consultant John Mullaney for first pointing out to me the simplicity of such a circuit for the special case where the dissipating resistor is of the same value as the transmission line impedance. This is the usual case when a dummy load is used.

Referring to the power-divider circuit in Fig. 17-8, it is apparent that the transmitter output is split into two parallel legs, each consisting of a reactive element and a resistive one (the transmission line is presumed to be matched and therefore resistive). Since these two branches combined must reflect a net resistive load to the transmitter, it follows that their reactances should be of opposite signs. It is immaterial which leg contains the inductance and which the capacitance; the choice may be dictated by values at hand, or other considerations such as DC paths for arc suppression circuits, etc.

Assuming that more than half the transmitter's power is to be shunted to the dissipating resistor R_D, a mathematical factor may be introduced:

$$M = \sqrt{\frac{P1}{P2}}$$

where P1 = power to be dissipated in R_D
and P2 = power to be delivered to the antenna.

Fig. 17-5. Front panel of presunrise power divider mounted outboard on air duct atop 5-kilowatt transmitter. This one, in conjunction with power reduction circuit integral to transmitter, gives choice of three output values. (Author photo by permission of WXGI)

The value of reactance for the P1 leg is given simply by:

$$X_C = \frac{R_D}{M}$$

and, for the P2 leg (inductive, in this case):

$$X_L = M R_D$$

since R_D must equal the transmission line Z.

From these simple relationships, X_L and X_C are found for this special case. Corresponding values of L and C at the operating frequency are readily found from the usual reactance formula. The elements should be variable to afford precise adjustment to suitable currents, as indicated by the dummy load, transmission line, and antenna (or common point) base current meters. Properly adjusted, any difference in transmitter loading between the full power and reduced power conditions will be imperceptible. It should be obvious that the dummy load R_D must be able to dissipate the undesired power plus modulation, and be suitably ventilated.

AM ANTENNA SYSTEMS: LIGHTNING AND THE FOLDED UNIPOLE

Seasonal thunderstorms are commonplace in most areas of the country. The lightning hazard posed to personnel by an antenna tower has been discussed earlier, but the greater chance of damage to equipment and consequent lost air time also requires some precautions. The conventional AM tower is series-fed and insulated from ground, with a static drain, usually a high-reactance RF choke, included in the associated tuning unit. During certain phases of construction, the static

Fig. 17-6. Partial interior view of power divider of Fig. 17-5, showing changeover relay, which is interlocked with transmitter control circuits so that it will not operate while carrier is energized. (Author photo by permission of WXGI)

Fig. 17-7. Another interior view of the power divider of Fig. 17-5, showing the L and C components. Variable vacuum capacitor is located behind the fixed padding capacitors. (Author photo by permission of WXGI)

drain may be disconnected. It is important to ground the tower temporarily at such times; even in perfectly clear weather, a highly dangerous static charge can accumulate on a totally floating tower. The series-fed tower always is equipped with an adjustable discharge gap across the base insulator. This should be set for a gap of from 1/8 to 1/4 inch, or just as close as possible without its firing under modulation peaks. This is the principal path to ground for lightning strikes, and it must carry the extreme current surge with a minimum of voltage drop.

Another approach to minimizing lightning damage in storm-prone areas is to employ a grounded tower with a shunt-feed arrangement. An interesting variation of this method is the folded unipole antenna, first developed for broadcast use by consultant John Mullaney, who was seeking signal advantages rather than lightning protection. The folded unipole utilizes several "folds" of heavy wire suspended parallel to and insulated from the tower faces and fed from their lower ends. These folds are electrically connected to the tower at a height determined by measurements taken when the radiation resistance is determined. As a rule, one of several resonant modes is sought, where the reactive component j = zero. The tower base is directly grounded for the unipole, either by heavy shorting straps across the base insulator, or if a new installation, the absence of one. Guy cable insulators are necessary, however,

The earliest broadcast unipoles used six folds, two to each face of a triangular tower. Since the Q, or bandwidth, depends in part upon the number of folds, there is a practical minimum number. More recent installations have reduced it to three. Fig. 17-9 illustrates a pioneer broadcast unipole installation (there is some controversy over whether it is the nation's first or second) as it is today. Originally a six-fold system, the photograph shows the present arrangement of

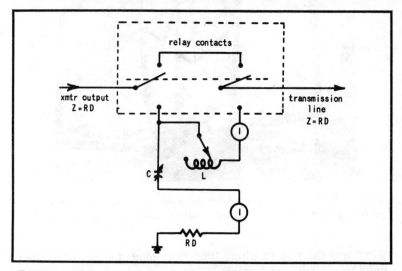

Fig. 17-8. The power divider, by shunting excess power into the dissipation resistor R_D, permits adjustment of presunrise power delivered to the antenna to the proper value. For the special case where R_D equals the transmission line impedance, calculation of design values is simple (see text). The relay operating coil should be interlocked with the transmitter control circuits to prevent its operation when the carrier is on.

Fig. 17-9. Unipole antenna folds are connected together at their lower ends to form a common feed point. (Author photo by permission of WXGI)

three and the way in which they are connected at their lower ends to a single feed point. This particular antenna system was converted to a folded unipole solely to reduce recurrent lightning damage in a local "hot spot." During the past nine years, total lightning losses in this installation amount to one RF line current meter in a transmitter and two chipped guy insulators.

For many installations, however, the lightning protection feature is but a fringe benefit of the unipole configuration. It was developed principally to provide improved radiation characteristics when towers must be less than optimum height. Its current distribution delivers a more favorable radiation angle, and its higher impedance (which can range from 250 to over 1,000 non-reactive ohms) reduces circuit losses. The ground system requirements, for example, are less stringent; the inevitable ohm or two of radial system resistance is an insignificant fraction of the total system. Further, the ground system for a conventional series-fed radiator must provide a near-perfect capacitive foil for the tower, while the unipole obviously possesses far greater fold-to-tower capacitance than fold-to-ground, thereby de-emphasizing further the critical role of the ground system.

Other fringe benefits accrue from a tower's being grounded at its base. No lighting system chokes are necessary if the AC wiring on the tower is bypassed for RF at the base; similarly, transmission lines serving other antennas on the structure—FM, mobile units, etc.—pose no isolation problems. Other than the somewhat increased first cost for materials and construction, the folded unipole offers few disadvantages. The new operation faced with limited tower height or severe lightning hazards should investigate it in depth.

THE LIGHTNING RETARD COIL

A commonplace lightning-protective device for any AM antenna is the retard coil, consisting of two or three turns in the antenna feed line. Fig. 17-10 illustrates how one may be formed in a tower feed using copper tubing. While it seems that such a small inductance would have a negligible effect on the basically DC discharge of a lightning strike, the engineering fraternity insists that it is beneficial. On this premise, the inclusion of a lightning coil can do no harm, since at signal frequencies its small inductance is obviated by the tuning unit adjustment.

THE REMOTE ANTENNA CURRENT METER

The antenna system component most vulnerable to lightning damage is the thermocouple RF ammeter, required for all AM installations. The thermocouple element has a very

Fig. 17-10. A small inductance, formed by a few turns in the feed line, can aid in limiting damage from lightning surges in an antenna.

limited overload capacity, and even a modest and short surge can burn it out. The resultant open circuit puts the station off the air until someone is brave—or foolhardy—enough to trek to the storm-enshrouded tuning unit and install a jumper.

Recognizing this, the FCC permits a make-before-break switch for the base current meter, so that it is out of the circuit except for those infrequent times of actual observation. However, the <u>remote</u> antenna current meter is another matter; a similar switch, requiring a trip to the tuning unit to operate, would defeat the purpose. It can be done, of course, with a suitable and expensive relay, energized from a remote point, but most stations use alternate methods that don't require a thermocouple in the signal circuit.

It is permissible to use either an inductive or capacitive coupling to the metering point to drive a diode, the DC output of which deflects the remotely-located voltmeter calibrated in terms of RF current. This method has the advantage of linear rectification and therefore stable current readings that don't reflect modulation. However, in my experience, such circuits have been prone to excessive calibration drift due to diode temperature effects and stray capacitive coupling.

Another permissible method is the use of a current transformer on the order of that in Fig. 17-11, the secondary of which feeds a conventional thermocouple of reduced current capacity. The thermocouple output operates the remote meter through a suitable line from tower to transmitter building.

THE BEEPER TELEPHONE

Once strictly taboo, the use of ordinary telephone facilities for broadcasting has become a standard practice. The simplest installation method is to order an ordinary beeper terminal installed by the telephone company, which then is fed to an open console input. Though it is the simplest, it may not be the best. And in some circumstances, it may not be necessary. The periodic "beep" applied to a telephone line is intended to alert the phone caller to the fact that his conversation is being recorded, and for live broadcasting it is not yet required by federal law. In fact, some interpret the law to indicate that a beeper is not mandatory for recorded intra-state calls unless it is so stipulated by local state law. In any event, more and more stations are airing phone calls uninterrupted by annoying beeps. The technicality raised by temporary recording in delaying calls from the air for several seconds is not a violation of the spirit of the law, although making program tapes for repeat airings or logging purposes may be.

The broadcaster is not averse to providing the beeper signal for the individual caller's benefit, but it is unnecessary, distracting, and superfluous to the radio listener, especially for prolonged periods. It theoretically is possible to deliver a beep to the phone caller without its being aired, through a process of adding an equal beep of opposite phase to the signal entering the console. To do this, the telephone company's beeper terminal must be entered to tap its oscillator for a sample signal that then can be buffered, amplified, inverted, and balanced against the beep appearing on the output to the console. The simple combining network shown in Fig. 17-12 will permit injection of the cancellation signal with a minimum of circuit interaction. However, the problem of total signal cancellation is not a simple one, and some re-balancing likely will be necessary for calls from various locations. Even if a total null is not always achieved, the intrusive nature of the "beeps" can be reduced.

The telephone company may take a dim view of a station's

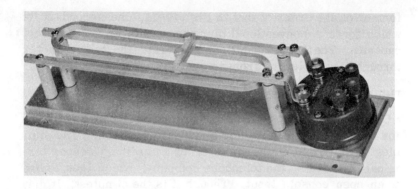

Fig. 17 -11. An antenna current transformer. The thermocouple across the secondary operates the remote antenna ammeter, which is suitably calibrated to indicate the primary current. (Courtesy of Collins Radio)

modifying its beeper terminal, since it is the prescribed interface between utility circuits and subscriber equipment. Regulations prohibiting a subscriber from attaching his own apparatus to the telephone exchange lines are intended to avoid the serious degradation and inconsistency of service that inevitably would result if the practice were permitted to become widespread.* However, regulations notwithstanding, certain violations usually are overlooked by the telephone company, so long as no detriment to service results. It is widely known that radio amateurs commonly use "phone patches" to extend their facilities to any subscriber, and some radio stations devise their own phone-to-console feed arrangements without telco-installed beeper units. Presumably, any competent broadcast engineer can concoct a method that will neither degrade phone service or damage telephone company equipment; the matters of legality and severity of the phone company's reprisals are considerations for management to weigh.

Whether with beeper or without, the audio quality delivered to the console by incoming phone calls leaves much to be desired. While there is no way to process them into high fidelity, a little simple equalization can effect a worthwhile improvement. Aside from distortion, which is very high in some heavily misused telephone "transmitters," the factors

---

*The FCC recently rescinded the Federal ban on attachment of private devices to subscriber lines.

limiting the audio quality of incoming calls are line losses and "transmitter" frequency response. Being carefully engineered for maximum intelligibility in normal telephone usage, the "transmitter" (or telephone microphone) responds to a communications bandwidth of about three kilohertz. Over this range, it has a rising characteristic from 250 or 300 Hz to perhaps 1,500 or 2,000 Hz, dropping sharply beyond these limits. This means that to improve the naturalness of amplified speaker reproduction, the low frequencies must be emphasized to offset the "communications" quality.

The effect of line losses, however, is greatest at the higher frequencies. Like any unequalized program line, the usual telephone circuit transmits high frequencies poorly. The net result of the combination of telephone transmitter characteristics and line losses is a "humped" mid-range at the receiving end, suitable for good intelligibility with an ear receiver but both thin and muffled when heard on a speaker. An empirically derived equalizer that has brought favorable comment from many is diagrammed in Fig. 17-13A. Used with a metropolitan telephone system where subscriber lines of small gauge wire

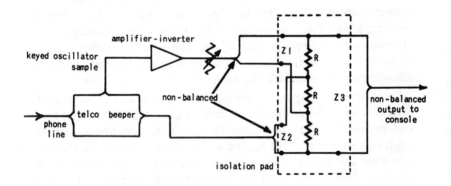

Fig. 17-12. In this circuit, a sample of the telephone beeper's oscillator output may be phase-inverted and level-matched to provide cancellation in an isolation pad before airing. This isolation pad has many potential uses. It can be used in reverse to feed a common source to two circuits which remain isolated from each other; or, as here, it can mix two outputs into a common feed without interaction, suggesting a convenient monaural monitoring output from stereo channels. The circuit can be re-drawn as a symmetrically balanced bridge giving theoretically infinite signal isolation between Z1 and Z2 when Z3 = R. (Z1 and Z2 do not have to equal R for balance, but they should for matching purposes.)

often attain maximum length (thereby providing minimum quality), this equalizer emphasizes both ends of the transmission pass band. Its frequency response is shown by Fig. 17-13B. It is of course a compromise, since calls from various local locations strictly require different equalization. However, it has worked well with its particular telephone system, and the excessive line hum anticipated from the bass boost has been evident only occasionally. (This particular circuit was composed of available "junk box" components; one designed from scratch with new parts would be more sophisticated.)

The discussion of telephone quality has centered thus far on the reception of an incoming call. The outgoing side of the conversation, from the station's phone, presents different problems. In any system the disparity of levels between the local and the distant phone requires drastic compensation. Ordinarily, the signal arriving from the far end will be from 15 to 30 db lower than that produced by the local phone. Further, while bass equalization will improve the frequency characteristics of the local telephone transmitter, the high boost given by the circuit of Fig. 17-13 adds to its inherent rising characteristic, untempered by the losses of several intervening miles of wire, to produce a very harsh sound in which the distortion products are emphasized beyond all reasonable proportion. Thus, the equalizer shown here is suitable for airing incoming communications, but not for simultaneously handling the local end of conversations.

Certain operating techniques minimize the level and quality differences between local and distant phones. Assuming that the announcer on the phone is operating the board, or is equipped with a control knob for the phone circuit, he merely turns the telephone feed very low during those intervals when he is speaking, and raises it for the telephone reply. His own voice is heard on the air only via the regular broadcast microphone, although he must simultaneously speak into the telephone to be heard by the caller. With a little practice, this simple manual technique is quite effective. Where the local announcer does not have control of the telephone air feed, a fast-acting AGC amplifier is a practical necessity, since no third party can anticipate the course of a conversation. This will not eliminate the poor quality of the local phone, but it will improve the level balance.

The sophisticated way to solve the aired telephone problem

is to substitute broadcast equipment for the telephone instrument at the station end. The caller hears a feed from the studio microphone, which has the added advantage of making all participants at the studio audible to him, while his voice receives optimum equalization for the intervening transmission path before it goes on the air. To do this properly a feed from the studio microphone(s) is taken ahead of final mixing and fed through a hybrid transformer to the telephone line. The hybrid connection eliminates the studio microphone signal (and the beeper, too, if desired) from the telephone's air feed, so that it can be mixed normally and with full quality.

One other control room telephone facility is highly useful for those occasions when it is desired to play a production spot over the phone for a client. Better than by holding a telephone instrument near a monitor speaker, a direct electrical connection provides superior quality and, therefore, more favorable client impact. A jack at the patch panel, assigned to outgoing telephone feeds, simplifies connection of a tape output at suitable level directly to the telephone system. A little pre-equalization for line losses might be included.

REMOTE LOOPS

Incoming leased remote lines, unlike telephone exchange lines, are available for direct connection to subscriber equipment. Apart from prohibitions against excessive levels and dangerous voltages, there are few restrictions on the manner in which such lines are used. Since telephone lines are critical as to electrical balance, it will eliminate many noise problems if all incoming (audio) lines are terminated with a transformer known in telephone parlance as "repeat coils." Thus isolated, no big difficulties arise from their inadvertent connection to unbalanced circuits. Also, in transmitter plants the repeat coils aid in isolating the strong RF voltages common to nearby lines.

Remote lines of any appreciable length require equalization. As the number of telephone subscribers increases and cable wire sizes get smaller, loss-per-wire-mile goes up. This means that the variable line equalizer common to most stations is adequate only for decreasing line lengths, beyond which telephone company equalization (which is done in segments) should be purchased. With an impedance of 500/600

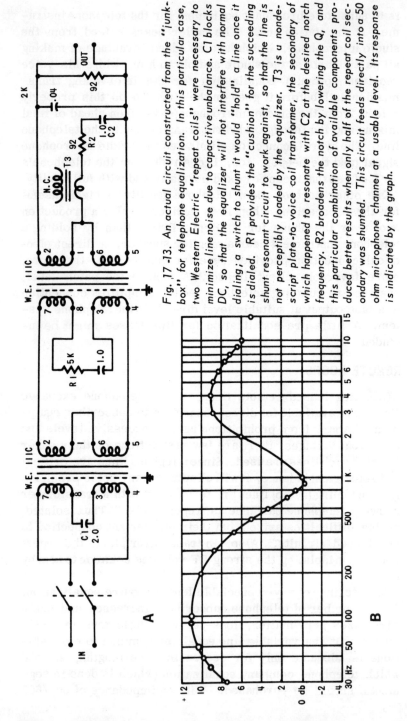

Fig. 17-13. An actual circuit constructed from the "junk-box" for telephone equalization. In this particular case, two Western Electric "repeat coils" were necessary to minimize line noise due to capacitive unbalance. C1 blocks DC, so that the equalizer will not interfere with normal dialing; a switch to shunt it would "hold" a line once it is dialed. R1 provides the "cushion" for the succeeding shunt resonant circuit to work against, so that the line is not perceptibly loaded by the equalizer. T3 is a nonde-script plate-to-voice coil transformer, the secondary of which happened to resonate with C2 at the desired notch frequency. R2 broadens the notch by lowering the Q, and this particular combination of available components pro-duced better results when only half of the repeat coil sec-ondary was shunted. This circuit feeds directly into a 50 ohm microphone channel at a usable level. Its response is indicated by the graph.

ohms being the broadcast standard, the industry has lost sight of the fact that metallic, non-loaded cable circuits provide better frequency response if they are terminated in 150 ohms. True, this increases the loss in level, which is exactly what the conventional parallel equalizer does, terminating in a very low impedance in the process. However, when telco equalization is provided, the proper station termination usually is 500/600 ohms.

Whether equalized by the station or the telephone company, the line in question should not be "loaded." Many long subscriber lines incorporate loading inductances to provide improved voice range transmission for normal telephone use, and occasionally an unoccupied loaded line will be assigned to a remote broadcast loop order. The loading coils make it impossible for the broadcaster to achieve good response with his own equalizer, but since they are common to relatively long subscriber loops telco equalization ordinarily is required anyway, so that loading rarely concerns broadcasters directly.

Another service that cannot be station-equalized is the carrier circuit. Inter-exchange channels derived from RF carrier modulation and demodulation are closely limited to passbands determined by the carrier equipment filters, and few of them deliver satisfactory broadcast quality. When it does become necessary to use a carrier facility, the broadcaster should bear in mind that it also has stringent level limitations. Whereas an ordinary metallic circuit can handle any audio level up to that which leaks excessively to adjoining cable pairs, a carrier circuit begins to overload audibly when program peaks exceed the standard line levels. Operators who consistently peg the meters on remote amplifiers only add to the poor transmission on such circuits.

The objectionable limitation common to both loaded and carrier circuits is that imposed on low audio frequencies. While a simple metallic line loses the least at the low end of the audio spectrum, loaded and carrier circuits are deficient below about 300 Hz. Because these sometimes are the only facilities within a station's reach, the Kahn Research Laboratories (81 South Bergen Place, Freeport, N.Y. 11520) recently introduced a novel system to improve them. Kahn engineers devised a method of transposing the frequencies below 300 Hz and transmitting them via a channel normally deficient in the low-end audio. The technique is based on the fact that a notch

265

can be cut from certain portions of the audio spectrum with no perceptible effect on voice reproduction. By making such a notch within the transmission passband, transposing the sub-300-Hz frequencies to the notch band for transmission, and then reconstructing them at the receiving end, voice transmission to 100 Hz is accomplished over a 300-Hz minimum facility. The improvement the system affords should be worthwhile, although each operation must evaluate it in terms of its rather high cost, which is typical of highly researched low volume products.

The methods of cueing remote crews vary from station to station. It used to be standard practice to order two lines for each remote; one for program and one for an order phone. This was a fail-safe system; if the program line failed, the order wire could be pressed into program service in a few moments. However, the cost of lines has led most modern stations to settle for one and provide remote cues in some other manner.

Most control consoles incorporate switch positions that feed program or cue back down incoming remote lines. Pads are included to reduce the level applied to the lines to the "legal" + 8 dbm, which, with line losses, often is not audible to the remote operator in noisy locations.

There are two solutions to the problem. The loss pads in the console can be reduced or removed, permitting higher levels to be applied to the remote line. Theoretically, this practice results in excessive spillover into adjacent telephone circuits, but in practice complaints of this happening are rare. Alternatively, the risk of displeasing the telephone company can be eliminated by modifying the remote amplifier so that the telephone line can be fed to one of its inputs for cueing purposes, giving the remote operator the benefit of an amplified signal. This is the preferable (and somewhat more complicated) method.

Console cue facilities are useful only with two-way lines. Any circuit containing a one-way repeater, as is typical of lines equalized in segments by the telephone company, will not transmit a reverse signal. For this reason, many stations have adopted the convenient pocket transistor radio as a cue facility for all remotes, taking their cues from station programming. This procedure works for any remote within range of a station's signal. For those beyond, either an order telephone or synchronized clock cues are necessary.

Occasionally a station will run afoul of local telephone company tariffs, which may impose a premium rate on lines extending beyond the city limits, where many control rooms are. Since a busy station can require eight or ten local remote loops, costs can mount unreasonably. One station's solution to this tariff problem was to arrange a termination point for local lines at an in-town location and then install its own stepping switch there. A single station line to the central termination point served to carry both the dial impulses from the station to actuate the selector switch and the program material from the selected line (not simultaneously). So long as only one remote at a time was necessary (this was before tape delay of simultaneous events was commonplace), this method worked well and economically. The fundamental requirement for this system's reliability is good design of the remote dialing arrangements.

Another station with a similar problem found that it could operate with only two remote loops to the telephone company, which in turn was so accommodating as to perform the necessary patching functions to connect various remote circuits. Although it ostensibly was against company regulations, patching was accomplished according to a timetable of as many as eight remotes a day with high—and welcome—consistency. Telephone company regulations and practices vary considerably from place to place. If he is to come to the best decision concerning incoming remote facilities, a clear understanding of the applicable ones is necessary to the engineer installing a new station.

Chapter 18

Operation and Maintenance

The Operating Log, commonly called the Transmitter Log, is intended to serve as a detailed record of technical performance throughout each operating day. In it are entered half-hourly readings of the important antenna and transmitter parameters, which must be recorded by an appropriately licensed operator or by approved and carefully maintained automatic logging equipment. There are specific Operating Log rules for AM and FM, respectively—Paragraphs 73.113 and 73.283 of the FCC Rules and Regulations. In general, all broadcast station logs are to indicate the carrier on and off times, including any interruptions requiring manual restoration; final RF stage plate current and plate voltage (before any corrections necessary to bring the operation within limits, and details of same); the beginning and end of program modulation; frequency deviation; and the daily observation of tower light operation.

TYPICAL OPERATING LOG

Fig. 18-1 illustrates a simple log form suitable for a nondirectional AM station. It need not be expensively printed; a simple duplicated form will suffice. The AM station with a directional antenna must add columns for phase monitor and sample loop current and phase indications, while the FM operation will replace the IA column with one for the I, E, or power level of the transmission line. Also, for a stereo operation, there must be an entry for the pilot subcarrier frequency.

The stability of modern broadcast equipment often seems to make a perfunctory duty of entering readings every thirty minutes, and many operators—particularly announcers whose licenses are but technicalities—are prone to simply

KWZZ OPERATING LOG

Day _Wednesday_ Date _April 17, 1968_

All times E**ST**

Carrier on **5:59 A** Off **6:00 P**

Modulation on **6:00 A** Off **6:00 P**

Tower lights checked **OK 6:00 P**
                        K.O.W.

Ep: Final plate kilovolts

Ip: Final plate amperes

IA: Antenna amperes

DEV: Hz deviation

Time	EP	IP	IA	DEV	Operators on/off; remarks
6:00A	5.30	1.36	8.57	+0.5	John Lleaux on 5:45A
6:30	5.30	1.36	8.58	+0.3	
7:00	5.30	1.36	8.58	0.0	
7:30	5.30	1.36	8.58	0.0	
8:00	5.28	1.35	8.55	-0.1	
8:30	5.28	1.34	8.52	-0.2	
9:00	5.30	1.35	8.56	0.0	
9:30	5.30	1.36	8.58	-0.1	
10:00	5.29	1.35	8.55	-0.3	
10:30	5.30	1.36	8.57	-0.1	
11:00	5.30	1.36	8.58	0.0	
11:30	5.28	1.34	8.54	-0.3	
12:00N	5.28	1.34	8.55	-0.5	John Lleaux off 12:00N
12:30	5.30	1.36	8.57	-0.3	Kilpatrick O. Watts on 12:00N
1:00P	5.30	1.36	8.58	-0.3	
1:30	5.30	1.36	8.58	-0.4	
2:00	5.30	1.36	8.58	-0.3	
2:30	5.28	1.35	8.55	-0.5	
3:00	5.28	1.34	8.52	-0.5	
3:30	5.30	1.35	8.56	-0.6	
4:00	5.30	1.36	8.58	-0.5	
4:30	5.29	1.35	8.55	-0.7	
5:00	5.30	1.36	8.57	-0.6	
5:30	5.30	1.36	8.58	-0.7	
6:00	5.28	1.34	8.54	-0.8	Kilpatrick O. Watts off 6:00PM

Fig. 18-1. An Operating Log suitable for an AM non-directional station.

repeat the previously entered figures each half hour all day long. Although it is extremely difficult for an FCC representative to prove an entry erroneous unless he was present the moment it was made, any of them knows that no equipment operates endlessly without some small variations.

Each operator is to sign the Operating Log when he goes on duty and again when he goes off. Those signatures assign the responsibility for the veracity of the intervening entries, and careless logging could be construed as fraudulent documentation, which is a more serious offense than inadvertent misoperation. Nevertheless, this threat to the announcer-operator's license privileges and possibly to his livelihood sometimes seems an inadequate inducement for him to log conscientiously.

THE MAINTENANCE LOG

The Operating Log has been integral to broadcasting since the dawn of regulated radio. With the advent of rules permitting "contract" engineering, where the first-class engineer is not necessarily a full-time employee, an additional log has become requisite. It is the Maintenance Log, which attests to a daily inspection of the operating equipment, at least five days a week, by a responsible First Class Radiotelephone licensee.

FCC Rules and Regulations (Paragraphs 73.114 for AM and 73.284 for FM) detail the information to be recorded on the Maintenance Log. Where applicable, required entries include the weekly remote antenna ammeter calibration check; auxiliary transmitter tests; removal and replacement of defective meters and monitors; outside frequency checks; and any experimental operation. The daily check specifically includes the engineer's notation to the effect that all meter indications and operating parameters reflect in-tolerance performance. Any necessary repairs, and the time required to make them, are to be described. Many stations kept their own maintenance logs, often for all technical equipment, long before the FCC made them mandatory for the transmitter complex. Others have found, since their enforced adoption, that they turn out to be remarkably useful records of past performance and failures. Like the Operating Log, the Main-

KWZZ MAINTENANCE LOG

Date	6/3/68	6/4	6/5	6/6		6/7
Day	Mon.	Tue.	Wed.	Thur.		Fri.
Times of inspection Start/end	3:00/3:05p	3:20/3:25p	3:00/3:10p	12:55a/1:15a	3:40/3:45p	4:00/4:15p
Freq. check — Frequency Mon. reading			-0.5			8.51
Freq. check — Time/date Lab. reading			-0.3 6/3/68			8.47
Modulation Monitor OK	✓	✓	✓		✓	✓
Frequency Monitor OK	✓	✓	✓		✓	✓
Ep meter OK	✓	✓	✓		✓	✓
Ip meter OK	✓	✓	✓		✓	✓
True Antenna I					✓	✓
Remote Antenna I reads						
Remote Antenna meter OK	✓	✓	✓		✓	✓
Remote Antenna meter OK/corrected						Corr.
Overall inspection	✓	✓	✓	✓	✓	✓
Remarks / Repairs / Signature	None John Deaux	None John Deaux	Freq. check report of 6/3/68 logged John Deaux	Both modulator tubes replaced in xtmr. Adjusted for minimum distortion during equipment test transmission 1 05/A – 1 15/A John Deaux	John Deaux	John Deaux

Fig. 18-2. A Maintenance Log that provides fast, simple check-off columns for routine inspection entries.

tenance Log can be a simple duplicated form.   Fig. 18-2
shows one that has passed FCC muster.

THE "THOUSAND-HOUR" LOG

The usual transmitter provides comprehensive metering of
all its essential circuits. This feature is an invaluable aid in
its tuneup, but since a broadcast transmitter operates on a
single frequency and is tuned with great infrequency, those
meter indications not essential to FCC logging may go un-
checked for months at a time. Therefore, it can be a very
useful maintenance practice to log all meter readings periodically, giving a continuing record from which may be spotted
the slow changes that arise from gradual tube weakening,
component aging, etc. While some operations do so daily or
weekly, my experience has been that trends can be spotted
better over much longer intervals. Every thousand hours by
the filament-hour meter is a practical period; most slow
changes will show up but not reach critical departures from
the norm in that time. From previous entries it may be noted,
for example, that the buffer plate current has decreased from
6.7 ma to 6.5 ma to 6.3, suggesting that its associated tube
is losing its emission and due for replacement at the next
maintenance session. If the thousand-hour logs are kept on
file from the date of installation, the engineer has a concise,
comprehensive history of the transmitter's lifetime performance that can be most helpful in future diagnoses.

MAINTENANCE PHILOSOPHIES

There is no single maintenance technique that greatly ex-
cels all others. Various procedures are practiced among
different stations to achieve the goal of minimum failure and
maximum equipment life, and their relative degrees of success
are, in part, a matter of opinion. Individual circumstances,
age of equipment, available engineering time, and overall
operating philosophy all enter into the choice of maintenance
procedures that a given station will find most satisfactory.

There can be no argument as to the aim of good maintenance
—maximum technical reliability.   This objective can be assured by a rigorous, detailed and continuous program of
cleaning, testing, and adjustment. In even a small station
an engineer can devote his full time to such a routine. However, modern professional equipment represents a ruggedness

and durability that delivers consistently good performance with far less attention, and _excessive_ maintenance is a waste of engineering time.

Then there is the other extreme, wherein a given equipment item receives absolutely no attention until it fails completely. In this instance poor maintenance procedures have led to lost air time and perhaps damage to the equipment that could have been prevented by earlier corrective measures. This is a waste of station time, money, and equipment life. It is within the wide area between these two extremes that most operations find their workable maintenance programs, and many of the smaller ones do not require 40 weekly hours of engineering time. These either manage with contract engineers, or with staff engineers who double in other station duties.

The rigidity of maintenance scheduling required differs for the two cases. It has been my experience that the station engineer, who usually operates the equipment and intimately observes it daily, is in a far better position to note the little harbingers of forthcoming failure than is the contract man who rarely partakes in its actual operation. A great majority of equipment failures are preceded by little aberrations— drifting meter indications; internal noises; perceptible distortion; reduced gain; etc. —for days or even weeks before outright failure occurs. The engineer who lives with his equipment learns to spot these signs and take corrective measures.

There are failures that are not announced by operating symptoms, of course. Capacitor breakdown, transformer failure, rectifier flash-back—these are typical of troubles that may strike abruptly without the slightest warning. However, they also are troubles that, in general, are _not_ prevented by ordinary maintenance procedures. Few stations routinely replace all capacitors and transformers every 90 days or so on the small chance that one may fail. (Mercury vapor rectifier tubes are another matter, to be discussed further.) What this boils down to is the fact that the staff engineer can permit himself a more flexible approach to maintenance, using normal operation as a continuous testing process. The outside engineer must spend more of his time on formal testing procedures in an effort to spot the subtle indications that give warning of future failures. He may test all tubes every 30 days, for example, while the staff man may manage to spot most of those few that weaken enough to affect performance during as much as 90 days between routine testing, making individual replacements as the need becomes evident. (Actual tube burnout is relatively uncommon, even among old tubes. Most lose their emission first.)

It is worthy of note here that a "wait-and-watch" maintenance philosophy can result in less than ultimate performance some of the time. For the engineer to notice a defect, there must be some degradation of technical quality, although it usually will be imperceptible to the average listener. The station that is devoted to the ideal of absolute state-of-the-art quality 100% of the time necessarily will institute very rigid and frequent testing procedures and component replacement schedules based on limited life estimates. Its signal will be impeccable more consistently than will that of the less dedicated operation, but it also entails a considerable engineering cost. Each broadcaster has to weigh the ideal against the practical in terms of his ability and willingness to approach the point of diminishing returns. The increasing use of transistors in broadcast equipment has reduced maintenance needs, since they do not deteriorate gradually as do tubes. Thus far, transistor failure in commercially designed broadcast equipment is relatively unusual.

The mercury vapor rectifier, once common to all broadcast transmitters, is being replaced by solid-state rectifiers with their attributes of greater efficiency, lower heat, and reduced replacement needs. However, many mercury vapor tubes continue in use, and engineers differ in their replacement practices. There have been many discourses on the subject of predicting failure probabilities, but the fact remains that such tubes are pretty unpredictable. Some may operate for 20,000 hours, while identical tubes in the same circuit may fail in a few hundred. There have been testers marketed that measure the ionization voltages, designed around the premise that an increased firing potential indicates imminent failure. Apart from the confusing fact that the tester reads differently for the two filament pins (the AC voltage used by the tester either adds to or subtracts from half the AC filament voltage), I have found that some mercury vapor tubes that test bad will continue to operate for many thousands of hours, while others that test good may fail early. The same is true for the criterion of color. A new tube will produce a healthy violet ionization glow, while an old one gradually turns weak and green-hued, which is considered to be a suspect condition. Again, many old green-glowing tubes continue to function year after year.

The mercury vapor tube's function is a particularly critical one, delivering power to the transmitter's output stages. Since they usually either work normally or not at all, the failure of one puts the station off the air. On the other hand, a 5-KW transmitter may use as many as a dozen, ranging in cost up to about $20 each, for which unnecessary premature replacement adds up to appreciable expense. Again, the availability of an engineer enters into consideration; if a staff man usually is at hand to make a replacement, the air time lost by operating mercury vapor tubes to the failure point may be kept short. If a contract engineer must be located after a failure occurs, though, it may be prudent to routinely replace them every 5,000 hours or so in the interest of sustained operation.

Tube replacement is but one aspect of maintenance. While it may be permissible for the staff engineer to be a little haphazard in certain of his testing procedures, it is not so where mechanical devices are concerned. A regular routine for lubrication and adjustment of turntables, tape equipment, and other mechanical devices is desirable in all situations. After excess wear is noted in a turntable's main bearing, it's too late for lubrication to correct the trouble. And when a record stylus audibly needs replacement, it already has inflicted some damage to the station's record library. In the realm of mechanical equipment, good and regular preventive maintenance procedures are necessary if it is to give good service life in any operation.

The mundane matter of cleanliness is another area of differing philosophies. Not that any respectable engineer advocates dirty equipment, to be sure, but the desire for chassis surfaces clean enough to eat from seems to become an obsession in some operations. It is not uncommon to find an installation where invisible and inaccessible corners are kept white-glove clean, while the electronics within are performing far below par. This is an example of misdirected maintenance. With many stations located in dusty environments, dirt is a constant reality. A light film of dust on a chassis does not degrade its performance in the least, and the engineer with limited time (as is usually the case) might better attack the dust less often and the equipment performance more so.

This is not to suggest that dirt is functionally harmless to all equipment. Certainly relays, switches, and other contact systems must be kept dust-free. High-voltage conductors and insulators precipitate dust from the air rapidly, and an accumulation may provide a path for arc formation. Heavy deposits of dirt may interfere with proper equipment cooling, and certain other components may be dust-sensitive. It is to suggest, though, that dirt in those places where it is functionally harmless may be tolerated to a modest degree in favor of improved technical maintenance when an engineer's time limitations force a choice. Certainly, dirt conditions are a valid item on any maintenance list, but in some cases it is given an unwarranted priority. Also, some equipment seems to be designed for difficult cleaning access. Extensive dismantling of equipment for routine cleaning may shorten its life more from repeated disassembly and reassembly than would the dirt if left to accumulate (again, excepting where dirt is functionally detrimental). For those situations, it may be preferable to leave the cleaning for those times when it becomes necessary to dismantle the equipment for other reasons.

EQUIPMENT PROOF OF PERFORMANCE

There are two "proofs" commonly referred to in broadcasting. One is the antenna proof, periodically required for all AM directional antenna systems; the other is the equipment proof, required annually of all broadcast operations. The equipment proof of performance is nothing more than a series of measurements taken on the overall performance of the broadcast system, from microphone input to transmitter output. The FCC regulations stipulate the limits within which such parameters as audio frequency response and distortion, inherent noise, and harmonic radiation must fall. They are set forth for AM stations in Paragraph 73.47 and for FM in 73.254 of the Rules and Regulations.

While the Commission requires such measurements to be made only once a year, the well-run station will conduct them far more often. Practically none will remain within proof tolerance for an entire year without attention, particularly high-level AM transmitters, in which adjustment of the modulator stage is critical and frequently necessary as tubes age. It is not in keeping with the emphasis here on professionalism to suggest that an annual proof is sufficient. Ideally, such tests should be conducted every 30 days, but perhaps every 90 days is a realistic compromise. It is not necessary, during the interim between annual FCC proofs, to conduct overall tests; a regular rotation among specific equipment items in the chain, so that a circle is completed periodically, should serve to keep them all working in acceptable harmony. The required annual tests are, of course, made of the total system simultaneously.

FREQUENCY CHECKS

The matter of proper carrier frequency is one of the Commission's greatest concerns, and one of its least problems, insofar as broadcast operations go. In over two decades in the business, I have known a broadcast frequency to drift beyond tolerance just once, and that was due to a crystal fracture that put its frequency beyond range of the station's monitor! Modern broadcast crystals are exceptionally stable devices, as the chart in Fig. 18-3 shows. In this case the crystal is an ovenless vacuum type, and no adjustment of any kind was made to the frequency-determining circuit over the span of the chart. According to the trend indicated by averaging the monthly outside measurements, this particular AM station will be verging on out-of-tolerance carrier frequency sometime around the year 2,000! The associated 20-year-old frequency monitor exhibited far less stability.

Despite modern carrier stability, FCC regulations require a periodic frequency measurement independent of station monitors. The period usually is taken to be 30 days, although I once arbitrarily set it at 90 in a small 250-watt operation, where the outside check had to be made between 4:00 and 4:14 AM on the second Monday of the month so that the signal could be squeezed out of the competition on 1450 kHz at the measurement laboratory several hundred miles away. (There were times when the signal was inaudible in Long Island and drew DX mail from New Zealand.) My 90-day figure drew raised eyebrows but no recriminations from the Commission. However, the 30-day interval is to be preferred, and it may be that a special early morning transmission time will be required. Some fortunate AM stations are near enough to ap-

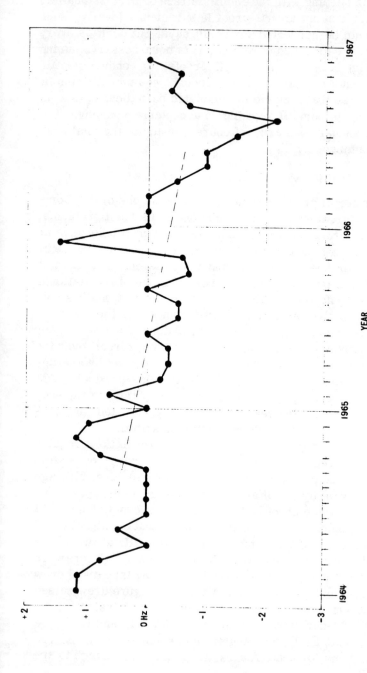

Fig. 18-3. Graph of actual monthly frequency check reports for a transmitter using an ovenless, vacuum-type crystal. No frequency adjustments were made during the three years shown. Stability of modern equipment is indicated by the trend of the average (dotted line); if transmitter is not corrected in the meantime, it will be close to tolerance limit sometime around the year 2000.

proved frequency monitoring stations to be measured by their daytime groundwave during normal broadcast hours, much to the benefit of their Chief Engineers.

FM frequency measurement is another problem, since few stations are close enough to them to be checked by fixed measurement laboratories. The solution lies in traveling measurement experts, who periodically come equipped with portable frequency standards to check FM (and TV) stations on site. In some cases, signals from the Bureau of Standards station(s) WWV can be used for calibration of local carriers. In general, frequency stability should be the least of a station's technical problems.

SPARE PARTS STOCK

The new radio operation usually begins with a small stock of spare parts, which should be sufficient for new equipment. Tubes is the major category, perhaps, although increasing transistorization is resulting in diminished tube needs. Certainly at least one of each tube type used should be stocked. Where several of one type are used, it is not necessary to stock the full number of spares; usually from one half to two thirds of that number is adequate. The Commission still expects a station to stock adequate spare transmitting tube types, probably on the valid assumption that they may be needed for replacement purposes at hours when local jobbers, even if they stock the tubes, are not open. Similarly, complete tower lamp spares are traditional, with the stated objective of replacement of tower light outages as expeditiously as possible. In fact, when a tower light failure occurs, the station makes the necessary report to the nearest Federal Aviation Agency facility and awaits a tower man's convenience to replace it, anyway, but the investment required for spare tower lamps is quite small.

As for components, new equipment should operate for several years before spares are needed. Thus a beginning station has time to build up a stock of resistors, capacitors, and related parts painlessly, month by month, before their probable need. If the engineer has the time and approval to develop circuits of his own, he will accumulate a stock of assorted component parts. Otherwise, it may be advisable to invest in a few inexpensive assortments of resistors, capacitors, and hardware against the time when they will be vital to equipment repair. Stations beginning with used equipment will find it expedient to acquire a good stock of spare parts at the outset.

POWER TRANSFORMERS

It is not customary, nor usually necessary, for a station to stock spare power transformers. In general, they are prone to give continued service for as many years as the equipment is considered serviceable. Yet one will fail unpredictably, upon occasion, and that may be highly crippling to the operation.

It may be worthy of consideration to examine the power transformer requirements of a station's vital equipment and stock a spare that can pinch-hit in the unlikely event of failure. Power for the main control console, for example, is vital to most small operations, and a transformer that would operate it is cheaper than a whole spare change-over power supply that may be used once every five years. It may be that the same spare transformer can be selected so that it can serve for any of several equipment items, since no two are likely to fail simultaneously. Similarly, a transmitter may use several identical filament transformers, for which a single spare should suffice. There is one power transformer in every station that is at once vital and prohibitively expensive to stock as a spare: the main high-voltage transformer in the transmitter. Fortunately, failure of this transformer is rare, but it also is totally crippling.

A little planned forethought may minimize lost air time if such a disaster should occur. Recognizing the critical nature of the problem in a station that had a history of losing lesser power transformers, I once found that pre-planning paid off well when it finally happened. At a 6:00 AM sign-on one morning, it became evident that something was drastically wrong. After my arrival at the scene and determination that the transformer was indeed gone, I went to the local power company engineers and asked their aid in providing pole transformers of suitable voltage and current ratings. With their gracious cooperation in delivering two (to provide the necessary center-tap) and connecting them backwards, as step-up transformers, plate voltage again was available for the one kilowatt transmitter. (It must be noted that the original high-voltage transformer in this transmitter included a lower voltage bias winding that could not be obtained from the power type, and an area "ham" operator obligingly came forward with a suitable separate transformer.)

In the station referred to in the previous paragraph, transformer failure was phenomenal. Over a span of less than three years, power transformers failed in the control console and the frequency monitor, as well as a filament transformer, the modulation choke, and the aforementioned high - voltage transformer in the transmitter. It was not a matter of inferior equipment design, and it took some time for the operators to realize that a combination of excessive transmitter room heat and lightning surges must be blamed. With a rural location, the supplying power line was subject to lightning surges that were not perceptible, but which must be blamed for perforation of the insulation on transformer windings. Then, thus weakened they succumbed to high operating temperatures.

There are available today surge arrestors that, installed on an incoming power line where it enters the building and connected to a good ground, very effectively bypass the sharp transient spikes induced on power lines by lightning. They are deceptively small solid-state devices that the power company may install upon request; if it will not, they are quite inexpensive and can be installed by the customer. For less than the cost of a single small power transformer, the entire station complex can be protected from the damaging effects of lightning-induced surges. In one station, situated close to a power distribution substation so that the power source is "hard" because there is little intervening line resistance to swamp out switching transients, the precautionary installation of surge arrestors by the power company evidently produced a small, unexpected bonus. The panel pilot lamps in the transmitter were short lived, sometimes lasting only a week or two. It cannot be coincidental that, following the addition of the surge resistors to the power line, pilot lamp life suddenly increased to an average of several months, even in the winter with its absence of lightning. Presumably, the surge arrestors are deleting transients arriving on the power line from substation switching processes, and the visibly increased lamp life suggest that other components, too, are receiving less stress.

THE DUMMY LOAD

Every station should have a dummy load for its transmitter(s);

yet many do not. Particularly in the case of a daytimer; a dummy load is a great convenience, permitting the engineer to tune up and adjust the transmitter during the early evening hours when antenna energization is forbidden. Even for the full-time operation, a dummy load can be useful for determining whether a loading problem lies in the transmitter or in the transmission line or antenna.

For lower-powered AM transmitters, a combination of light bulbs can be devised to serve as a dummy load. This is not an ideal situation, since a lamp filament is not a constant resistance device, but it can be tolerated for economy's sake. In one case, two routinely retired 500-watt tower lamps located atop the transmitter were used as a dummy load. Here the normal transmission line impedance (and therefore the adjusted transmitter output impedance) of 65 ohms was not far mismatched by the two in series, since a 500-watt, 125-volt lamp must have a hot resistance of about 31 ohms. With 50 ohms a more common output impedance, some other series-parallel arrangement would be necessary to match other transmitters. Some mismatch can be compensated for within the normal output adjustments afforded by most transmitters. When the total lamp wattage is equal to the rated transmitter output, the filaments will withstand normal program modulation, but care must be exercised with tone testing, since a lamp may burn out under the sustained overload, unload the transmitter abruptly, and cause arc damage to some of the output stage components.

While the incandescent lamp may serve as an impromptu dummy load for lower-powered AM transmitters, it is not satisfactory for the power divider circuit discussed in Chapter 17 because of its varying resistance. For divider applications, as well as for higher-powered transmitters in general, a commercially designed dummy is preferable.

FM transmitters, too, may be fed into dummy loads. However, at FM frequencies the light-bulb arrangement may not work satisfactorily because the physical arrangement possesses too much reactance. Commercially made dummy loads, with coaxial line fittings and carefully engineered impedances, are preferable. Many FM stations use dummy loads with power calibrating devices to determine the transmission line parameters by which their operating powers are measured. These, of course, serve admirably for routine dummy load applications.

THE DIAGRAM FILES

Every item of broadcast equipment comes with an instruction book and diagram, which should be kept conveniently available for its useful life. There is little that is more frustrating to the engineer than to encounter equipment trouble and be unable to locate an appropriate diagram. Simple as it would seem to be to keep track of instruction manuals, they do become misplaced and even lost with surprising ease. In part, this is due to the lack of method in using them. A single place (such as an assigned file drawer) for them to be kept in at all times they are not in actual use is most helpful. Making it a habit to return each one the moment it has served its purpose assures that each will be in its place the next time it is needed.

Stations with separate transmitter sites need two files, since it is necessary that an instruction manual be on the same premises as the equipment it covers. Sometimes, however, it is convenient to have, say, the transmitter book available at the studios for reference in ordering parts, designing modifications, or interpreting remote control readings. One method that accommodates this need is that of duplicate copies of all instruction manuals, which also serves as a backup system when one becomes lost or destroyed. In many cases, manufacturers will supply extra copies gratis; in others, there may be a nominal charge.

It is not unusual for an engineer to make some modification in an item of equipment for any of several good reasons. Somehow, it is all too easy to overlook indicating those modifications in the manual's diagrams and test, leading to future confusion and misunderstanding. It's usually a matter of inconvenience at the moment and all good intentions to indicate the changes at the first spare moment, which somehow fails to arrive until the incident is forgotten. To prevent this, the engineer needs to develop some system that works for him as a continual reminder to enter the modifications into the manual.

OPERATING PROCEDURES

Entire books might be written on the variety of operating

practices and procedures to be found in broadcasting, and it is not the intention here to delve into the subject in depth. However, there are some aspects that sooner or later become somewhat controversial in every operation that may be worthy of comment. One of these is "gain riding"—the process of maintaining uniform volume levels on the air. While modern AGC amplifiers have relieved the board operator's burden somewhat, sloppy and inattentive gain operation remains a common and audible broadcasting fault. It is not surprising that this should be so, in an era when the board operator also is the announcer, log keeper, phone answerer, transmitter attendant, and receptionist. Nevertheless, a few firm house rules may be effective in improving the situation somewhat.

The widely varying levels to be found on records also contributes to the problem. It is natural for an announcer to bring a turntable pot up to a consistent position each time a record is started, and then turn to his next duty. The fact that a late 45 RPM disc may be cut 15 db "hotter" than a 10-year-old LP escapes his notice until it is half played, when he may make a half-hearted correction. Even with AGC, this does not give a smooth air sound. More common, however, is the announcer's psychological urge to operate his own microphone at a higher level than that of the surrounding program material. This is a commonplace trait, together with leaning into excessive intimacy with the microphone, and it should be strongly discouraged by the engineer (unless the announcer at fault is the boss!). There is no good reason to tolerate the practice, since it really does more harm than good.

If nontechnical operators are to become conscientious about gain riding, they must be observed and repeatedly corrected by the engineer. (This adds another spike to the contention that a staff engineer offers a station many advantages over the outside contract man.) In extremely stubborn cases I have known engineers to devise loud peak alarms in the control room that chatter raucously when excessive levels are permitted. This is said to break even the most persistent announcer-operator.

Another area of operator controversy concerns the use or nonuse of headphones by the board operator. Some announcer-operators rely on the phones like a cripple on crutches, feeling downright undressed without them. Others find them to be very onerous devices, to be avoided at all costs. While they may not be a vital necessity, headphones can serve a very useful purpose. Since the control room speakers are muted when the microphone is opened, the operator without phones doesn't really <u>know</u> what's going on the air at such times. It's a little like driving down the street with one's eyes closed for long intervals. Conversely, the operator wearing phones hears all that goes on. If he is unwittingly making audible noises with a creaky chair, he hears it and can take remedial action. He will be aware of any sloppy switch operation producing mechanical noises and hopefully will develop greater manipulative finesse. He can improve his own air performance, too, by hearing and eliminating excessive breath noises, "popped p's," etc. If an inadvertently open channel picks up material not intended for the air, he may catch it in time to kill it before anyone is embarrassed.

More importantly, the announcer's production is enhanced by headphones as he talks over record openings or closings, since he can monitor exactly what is playing under his voice and pace himself accordingly. This technique of opening the microphone before a record ends and not closing it until another has begun has an important added advantage: it minimizes apparent noise in the control room. This is because background noise in most control rooms is not especially obtrusive while the program material is underway, but it becomes very noticeable in contrast to utter silence. The operator who waits for the last note of a record to end before he opens his microphone gives the listener an instant of silence, which then is noticeably interrupted by background noise when the microphone is abruptly opened. Later, if he closes his microphone before the first sound of the ensuing record is heard, the contrast of silence again is heard. The practice of introducing control room noise under the sound of the record and maintaining it unabated until the early notes of the following one is very effective in "hiding" it from the listeners' awareness. This microphone operating technique best can be done with the aid of headphones.

The phones resorted to by some operators are enough to sour any operator. To begin with, they should be of good technical quality (I prefer crystal phones for their clarity, light weight, ability to expose noise and distortion, and negligible circuit loading). Also, headphones can be singular—a single phone. Most operators who use phones cover but one ear anyway, and the lighter weight and simpler removal of the single unit recommends it. Additionally, differences in personal preferences dictate a volume control for the control board headphone. Given a unit of good quality, light weight, and controllable volume, it should not be too difficult to encourage board operators to use it. In cases of extreme reluctance, it may be feasible to mount a small speaker somewhere on the dead side of the microphone and feed it with level well below the feedback point. This will make a suitable monitor for the operator to hear his cues with the microphone on, although it will not show him delivery defects or audible physical activities.

The potential state of the broadcasting art today is extremely high, both technically and artistically. Whether in practice the medium advances at the rate of broadcasting's early evolution, or whether it settles for a statis of mediocrity will be entirely up to those who man the profession. We cannot look to the public for leadership in an area where they have no expertise; we cannot look to the FCC for guidance when it is tied to political tradition and conflicting influences; we must exercise our own initiative with an unyielding dedication to increasing professionalism.

Index